# Doreen Massey
Selected Political Writings

**Lawrence Wishart Selected Political Writings Series**

The Selected Political Writings Series features edited collections of political writings by key figures from Lawrence Wishart's heritage, spanning fields from cultural studies to economics.

Titles in this series:

1. *Stuart Hall: Selected Political Writings* (2017)
2. *Robin Murray: Selected Political Writings* (2020)
3. *Doreen Massey: Selected Political Writings* (2022)

# Doreen Massey
## Selected Political Writings

Doreen Massey

*Edited by David Featherstone
and Diarmaid Kelliher*

Lawrence Wishart
London 2022

Lawrence and Wishart Limited
Central Books Building
Freshwater Road
Chadwell Heath
RM8 1RX

Typesetting: e-type
Cover design: Oliver Munday

First published 2022
Essays © Doreen Massey Estate 2022
Introduction © David Featherstone and Diarmaid Kelliher
'The great male moving right show' © Doreen Massey estate, Lynne Segal and Hilary Wainwright
'Beyond the coalfields: The work of the Miners' Support Groups' and 'Keep Moving On' © Doreen Massey estate and Hilary Wainwright

The author has asserted her rights under the Copyright, Design and Patents Act, 1998 to be identified as the author of this work.

All rights reserved. Apart from fair dealing for the purpose of private study, research, criticism or review, no part of this publication may be reproduced, stored in a retrieval system, or transmitted, in any form or by any means, electronic, electrical, chemical, mechanical, optical, photocopying, recording or otherwise, without the prior permission of the copyright owner.

British Library Cataloguing in Publication Data.
A catalogue record for this book is available from the British Library

ISBN 978-1-913546-04-5

# Contents

| | |
|---|---:|
| Acknowledgements | vi |
| Introduction (David Featherstone and Diarmaid Kelliher) | 1 |

**Rethinking Region and Economy**

| | |
|---|---:|
| 1 A Politics of Location | 21 |
| 2 The Shape of Things to Come | 37 |
| 3 Heartlands of Defeat | 60 |
| 4 A New Class of Geography | 70 |
| 5 Vocabularies of the Economy | 83 |

**The New Urban Left and the Miners' Strike**

| | |
|---|---:|
| 6 The Great Male Moving Right Show (with Lynne Segal and Hilary Wainwright) | 99 |
| 7 Beyond the Coalfields: The Work of the Miners' Support Groups (with Hilary Wainwright) | 111 |
| 8 Keep Moving On (with Hilary Wainwright) | 133 |
| 9 Equal Opportunities: The GLEB Experience | 138 |

**Politics of Place**

| | |
|---|---:|
| 10 A Global Sense of Place | 151 |
| 11 Places and their Pasts | 164 |
| 12 The Geography of Power | 178 |

**Learning from Latin America**

| | |
|---|---:|
| 13 Nicaragua: Reflections on some Socio-Spatial Issues in a Society in Transition | 187 |
| 14 Space and Power in Theory and in Political Practice | 199 |
| 15 Learning from Latin America | 214 |

**Occasional Writings**

| | |
|---|---:|
| 16 Liverpool's Football Activists Are Part of a Wider Social Movement | 227 |
| 17 Exhilarating Times | 230 |

# Acknowledgements

We would like to thank the many people who have supported this collection of Doreen Massey's political writings. Foremost we would like to thank Doreen Massey's sister Hilary Corton for granting permission to reprint these essays and her enthusiasm and support for the project. John Allen provided significant support and cast a friendly eye over the introduction. Lynne Segal and Hilary Wainwright kindly allowed us to reproduce work which they co-authored with Doreen. Conversations with Sally Davison and Mike Rustin were helpful at the inception of the project. Nuria Benach and Ryan Centner both provided useful advice. At Lawrence and Wishart Jumanah Younis has been an exemplary and supportive editor and Eamon Foreman has been refreshingly engaged in terms of his approach to marketing the book. Mo Hume provided useful comments on the introduction and Dave Featherstone would like to acknowledge the support she has provided through the process of editing this book during Covid times.

# Introduction

## David Featherstone and Diarmaid Kelliher

Doreen Massey was a key feminist and socialist thinker who brought a radical focus on geographical inequality to the forefront of left politics. She was also a political activist who participated in and documented movements from the diverse solidarity campaigns during the 1984-85 Miners' Strike to the alter-globalisation movement of the 1990s and 2000s. Through this organising she combined a focus on class with concerns about gender, race and sexuality that were groundbreaking for her time. As one of the most influential human geographers of the post-war period, Massey was a committed public intellectual and her ideas had a direct impact on, and were shaped by, political initiatives including the progressive Labour administration of the Greater London Council in the 1980s and Hugo Chavez's Bolivarian Revolution at the turn of the twenty-first century.

While Massey offered important insights into policy issues facing left-wing governments, this was not the limit of her concerns. As she once observed, 'there is a "political" audience far greater than politicians'.[1] She believed that there was a crucial role for ideas in influencing ways of thinking more widely in society, in 'the construction of popular and political geographical imaginations'.[2] While often engaged directly in the pressing matters of the time, the pieces collected here speak powerfully to contemporary issues surrounding regional inequality, the politics of place, geographies of class, and strategies of the left.

Born in Manchester in 1944, Massey lived most of her adult life in London until her untimely death in 2016. England's north-south divide shaped her political and intellectual life. Massey's writings are essential reading in a context where the current Conservative government's opportunistic 'levelling up' slogan has signalled a revived attention in British politics to regional inequality. Her writings argue that it is necessary to understand the broader processes that have produced these geographical divisions. They provide important insights for developing a left politics that can counter the intense concentration of wealth in London and the south-east of England.

These regional imbalances have often been the lens through which class has resurfaced in British politics in recent years, usually in extremely reductive forms. During the 2016 EU referendum and in the aftermath of the 2019 General Election, 'ordinary working-class people' were conjured by politicians in ways that assumed the working class to exist only in an ill-defined 'north'. Moreover, this rhetorical working class was often portrayed as white, male, and straight, characterised by social conservatism and a parochial attachment to their local areas.[3] Partly as a result, there is understandable unease in much of the left about the potentially reactionary implications of a politics of place.

Massey's writings are a necessary corrective: they chart the complexity of class formation in Britain with an attentiveness to what would now be termed intersectionality. Further, she traced the transformation of labour wrought by deindustrialisation and the rise of neoliberalism. This dynamic approach is crucial for understanding uneven geographical development within the UK and beyond, moving past the simplistic attribution of the working class to 'the North'. She also provides powerful resources for understanding and developing politics in particular places that are also part of broader connections and solidarities. Together with a direct political analysis of the strengths and weakness of various progressive local government initiatives, her work gives an invaluable insight into radical, local municipalism, and an opportunity to navigate a politics of belonging that avoids reinforcing borders.

This collection draws together a selection of what we have defined as Massey's 'political writings'. Given that almost all her writings were animated by political questions this might seem an anomalous exercise. However, we have selected essays and articles that were intended to have a broader political impact, to speak to audiences beyond the academy, and to intervene in particular pressing debates and problematics. Most of these writings were published not in academic journals but in a range of left publications, and hence formed part of a broader left political culture. It is significant in this regard that one of her most famous essays, 'A Global Sense of Place', was published in one of the last issues of the political magazine *Marxism Today*, rather than a geographical journal.

Massey's contributions in *Marxism Today, New Socialist* and elsewhere were not just theoretical, although they were often powerful in this regard. They frequently engaged in the empirical detail of mapping the geographies of economic transformation, the structure of class, and the shape of labour organisation. Massey made clear why thinking spatially was so crucial to left political analysis and strategy. As a result, her writings have been and remain a powerful resource for the contemporary left, and set a compelling example for politically engaged academics and spatially minded activists.

This book seeks to make these writings accessible and to ensure they are better known. Nonetheless, it is very much a selection from her political writings, rather than a comprehensive collection.[4] The work included here gives a sense of Massey's varied political interventions and interests, spanning reflections on the Sandinistas' spatial policies to a discussion of campaigns by fans of Liverpool Football Club (of which she was a devoted supporter, despite her Mancunian origins!). They provide a vivid impression of Massey's style as a left public intellectual who engaged with diverse issues and events, animated by a concern to analyse the central problems of the day but also propose ways forward for a plural, open and radical left.

## Rethinking Region and Economy

The opening section of the book, 'Rethinking Region and Economy', begins with 'The Politics of Location', originally published in 1983, and ends with Massey's essay 'Vocabularies of the Economy' from 2013. In 'The Politics of Location', Massey took on the intensifying regional inequalities which characterised the Thatcher regime. Locating this intervention in a broader critique of regional policy in the UK, she argued that it was 'the fact that inequality might provoke political and social unrest' which motivated such policies. Critiquing 'politics which are simply reactive', she stressed the need for alternative agendas and socialist approaches (p23).

There are resonances here with 'Vocabularies of the Economy', first published in *Soundings,* where she contends that 'The vocabulary we use, to talk about the economy in particular, has been crucial to the establishment of neoliberal hegemony' (p84). She argues that discourse constitutes political realities and is therefore a crucial battleground for challenging how neoliberalism shapes ways of thinking and relating, and structures relations between places. This essay was published as one of the instalments of *The Kilburn Manifesto*, co-authored in 2013 with fellow *Soundings* editors Stuart Hall and Michael Rustin. They argued that, following the 2008 financial crisis, 'the economic model that has underpinned the social and political settlement of the last three decades is unravelling, but the broader political and social consensus apparently remains in place'.[5]

Most of the pieces included in this section are from the 1980s, and provide a compelling lens on the period in which this neoliberal consensus was being formed. They apply the broad intellectual approach to the spatial-political dynamics of that decade that Massey was developing at this time in key texts such as *Spatial Divisions of Labour* (1984) and in co-authored work with colleagues including Richard Meegan and John Allen on unemployment and regional inequality.[6] This work combined a critical engagement with Marxist political economy and a commitment to spatial thinking with insights from socialist feminism. This produced an approach which both traced geographical shifts in the economy and simultaneously sought to unpack and critique dominant ways of approaching economic relations.

Many of the writings in this section trace the geographical divisions which were entrenched by neoliberalism in the UK and foreground attempts to struggle over and contest these changes. In 'A New Class of Geography', published in *Marxism Today* in 1988, Massey gives a strong sense of the classed dynamics that shaped these intensifying inequalities. She insists that 'the unequal geography of Thatcherism is closely tied in with the government's championing of the cause of certain already-privileged groups. These groups are the basis of the higher levels of *average* prosperity in the outer areas of the south and east of the country' (p70). Such interventions are particularly relevant in the context of 'levelling up', a discourse which positions regional inequalities as abstracted from broader relations of power that focus and entrench wealth in London and the south-east of England. Further, prominent Labour politicians, such as the Mayor of Manchester Andy Burnham, are now accepting and drawing on discourses of 'levelling up'.[7]

These pieces also engage with, and analyse, some of the significant political defeats of the left in that decade. The essay 'Heartlands of Defeat' provides a geographical engagement with the election result of 1987, when Thatcher's Conservatives won a further landslide, largely entrenching their historic 1983 victory. Massey argued that while Labour had 'further strengthened' its support 'within its traditional strongholds' (p60) and increased its vote among certain groups of women, for the most part it had failed to extend its electoral base. Her analysis gives a sense of how the election intensified the regional polarisation of the UK, particularly given the failure of Labour to win towns in the South East and the South more generally.

However, her engagement with the electoral defeats of the 1980s is also marked by attempts to shift the terms of debate and to consider how the left might come to intervene in the transformations being wrought in spatial, political and economic terms. Thus in her 1983 essay 'The Shape of Things to Come', with its fine-grained analysis of class composition and the gendered politics of work in the early 1980s, she identifies 'that the movement always seems to be on the receiving end of such processes: never to hold the initiative' (p58). But referencing the factory occupations by women in Plessey-Bathgate, of Lee Jeans and Lovable in central Scotland, she notes that 'the situation is *not* all gloom and doom.' She argued that 'there are already attempts to respond, to take back some of the initiative' (p59).[8] Crucial here was Massey's political engagement with the New Urban Left and the 1984-85 Miners' Strike.

## The New Urban Left and the Miners' Strike

Visiting Berkley in the early 1980s, Massey has been remembered as making quite a different impression from what was expected of a

British academic, 'with her "cropped blond hair – short, loud, [and] punk," with talk of miners' strikes and combustible class politics'.[9] But it was not a simplistic class politics; her work was often alive to the potential for solidarities across difference. In this respect, while she detailed the structuring effects of spatial divisions, Massey never saw these as final, but was always attentive to the ways in which they could be reworked and challenged through political organising and solidarity. This is something that shaped much of her writing and political involvement, but comes through particularly strongly in her essays on the 1984-85 Miners' Strike.

Involving over 150,000 miners and lasting twelve months, the Miners' Strike was one of the most significant industrial disputes in post-war Britain. The miners were resisting plans for widespread pit closures and to protect their communities, but the strike took on a wider importance. It came to be seen as something of a showdown between the labour movement and the anti-trade union Conservative government. Partly as a result, the strike inspired a large solidarity campaign. Writing with her friend and GLC colleague Hilary Wainwright, they argued that alongside what some thought of as an 'old fashioned' industrial dispute, 'a massive support movement has grown up – almost unreported – with as broad a social and geographical base as any post-war radical political movement' (p111).

Massey and Wainwright detailed 'the support from marginalised and oppressed groups', from racialised minorities, LGBTQ+ people, women's groups, and others (p116). They were attentive to the geographies of support and how these reflected social processes such as the 'crisis of the inner city', which Massey would analyse extensively in its own right. The lessons drawn from this movement were profound: 'not a question of *either* industrial action *or* the new social movements, nor ... of just adding the two together. What is important is a recognition of mutual dependence and a new openness to influence, of the one upon the other. What this strike has demonstrated is a different direction for class politics'.[10] In this regard, for Massey, what we can see in the analysis of the Miners' Strike was that class politics had the potential to be reformulated in a way that moved beyond narrow, exclusionary and conservative forms, while also responding to new social and political realities.

This project of sustaining but re-thinking class politics was evident in her thinking more generally. *Marxism Today*, a journal Massey frequently wrote for in the 1980s, has often been seen as paving the way for New Labour and a wider retreat from class on the left. But Massey's engagements in the magazine were part of a current of left thinking that saw a very different way of 'modernising' the Labour Party to those that became hegemonic under New Labour. Massey's writings, and those of colleagues who would become involved with her in *Soundings*, saw such a project as being shaped by links between the labour movement and an emerging set of popular struggles associated with feminism, lesbian and gay liberation, and anti-racism. This offered elements of a progressive left alternative to the New Labour project, sharing the broad critique developed by Stuart Hall, both in *Soundings* and in his essay 'The Great Moving Nowhere Show' in the revived issue of *Marxism Today* published in 1998.[11]

The Miners' Strike was one of a number of key campaigns that stimulated Massey's political writing. She explained that aside from, perhaps, the French Marxist philosopher Louis Althusser, her key influences and inspirations were not 'intellectual in the usual sense'; rather, 'the stimulus for asking questions and the ways in which debates got framed, has come out of being part of political movements … and more generally an engagement with politics'.[12] Among the specific moments she mentioned was her own involvement with the Greater London Council (GLC) in the early to mid 1980s, during the leadership of Ken Livingstone. This was an important period in which political activists, trade unionists and left-wing academics sought to build an exemplary alternative to Thatcherism through the local state.

Massey was particularly involved in the Greater London Enterprise Board (GLEB), established in 1982, which used the resources of the local state to provide financing for local businesses, based on tripartite agreements between employers, unions and the GLEB itself. The work of the GLEB perhaps most directly speaks to the contemporary concerns of Community Wealth Building (CWB) councils in Britain, with notable examples including Preston and North Ayrshire.[13] CWB councils have attempted to use the spending power of local public institutions to ensure that wealth circulates in the community rather than being siphoned off elsewhere. The approach has often been developed in areas scarred by the long-term impact of deindustrialisation and hit by brutal cuts to local government budgets since 2010. Not only is the intention to keep wealth in the area, but also to ensure it is distributed and controlled in equitable ways, echoing – if in different contexts – the GLEB's attempts to create good jobs and promote social goals through economic development using local state resources.

There is much in the history of the GLC in the 1980s that is rightly celebrated, and it continues to inspire left political activists.[14] However, in her writing on the GLEB here, Massey refuses to be self-congratulatory, emphasising the tensions between the GLEB's commercial and social imperatives. In this respect gender played an important role in Massey's broader political analysis. Shaped by her involvement with socialist feminism, this involved reconfiguring notions of the economy in ways which critiqued narrow, male-dominated approaches to development. This was evident in her critique of the GLEB's approach for fundamentally staying within the boundaries of the capitalist economy: 'Any economic strategy which aims to go beyond the formalities of equal opportunities, to produce an anti-sexist programme of intervention, will have to think about the very shape of the economy itself, and about the division between what is currently called economic and what is currently called social.' With municipalism gaining renewed traction on the left, these arguments are important to ongoing questions around the terms on which different groups participate in such initiatives.[15]

Nevertheless, as her essay with Lynne Segal and Hilary Wainwright 'The Great Male Moving Right Show' shows, she saw the 'new urban left' as offering a political alternative that contrasted with the negative assessments of the left developed by Stuart Hall, Eric Hobsbawm and others in the early 1980s. Massey, Segal and Wainwright argued that 'new ideas', experiments and visions were being created, 'even in the midst of Labour's defeat.' Recognising that these were 'only a beginning' and 'far from perfect', they nonetheless saw the potential for national strategies that were more than the simple sum of local experiments (p109).

This account of the urban left of the early 1980s makes it clear how much this was the New Left in power, an alternative to free-market capitalism but one rooted in a critique of older models of social democracy as well. In the focus on co-operatives, worker control, and popular planning we can see the attention to broad notions of economic democracy that continue to influence municipal socialists.[16] This diverse approach to public ownership continues to resonate in the trend towards re-municipalisation; that is, taking back into local authority control various services and assets that had been privatised. But it is also evident in autonomous initiatives such as Cooperation Town, and in the flourishing of mutual aid groups across the UK, in and beyond the context of the pandemic.[17]

If the ambitions of the 1980s urban left can sound somewhat utopian – and Massey recognised that rhetoric and reality did not always match up – the centrality of measures like expanding good quality, cheap public transport in London and Sheffield demonstrated how concretely these ideas could shape urban life and politics.[18] While Massey saw hope in both the Miners' Strike and support movement, and the new urban left – and drew attention to their significant overlap – she was certainly not glibly optimistic. She would later reflect on the defeat of both movements in the mid 1980s as central to the consolidation of Thatcherism.[19] This defeat was not just political in the narrow sense, it was about the re-shaping of society more broadly: about deindustrialisation, union decline, and the dismantling of local politics.

While local authorities had provided a crucial avenue for developing an alternative both to Thatcherism and mainstream Labourism in the early 1980s, this had been shut off by the end of the decade. Where Massey was directly involved in the GLC under Livingstone – abolished alongside the Metropolitan County Councils in 1986 – recommendations for a socialist urban policy no longer had significant political space to be developed. What the early 1980s had provided, however, was an opportunity to put ideas into practice, to see what actually worked and did not, and to reformulate ideas in response.

## The Politics of Place

The writings on place from the early 1990s in *Marxism Today* and *History Workshop Journal* shift in tone. Here, Massey is less concerned with the specifics of policy recommendations or day-to-day politics, and more focused on how to conceptualise the local in a period of 'space-time compression', or, as it would more commonly be described, globalisation.[20] This perhaps reflected a move away from the immediate political engagement that Massey had through the GLC, but it was marked by the defeats of the 1980s in a more profound way. The Docklands of east London were a central part of the GLC's attempt to use popular planning to respond to deindustrialisation, to provide an alternative to the neoliberal Enterprise Zone approach of the Thatcher government. The transformation of the area into a key global financial hub made clear which vision had won. In the absence of more hopeful alternatives, reactionary ideas had greater opportunity to take hold.

While the GLC's approach had depended in part on understanding this part of the city as a 'working-class' area, in Massey's writings there is concern that the Docklands had become essentialised and racialised as a 'white working-class' place. In this respect, 'Places and their Pasts' offers an important critique of racialised narratives of class that have been entrenched in current media and political discourse. Her essay holds out the importance of constructing different articulations of class and race, more in line with Paul Gilroy's focus on ideas of 'ordinary multiculture',[21] which influenced Massey's writings in *World City*. These were also pressing political questions given that in the same year in which both the *History Workshop* and *Marxism Today* articles were published, the fascist British National Party enjoyed its first electoral successes, with Derek Beackon becoming councillor in the Millwall ward of the Docklands.

These essays should therefore be understood in the context of an immediate political problem: that a sense of belonging was being tied to reactionary political projects. While the form this has taken has mutated in the decades since, it certainly has not gone away. For Massey, it is important to recognise that people have a need for attachment and belonging, but she refigured the terms on which such placed commitments were negotiated and understood. Elements of the Labour Party and influential media commentators continue to read such injunctions in simplistic ways, in thinking that only British nationalism and militarism can speak at this emotional register. For Massey, a deep connection to place does not have to be insular. It can be 'place-based' but not 'place-bound', alive to the global relations and multiplicities that shape parts of the country as different as Kilburn High Street and ex-coal mining villages.

But how does the left actually develop a politics of place that gives such a view a popular resonance? The importance of history in shaping how places are understood provides one possibility. As Massey says, the strategy of promoting alternatives pasts, of developing radical histories can be part of this project. The Cable Street mural in east London, or the statute of Mary Barbour, one of the leaders of the 1915 rent strikes, in Govan in Glasgow are an attempt to give specific meanings to such places rooted in progressive pasts. Still, Massey cautions that even such projects risk idealising how things once were, and argued that these histories should be thought about in ways which acknowledged that they were shaped by different connections and linkages.

Of course, in these essays Massey is also thinking about the wider issues thrown up by the debates on globalisation. She anticipates much of the recent focus on mobility politics here.[22] Massey emphasises the need to understand the socially differentiated nature of mobility; that is, it is not simply the case that globalisation means that movement of all kinds has increased, but that mobility continues to be shaped by class, gender, race and nationality, among other factors. Crucially, she argues that control over movement is patterned by differential power relations. These ideas were revived more explicitly in her work on the geographies of power at the height of the so-called anti-globalisation movement. Here, Massey aligns herself clearly with *alter*-globalisation: not for or against global relations, but highlighting the need for conflict over the terms on which it takes place. The essay republished in this volume importantly emphasises the limitations that come from the left fetishizing the local in response to globalisation.[23] For instance, she argues that the principle of subsidiarity – essentially arguing that decision making should be as local as possible – can fail to take account of wider goals such as redistribution.

For Massey, a narrow focus on the local fails to account for the broader impact of decisions beyond the place in which they are made. There is a sense in Massey's later writings that some of the arguments of a 'Global Sense of Place' and 'Places and their Pasts' have become mainstream, at least in London, where an understanding of community as heterogeneous has become dominant (if not, considering the renewed strength of the BNP in east London in the 2000s, unchallenged). Yet, Massey argues there has been a failure to think about the impact of London beyond its boundaries. London is not just a locality shaped by global relations, but one of those world cities that is itself central to sustaining an international economic system that results in brutal inequalities. For Massey, there needs to be 'a way of thinking multiculturalism outwards'.[24] Contemporary political debate around London is still too often caught in a simplistic binary: either the diverse, progressive city or the root cause of Britain's vast geographical inequalities and a key node in global financial capital. Massey rather emphasises that it is all of this, that these factors are fundamentally connected, and that we need a politics built on this understanding.

## Learning from Latin America

In 2000, nearly fifteen years after the GLC's abolition, Ken Livingstone was again elected to lead a London-wide authority, if a much diminished one. One of the initiatives during Livingstone's tenure as London Mayor that inspired Massey, reflecting the call for a municipal politics that looked beyond the city's boundaries, was the attempt to forge connections with the socialist project in Venezuela. In *World City* she argued that the logic of these connections challenged neoliberal ideas of profit and competitiveness that generally structured relations between cities. Thus she argued that 'the proposal ... is for a barter arrangement in which Venezuela would send cheap oil to London in return for advice and experience in the areas of transport planning, housing, crime, waste-disposal, air quality and adult education'.[25] This approach was, she noted, intended to be redistributive in both cities.

Massey saw internationalism as a set of interventions in the relations between places rather than a disembodied intellectual discourse. Her own political involvement was shaped by such a conception of internationalism. As Rogério Haesbaert and Ana

Angelita Rocha note she had 'strong international ties, especially with Latin America, particularly Nicaragua, Mexico, Brazil and Venezuela'.[26] In 1985 she spent approximately a year working at the Nicaraguan Institute for Economic and Social Research in their Department of Urban Research. This was in the period when the Sandinistas, left-wing rebels who led an uprising against the Somoza dictatorship, attempted to build a democratic socialist alternative in the context of significant attack from US- backed Contra fighters.

Her paper 'Some Reflections on Socio-Spatial Issues in a Society in Transition', originally published in the radical journal of geography *Antipode*, draws on research she did while at the Nicaraguan Institute and highlights her political commitment to the Sandinista project. The paper engages with some of the key challenges of socio-spatial transition, and offers useful discussions of the spaces of rural-urban migration and informality. Her work challenged some of the then orthodox ways of thinking about these relations. The paper was also part of a broader set of conversations together with friends and comrades such as David Slater about the forms taken by socialist alternatives at this time.

Slater had argued in the preceding issue of *Antipode* about the importance of the Nicaraguan experience as a democratic socialist project, counterposing this with forms of Leninist authoritarianism.[27] Looking back at these articles from the vantage point of 2021 it is clear that this experience has not delivered on the promise that Massey and Slater saw in this political alternative. As Karen Kampwirth noted, the FSLN has evolved 'from a revolutionary party to one that was often a personal vehicle for Daniel Ortega and his family'.[28] It has also become a party which is increasingly underpinned by authoritarianism, and inflected by a strong opposition to feminist demands and concerns, a significant contrast to some of the engagements between gender and revolutionary politics which emerged in the 1980s.

While her writings on Nicaragua resulted from her own direct involvement, Massey's engagement with the 'Bolivarian Revolution' in Venezuela was prompted by Hugo Chavez's interest in her ideas of 'power-geometry', though she continued to have dialogues with geographers from the continent. Introduced to Massey's ideas by his 'closest geographical advisor' Ricardo Menendez, the 'geometry of the people's power' [geometría del poder popular] was adopted as one of the motors of the Bolivarian revolution. However, as Ryan Centner notes, this was arguably done in ways which were not attentive to important aspects of Massey's approach to spatial politics, including her feminism. For Centner, 'in the Caracas context, the notions of "right to the city" and "power-geometry" are denuded of their complexity, and certainly the nuances of theoretical lineage'.[29]

In her essay 'Concepts of Space and Power in Theory and in Political Practice' Massey provides her own reflections on these experiences, arguing that 'a geographical concept is being put to positive political use. Indeed … part of what lay behind the proposal was an impressive recognition of the existence and significance, within Venezuela, of highly unequal, and thus undemocratic, power geometries'.[30] Her essay probes some of the tensions involved in this process. Thus she argues that in Venezuela, the concept of power-geometry was being 'mobilised specifically in the sphere of politics', but that there also needed to be recognition that 'there are geometries of power in all instances of society', which tend to be mutually reinforcing. She also insists that places needed to be thought of in more dynamic ways in relation to the political processes of building a new power-geometry and a recognition that they would be 'an evolving *result* of the process of building participatory democracy' rather than having a 'presumed already-existing coherence' (p209).

Nonetheless, during an interview in Glasgow in 2009, she spoke of her interest in initiatives such as the setting up of the communal councils, Consejo Comunal, which would exist in parallel with 'the structures of the representative state'. Massey was clearly passionate about the possibilities of these emerging participatory alternatives.[31] In this respect, her exasperation at having to defend the political achievements of the so-called 'Pink Tide' in Latin America inspired the final essay in this section, 'Learning from Latin America', which was published in *Soundings* in 2012. This argued that far from simply being the subject of left critique, the governments in Bolivia, Brazil, Ecuador and Venezuela were in fact something the left in places such as Britain could learn from.

She uses the essay to invert some of the ways in which the relations between the 'global South' and 'global North' are frequently configured, posing the importance of recursive engagements and exchanges of ideas. As Perla Zusman argues, 'It is not common for

European intellectuals to show interest in the Latin American experience and to reflect upon it as a model for developing a different kind of relation between European countries themselves'.[32] Thus she argues that these left projects were shaping innovative engagements with questions around democracy, the media, and space, which had significant lessons for the European left. Her stance towards the Latin American left could be thought of in terms of what Priyamvada Gopal calls 'reverse tutelage':[33] ways in which the work of scholars and political activists involved in anti-colonial movements and politics unsettled and expanded the worldviews of leftists in contexts like Britain (though in Massey's essay there's a slight tendency to homogenise Latin America itself).

Massey saw great promise in the way that the left in Latin America articulated itself in populist forms. This engagement shaped Massey's enthusiasm for Jeremy Corbyn's leadership of the Labour Party and the potential it represented for a left populist project that drew together different progressive demands. In 'Exhilarating Times', a *Soundings* editorial and one of the last pieces she wrote before she died, she outlined how the election of Corbyn as Labour leader offered the kind of political rupture and opening of possibility that she, and others, had long been working for. She observes that *Soundings* had been 'arguing for a long time that Labour should "take a leap," that it should challenge the dominant terms of debate' and she noted that the 'whole point of the Soundings Manifesto, likewise, has been to argue the political necessity of challenging the currently hegemonic common sense and to establish new ground' (p229).

Her editorial makes it clear that she was less interested in the personality of Corbyn than the broader promise for a renewed left political space that his election as Labour leader represented. This emphasises Massey's hopeful style of political engagement, which is a key disposition running through the book. Her provisional assessment of Corbyn, which predicts some of the challenges he would face while signalling the potential political spaces that would be opened up by his leadership, feels like a fitting essay to end this collection. As she argues:

> We are not talking here of already achieved political gains. Far from it. 'Shifting common sense', 'changing the terms of debate'

and 'shaping a new political terrain' can only be part of a long and multifaceted political project; and, most importantly, any new common sense must be able to reach out to, and in some way engage, parts of society way beyond the self-described left. But seeds are being sown. There is somehow a feeling of possibility (p230).

## Note on terminology

Some of the essays reproduced here use outdated terminology to refer to Black people and people of colour. We have taken the decision to reprint the essays as they originally appeared since we have not conducted any other post-hoc editing of the texts. However, we have included this note to alert the reader ahead of time since we acknowledge that such language can be jarring.

## Notes

1. Doreen Massey, 'Geography on the Agenda', *Progress in Human Geography*, Vol. 25, Issue 1, 2001, p12.
2. *Ibid.*
3. See L. Schwartz, 'Working Class Heroes?', www.historyworkshop.org.uk/working-class-heroes, 24 November 2021 and S. Valluvan, *The Clamour of Nationalism: Race and Nation in Twenty-First-Century Britain*, Manchester University Press: Manchester, 2019.
4. Here we have brought together well-known and easy-to-access pieces, with pieces from journals like *The New Socialist* that have not to our knowledge been digitised. Our hope as editors is that it stimulates further interest in this aspect of her work; Massey's archive at the Royal Geographical Society-Institute of British Geographers is a resource that will be important for deepening appreciations of her political activity.
5. S. Hall, D. Massey and M. Rustin, *After Neoliberalism? The Kilburn Manifesto*, Lawrence and Wishart: London, 2015, p9.
6. D. Massey and R. Meegan, *The Anatomy of Job Loss: The How, Where and Why of Employment Decline*, Methuen: London, 1982 and J. Allen and D. Massey (eds), *Restructuring Britain: the Economy in Question*, Sage: London, 1988.

7   See for example A. Burnham, 'Boris Johnson now has the chance to make "levelling up" mean something', www.theguardian.com/commentisfree/2021/oct/06/andy-burnham-boris-johnson-levelling-up-north-of-england, 6 October 2021.
8   On these occupations see A. Clark, *Fighting Deindustrialisation: Scottish Women's Women's Factory Occupations, 1981–1982*, Liverpool UP: Liverpool, 2022.
9   J. Peck and T. Barnes, 'Berkeley in Between: Radicalising Economic Geography', in T. J. Barnes and E. Sheppard (eds), *Spatial Histories of Radical Geography; North America and Beyond*, Wiley: Chichester, 2019, p228.
10  *Ibid.*, p168.
11  See S. Hall, *Selected Political Writings: The Great Moving Right Show and Other Essays*, S. Davison, D. J. Featherstone, M. Rustin, and B. Schwarz (eds), Lawrence and Wishart: London, 2018.
12  D. Massey, S. Bond and D. J. Featherstone, 'The possibilities of a Politics of Place Beyond Place: A Conversation with Doreen Massey', *Scottish Geographical Journal*, Vol. 125, No. 3-4, 2009, p403.
13  See M. Brown and R. F. Jones, *Paint Your Town Red: How Preston Took Back Control And Your Town Can Too*, Repeater, 2021.
14  For more on the history of the GLC visit www.glcstory.co.uk.
15  Brown and Jones, *op. cit.*, p121.
16  See A. Cumbers, *Reclaiming Public Ownership: Making Space for Economic Democracy*, Zed Books: London, 2012 and D. Payling, '"You have to start where you're at": Politics and reputation in 1980s Sheffield', in E. Smith and M. Worley (eds), *Waiting For Revolution: the British Far Left From 1956*, Manchester University Press: Manchester, 2018, p20.
17  E. Jupp, *Care, Crisis and Activism: The Politics of Everyday Life*, Policy Press, 2022.
18  A. Cochrane and D. Massey, "Developing a socialist urban policy", in P. Alcock, A. Gamble, I. Gough, P. Lee and A. Walker (eds), *The social economy and the democratic state: a new policy agenda for the 1990s*, Lawrence and Wishart: London, 1989, pp132-154.
19  D. Massey, *World City*, Polity Press: Cambridge, 2007, p31.
20  For a critical discussion of Massey's writings in this regard see M. McGuinness, 'Geography matters? Whiteness and contemporary geography', *Area*, Vol. 32, No. 2, 2000, pp225-230.

21 Paul Gilroy, *After Empire: Melancholia or Convivial Culture?*, Routledge: London, 2004.
22 See M. Sheller, *Mobility Justice: the Politics of Movement in an Age of Extremes*, Verso: London, 2018.
23 D. Massey, 'London inside-out', *Soundings*, 32, 2006, pp62-71.
24 *Ibid.*, p69.
25 Massey 2007, *op. cit.*, p199.
26 R. Haesbaert and A. A. Rocha, 'Doreen Massey, 1944-2016', *Geographers: Biobibliographical Studies*, Vol. 38, 2019, n.p.
27 D. Slater, 'Socialism, Democracy and the Territorial Imperative: Elements for a Comparison of the Cuban and Nicaraguan Experiences', *Antipode*, Vol. 18, No. 2, 1986, pp155-85.
28 K. Kampwirth, 'Abortion, Antifeminism, and the Return of Daniel Ortega: In Nicaragua, Leftist Politics?', *Latin American Perspectives*, Vo. 35, No. 6, 2008, p127.
29 R. Centner, *Clashing power-geometries: geographic thought and the transformation of centrality in Caracas,* Geography and Environment Discussion Paper Series (5), Department of Geography and Environment, LSE: London, 2020, p19.
30 Massey 2009, *op. cit.,* p20.
31 *Ibid.*, p410.
32 P. Zusman, 'Doreen Massey and Latin America', in M. Werner, J. Peck, R. Lave, and B. Christophers (eds), *Doreen Massey: Critical Dialogues*, Agenda Publishing: Newcastle, 2018, p303.
33 P. Gopal, *Insurgent Empire: Anti-Colonial Resistance and British Dissent,* Verso: London, 2019, p8.

# Rethinking Region and Economy

# 1
# A Politics of Location

## 1983

**The problem**

Different stages in the economic and political development of a society have different implications for its economic and social geography. In the UK the birth of industrial capitalism saw the rapid growth of towns, especially in the north and west, and the impoverishment of agricultural areas and of agricultural labour in the south and east. The decline of Empire was marked by the decline of the major industries on which British world dominance had been built, and that in turn brought with it the collapse of the economies of particular regions. By the 1930s the areas on the labour of whose workers British capital ruled the world were suffering the highest unemployment and the most abject levels of poverty. Capital had moved on. At the same period, and over subsequent decades, investment in new industries was concentrated in the south-east and the midlands of England. That latest burst of growth too is now slackening. Manufacturing employment grew in Britain until the mid 1960s but since then has been declining. Britain's deindustrialisation has been faster, so far, than that of other industrialised capitalist countries. Another reorientation of the world economy is under way, and the UK is losing out as a manufacturing economy. And, once again, a shift in the international economy, of Britain's place within it and of its own economic and political development, has brought with it a change in the national geography.

To simplify greatly an immensely complicated process, what is happening this time is that, with the decline of manufacturing, including many of those industries which have arisen only in the last fifty years, has come the collapse of the manufacturing heartlands of the country. The West Midlands has been particularly badly affected and has slumped in the space of little more than a decade from a booming central region to one with an unemployment rate well above the national average. The inner cities too have been hit, especially because much of the manufacturing investment there was older and often less profitable – and therefore most vulnerable when that wave of capitalist growth in its turn ran out of steam.

National economic and social development, and national economic and social geography, are thus closely linked. And for socialists, therefore, national economic and social policies should be closely linked with considerations of geography, of geographical distribution and of geographical equity. This is not to argue that spatial distribution supersedes social distribution, that all would be well if each region had its fair share of each class and social group. Nor is it to argue that 'spatial' policies are any solution – indeed our conclusion is if anything the opposite. But it *is* to argue that geographical distribution is important, both economically and politically, and it *is* to argue that whole areas – and the people within them – should not simply be developed, exploited and then just as suddenly abandoned as greater profits can be made in pastures new. It *is* to argue that one of the rights of capital which must be challenged is its right to locate where it will. There must be social control, with socially and democratically determined priorities, over the geographical organisation of the economy. We need a politics of location.

There is not much positive experience to go on. There has been a long history of spatial policy in the UK. Most obviously, there has been a 'regional policy', changing in form and intermittent in operation, since the 1930s. And in the last decade there has been the newly urgent concern to 'do something' about the plight of the inner cities. But almost all these policies have had a number of characteristics, shared underlying assumptions, which it is important to challenge.

Perhaps most significant, these policies have almost always been reactive. As an area or region has gone into crisis, some spatially specific response has been devised. In the 1930s the Special Areas Act and associated measures were too late to cope with the appalling conditions in the Welsh valleys and the north-east of England. In the late 1950s the renewed decline of ship-building provoked visits by Lord Hailsham to the unemployed of Tyneside, and regional development strategies were hastily concocted. In the 1960s the colliery closures were pushed through with the promise of Special Development Area status for affected areas and, in the 1980s, the closures of steelworks with the consolation of an Enterprise Zone. Most recently, the political threat posed by serious rioting in inner-city areas saw another Conservative Minister (this time Michael Heseltine) making another trip north (this time to Merseyside) with more promises and policies.

The history so far, then, has been very much a question of stimulus and response: the stimulus – the threat of trouble from an area suffering the effects of the withdrawal of capital; the response – elastoplast for the particular area in question. Two things should be noted. First, the stimulus has only rarely been the fact of inequality itself; generally, it has been the fact that inequality might provoke political and social unrest. During the long postwar boom in the 1950s the inequality in unemployment rates between the regions of the UK was actually greater, in a simple statistical sense, than in the 1960s. But the low absolute levels of unemployment meant that even the regions where the rate was highest were quiescent. The lack of political pressure enabled nothing to be done. And so the 1950s, the decade which in economic terms offered the greatest opportunity for an attack on geographical inequality and the regional problem, passed with scarcely any action being taken.

Second, though, and to return to the central argument, policies which are as simply reactive as this, which are so clearly post hoc responses, do not amount to planning or social control at all. Apart from a few honourable exceptions, mostly embodied in Commission Reports rather than in actual policies, we have never really attempted in Britain to take positively planned social control over the general geographical distribution of jobs.

There are other criticisms too. Emergency measures for 'problem areas' (note how, in a nice turn of phrase, it is the area that is seen to be the problem rather than its desertion by industry) are rarely related to other policies, in other fields, being pursued at the same time. Often in the past they have been undermined by programmes with which they have been in contradiction. The cut-backs in public services, for instance, have had especially serious effects (in terms of jobs as well as services) in many areas supposedly benefiting from special state aid. Policy towards nationalised industries has conflicted with that towards inner cities and peripheral regions. Further, these spatially specific emergency responses have for the most part taken the form of boosting the competitiveness of certain areas. The workers in one region are still left competing against those in another: all that has happened is that the relative advantages of these competing places has been altered. Once again, this is hardly planning or social control. Moreover, the solution has always been seen in terms of the private sector, in attempts to turn the area, through improvement or subsidy, into one in which private profits can be made. The role of the public sector has been indirect, confined to creating the conditions for renewed exploitation by private industry. The only exceptions to this rule have been occasional decentralisations of central government functions. All these things put together point to a final, and politically most important, characteristic. Policies so far have been fundamentally undemocratic. They have not grown out of the work experience and the requirements of the people of the areas in question. They have been run, very often, by central government or by special, unelected, bodies. There has been very little understanding, at grassroots level, of what the issues are and therefore very little coherent strategic political pressure. The emergency has already arrived before the issue is placed on the political agenda, and all too often anything has looked better than nothing. And the whole process has remained subject to the dictates of private industry.

## A new approach

A number of general principles, then, can be defined for a socialist policy on industrial location and the geography of economy and society. First, it must be positive planning built around long-term strategic objectives. Spatial policy must stop being simply a response to already existing problems. It must also be about long-term balanced growth. This in turn means that location policy towards industry, and spatial policy in general, must be fully co-ordinated with other arms of policy and, in particular, with national economic strategy. Spatial policy must not be a cosmetic afterthought, It is not a question of first making plans for national economic recovery and then thinking about the geographical implications of that strategy. The two must go hand in hand. And spatial planning must be co-ordinated with other aspects of policy too. There are very few areas of politics which do not have geographical implications.

A socialist policy on location must also abandon the method of forcing areas to compete against each other. At the best of times this is politically unacceptable because it simply plays one group of workers off against another to the benefit of capital. But in the cold climate which we face today it is simply absurd as advertisements, inducements and enticements – and (public) expenditure – are piled on top of each other in the competition for the few crumbs of new investment which are around. Abandonment of that approach will mean different things in different cases. In general, it will mean greater social control. For those companies which in the past have been able to sit back while the competing incentives mounted it must mean some degree of public control over their location strategies. There must not be a repeat, for instance, of the humiliating Nissan episode, when local communities and work forces were forced to bid against each other in an attempt to sell themselves to this multinational which had (or might have had) a few thousand jobs on offer. Further, one conclusion which the competitive approach has always neatly avoided is that some areas must lose. Instead of a race of leapfrogging bribes, this fact must be faced politically. Instead of handing out vain hopes, it must be recognised that there are many areas in the UK to which private capital will not soon return, even with the most massive 'inducements' and even with considerable public and state pressure (it will either not invest, or it will go abroad, thus holding back national employment growth). In these areas it is quite unrealistic to rely on private investment to promote economic recovery. Public investment, directly, must take the lead, combining the aims of improving the environment, rebuilding dilapidated infrastructure, providing much needed social and public services and creating employment. Here again, then, spatial policy links directly with the overall framework of a national Alternative Economic Strategy (AES).

Finally, a socialist politics of location must be democratic.

Indeed, regional and locational policies can themselves be a *means* for decentralising and democratising control over national economic policy. Already we are beginning to see, for instance, a hierarchy of alternative economic strategies, from the national AES, through metropolitan-level strategies, to mini-AESs in local boroughs. Such spatially defined strategies can also be an arena for linking industrial and community issues in the process of drawing up local plans and proposals. There are some obvious opportunities: power workers and local communities on plans for district heating; public-sector workers and local service provision. The present habit of tacking 'democracy' on to the end of economic policies will not do. Democratic forms and local and grass-roots organisations must be the basic building blocks of policy. And that applies to regional and inner-city policies as much as any other. Without that, we will simply perpetuate that unhappy legacy of the Labour Governments of the 1960s and 1970s, disillusionment with all forms of public intervention and social control.

These general principles imply also a very different organisational framework for spatial policy. Instead of just defining areas for different levels of subsidy or with different powers of economic policy-making, a range of varied structures needs to be devised to intervene in, and control, the different processes through which geographical inequality is produced and to provide a co-ordinated subnational basis for local economic planning.

At national level there should be at least two strands to this. First, there should be some mechanism for the scrutiny of major national policies which are not in themselves explicitly spatial. Their urban and regional implications should be evaluated against wider geographical policy. This evaluation should, of course, include in its remit the AES, especially in relation to strategic policies – for instance, in connection with broad decisions about which industries to promote and support and which industries might be restructured and how. Second, there will have to be a specifically spatial policy to deal with inter-regionally mobile jobs and investment and the internal organisation of multiregional and multinational companies. At subregional level a kind of geographical hierarchy of AESs is developing. The best-known examples are those built around the Enterprise Boards of the Greater London Council and the West Midlands. Attention must now be given both to the extension of these experiments and also to the development of methods of 'horizontal' and 'vertical' co-ordination so as to avoid the problems of competition between areas. It must also be recognised that different local and regional areas have very different advantages and problems, and that it is likely that the problems will demand very different solutions in different places. The same formula will not work everywhere.

The next two sections of this chapter cover two aspects of this structure. The first looks at the question of how to assume some control over interregionally mobile investment. The second looks at inner-city policy. Inner cities are good examples of areas likely to lose out in any competition for private investment in the near future, no matter how much that competition is 'fixed'. In both areas of policy it is shown how past political initiatives have suffered, each in specific ways, from the general problems outlined above, and in each the beginnings of an alternative strategy is presented.

## Interregionally mobile investment

One of the political results of the current high regional unemployment is nostalgia for the regional policy of the 1960s. Although not its only function, it was this policy which was mainly responsible for Government influence over the location of interregionally mobile jobs and investment. The argument here is that it would be quite wrong to resuscitate that form of regional policy.

In its specific ways, the regional policy of the 1960s and 1970s suffered from all the general problems of past spatial policies which have already been mentioned. Although at some periods backed by negative controls in central, congested regions, it was in general a policy based on a range of different sized carrots. Hence it was impossible for there to be any social control over industry, and areas were reduced to competing with each other. Nor, given the levels of information, the nature of the incentives and the nature of the advertising, was it a competitive system which led to a 'rational' distribution, even in industry's profit-oriented terms. The policy, then, was not one which could easily be squared with socialist political objectives.

But, anyway, did it work? The arguments over this have been long and complex, but some things are clear. First, obviously, it did not 'solve' the regional problem; differentials in rates of unemployment persist. Second, although its impact has been overestimated (some of the movement to peripheral regions might have happened anyway), none the less there is no doubt that regional policy did influence the location of some investment. Third, however, the conditions no longer exist for even that degree of success. The impact of the regional policy of the 1960s and 1970s was dependent upon the economic and political conditions of the 1960s and 1970s. In particular, it depended on a high level of spatially mobile investment and employment in the private sector. At present, under a monetarist national government, such investment is not available. And if economic growth were once again to be promoted, but through an AES, the mix between public and private would change. This would present enormous opportunities for a different sort of regional policy.

Not only did past regional policy not solve the old problems, however, but it was also instrumental in encouraging the emergence of new ones. Levels of unemployment are not the only possible index of spatial inequality, and during the 1960s and 1970s other indices emerged as increasingly important. Differences between regions in the types of jobs available changed and in some ways were exacerbated. The new high-status jobs in management, services, technology and R & D created over this period remained unaffected by regional policy and were located in the south-eastern parts of England. In complete contrast, most of the jobs moving to the old peripheral regions were of low skill requirements, low-paid, often part-time and of very low status. The north-south divide was being recreated in a changed form. Further, because the policy relied above all on attracting interregionally mobile investment, and because this in turn was mainly in large, multiplant firms, most of the jobs created in peripheral regions over this period were in branch plants controlled by headquarters elsewhere – often in the south-east. Any policy which operates by competition between areas, which focuses only on numbers of jobs rather than also on their quality and which ignores completely the internal organisation of multiplant firms will reinforce these increasingly important aspects of the regional problem.

What, then, should be done about this level of policy where interregional location decisions are made by major companies?

First, competition between areas must be ended. This aspect of policy should be brought within the scope of enforceable planning agreements. What this should not mean, however, is that management and 'someone from Whitehall' should sit down together drawing up plans in the manner of French indicative planning in the 1960s. Rather even than the tripartite structures of many forms of the AES, we should move towards a situation in which the Labour Party and government, at local and at national levels, support workers' plans. This way the rhetoric of democratising the AES can be given some real meaning. In other words, planning agreements should be linked with work-force plans for industries, where such exist. In most cases, of course, they will not exist. Such plans can be built up only over time. What will be important from the beginning will be to create a climate of possibility and of confidence in the fact both that plans can be drawn up and that the effort will be worth it. Apart from political support, a wide range of open and accessible resource centres would be an essential part of any democratically organised industrial strategy. This all relates, so far, to existing firms and sectors. In a case like Nissan there is no existing work-force. How, then, would a decision be made about the location of new investment? How, then, would the competing claims of London's docklands, Merseyside, South Wales be resolved? This is not only a question of criteria; it is a question also of thinking about the mechanisms through which such a decision should be made. Three things are clear. The criteria for making the decision should be public and should concern social issues as well as considerations of profitability. The procedures themselves must be entirely open; the space for behind-the-scenes deals and for clandestine competitive bargaining must be cut back as much as possible (and to say that these can never be entirely eliminated is no argument for abandoning the attempt to curtail them). Wherever possible, decisions should be linked with existing, wider sectoral plans – decisions about location should be part and parcel of decisions about production.

Second, there is the issue of ownership and control. At present, in discussions of spatial policy this is seen largely as a matter of the geographical location of control. The problem, it is argued, is that ownership and control lie outside the area in question. Now, the geographical location of ownership certainly does have its effects – it can make things far more difficult for trade union negotiators, for instance. But the answer is not to encourage 'local entrepreneurship' or to hark back longingly to the days when most regions had their 'own' capitalist class. Put like this (and such an attitude is, in fact, implicit in much recent policy that is supposed to generate 'indigenous growth'), it is anyway a strange demand for the labour movement to make. What is at issue, rather, is not only the geographical location of control but also its social location. It is not capitalists and top managers we want to restore to the regions but control over production. Once again, the geographical issue is bound up with the organisation of production itself. For socialists, bringing ownership and control back to the local level must therefore mean two things (at least). In connection with ownership it must mean a change in class location, establishing new forms of public and common ownership; with control it must mean the at least partial removal of such production from market forces and its evaluation by wider social criteria, including a plant's relation to the community in which it is located. (But here we move into the more local planning concerns of the next section.)

Third, what might be done about the vast variation in the kinds and quality of job available to people in different regions? Here again, previous policy prescriptions have completely missed the point; by focusing entirely on geography without seeing the link between that and the organisation of production, they have ignored the essential problem and their prescriptions have, from the start, been doomed to failure. To see the policy in simply spatial terms is to regard the aim as being to recreate Slough in Sunderland, Silicon Valley in Scotland. What such an approach fails to appreciate is that with the present organisation of capitalist industry, with the present form of technological development and division of labour within production, there will always be places where people do only boring production work if there are to be places where people do all the management and all the R & D. Not everywhere can be Silicon Valley. Nor would simply spreading the high-status jobs around the country do much to help those who anyway get stuck in the low-paid tedium and futurelessness of assembly. And this raises the real point. For it is the kind of technological development that we are pursuing, the kind of division of labour within production which this promotes and which we are allowing, that enables the new spatial division of labour between different areas. More equal, democratic and progressive ways of organising production itself must of necessity lead to less of that kind of geographical differentiation between areas.

The kind of science and technology implicit in the White Heat policies of the 1960s, combined with the lack of control over job quality in the regional policy of the same period, together enabled the emergence of the new form of regional problem. Only when we have a policy on production which recognises that technology is not neutral will we stand any chance of overcoming geographical inequality in employment. It is the Lucas Aerospace shop stewards' plan, which combines the advantages of high technology with an attempt to undermine the divisive hierarchy of skills within production, that points the way forward.

# Inner cities[1]

The inner-city policies of previous Labour Governments (embodied in the continuing Urban Programme and the Inner Urban Areas Act) shared many of the same assumptions and were subject to many of the same criticisms.

First, they were committed fundamentally to a private-sector solution. The role of the public sector was essentially to be one of providing the preconditions for private industry to make a profit, whether this was to be done by building advance factories, by loans and grants or by leasing land to private house-builders.

Second, the inner cities were simply set up as yet more 'assisted areas', in competition with others.

Third, there was a lack of co-ordination between measures specifically directed at inner cities and wider national policies. One of the most obvious cases was that of landownership; inner-city policy failed even to make use of existing legislation. Given its weak formulation, the Community Land Act was never going to be a serious aid in reducing the high price of derelict urban land. But the inner cities legislation failed to take advantage even of the possibilities the Act did offer of enabling local authorities to buy land at 'current use value' rather than at a price based on some potential higher-value use (such as offices). Instead, such was the desperation to attract industry that 90 per cent loans were offered to companies to buy land on the open market – a policy which could only keep land prices up.

Finally, it was a 'top-down' policy. Initiatives and decisions came from senior national and local government officials. Local involvement and control was concentrated in local government – members of the public were excluded from Partnership Area Committee meetings, for example.

This approach can be criticised on two different grounds. To begin with, it can be criticised 'technically': it is most unlikely to work. In the present cold economic climate it would take enormous injections of cash, and major reconstruction, to make these areas attractive again to the private capital which produced the present dereliction. And, given the way that policies have so far been formulated, to the extent that investment and jobs *were* attracted back to inner cities it would only be at a cost to other areas. Jobs for Liverpool at the expense of South Wales – and with private industry calling the tune.

But the more important criticism is political. It is not just that such policies won't work, even in their own terms, but that the approach on which they are based should be challenged politically.

First, in what sense is this an inner-city problem anyway? Past policies have tended implicitly to 'blame' the cities for their unsuitability for private-sector development and have therefore concentrated on area-based policies to 'improve' them. But the loss of jobs in urban areas is part of a much wider process. As we have seen, the present crisis of the British economy is bringing with it also a major geographical reorganisation, and some of the worst effects of that reorganisation are evident in the cities. Many of the major underlying causes of urban decline lie outside the cities themselves. Once again, area-based policies alone will not do.

But, second, that does not mean that employment will simply return to the inner cities with national economic recovery. Geographical characteristics *are* important; even were there to be an up-turn in the economy, new investment would not, first off and undirected, go to inner urban areas. There is, then, a need to pay specific attention to inner cities – a need for a politics of location. What must be faced politically is that without ridiculous levels of subsidy, in one form or another, to private industry, inner cities are the areas most likely to lose in the competitive approach to spatial policy.

But the central political question is: what – or who – is all this policy-making for? The revitalisation of what? Regeneration for whom? The restoration of whose confidence? What, in other words, would it mean to say that an inner-city policy had 'worked'? Both Tory and Labour policies have in the past given the issue what has been called a 'property definition' rather than a 'people definition'. It is simply assumed that if profits *could* once again be made in the cities, the problems would go away. It is important to look at who gains from present policies.

- The incentives approach to location means subsidies to private companies but with no *quid pro quo* in connection with the types of jobs, conditions of employment, or even, indeed, the numbers of jobs created.
- The rates and tax provisions of the Conservatives' Enterprise Zones and the loans for land purchase under Labour provide a potential bonanza for landowners.
- The more way-out schemes are just the same. Marinas are frequently proposed for London's docks. But then, as the schoolkid's poem asked: 'How many East Enders have yachts?'

Urban local government, like other forms of local government, has been bending over backwards to attract investment – development at any price and any kind of development. But this means that the city is thought of in terms of its function as land and location from the point of view of the market. To the extent that there is any real connection between such development and social need, it is usually coincidental. What is required is a rethinking of the whole issue, a redefinition of the problem.

To begin with, any strategy for the inner cities which is both to be socialist and to stand a chance of success needs to have the following characteristics.

- It should be public-sector-led. Instead of the public sector 'creating the conditions' for private capital, it must itself play the leading role in investment.
- It should be integrated with wider socialist aims, including initiatives in new forms of ownership and control; it should demand a real *quid pro quo* for any aid given to the private sector; it should stem from, and seek to build, a strong local base, with much of the local-level initiative being taken by local workers, tenants groups, trades councils, etc., a number of which have already produced local studies and plans.
- It should, in other words, shape itself around social needs rather than the requirements of private profit. We must begin to think what a socially useful city would look like.
- There must be real co-ordination of national and local policies.
- There should be co-ordination between employment and other policies. For example, there must be control over urban land markets (we need something much stronger than the Community Land Act); direct labour organisations must be rebuilt and expanded, and this in turn should be related to extended housing programmes, etc.
- This will require a far greater financial commitment than there has ever been in the past; it will require the use of funds at present controlled by financial institutions.

All this may sound ambitious. In one sense it is. But it is also what is necessary. Tinkering with local-area policies has been tried for over a decade, and virtually no impression has been made on the problem. But it is also a framework in which policies and action can be constructed now. We don't have to wait for the millennium before anything can be done.

Take an example: small clothing firms in inner London, where economic pressures are causing both loss of jobs and a worsening of working conditions. The need is to improve the conditions of workers while not at the same time adding to costs so much that jobs are lost altogether. This can be done through precisely the kind of co-ordination of policies suggested above. Thus at national level government could:

- give (temporary) trade protection to the worst-hit sections of the industry;
- reinforce, and implement, legislation relating to working conditions – such as health and safety provisions.

At the same time, at local level it could:

- provide cheap premises with better working conditions;
- in return, operate a good employer code.

Such an approach would not be competitive with other UK areas; it would both keep jobs and improve conditions; and it would ensure a return for aid to private companies. It could, moreover, be adapted and extended, depending on local political conditions. It could be combined with workers' plans for the industry (including, it is to be hoped, attacks on the entrenched sexual division of labour) – indeed, it would give such plans the space to operate realistically. The degree of control taken by workers or the local authority could vary from 0 to 100 per cent. It could be combined with local campaigns about homeworking – as is going on in London now.

In some areas a start on the 'local end' of such policies has already been made. The initiative is being grasped in some cities where the left now has significant influence. In the West Midlands and Greater London it is hoped that money from local authority and other pension funds will enable the public sector to play a larger and more positive role. Moreover, in both areas the principle of *quid pro quo* is being firmly established. In the West Midlands existing companies will be assisted only on the condition that some combination of local enterprise board control, workers' control or a planning agreement is accepted. It is important to realise that this scheme depends on the workers' agreement and initiative; such 'economic' policies are part of a wider politics.

This is what is most significant about these new ventures at local level: the initiative is coming from a wide variety of sources. In London, decisions on where the local authority should put its money are to be made in consultation with shop stewards, trade unions and trades councils. Sectoral planning is to be undertaken by workers in the industry together with the local authority. New forms of organisation are to be experimented with – and proposals are coming in from boroughs, from co-operatives, from trade unions. Mini-AESs are being devised even at the level of individual London boroughs. The importance of all this as a complete rethinking of the 'inner-city problem' was symbolised by a river trip down the Thames. At each stage of the journey local groups argued how they thought their area should be revived. The trip was laid on by the GLC, but the idea came from a local group. The last time such a voyage took place it was so that the GLC could point out to the property sector the 'potential development sites' along the river!

On their own, obviously, these initiatives cannot reconstruct an employment base for the inner cities. Compared with the scale of the problem, they are tiny. Even with the pension funds, their cash resources are small. Moreover, most production today is organised on a basis which goes far beyond the remit of the local authority, so there are severe constraints on the kinds of company and industry over which individual local areas can have effective control or which they can sensibly organise.

And this, of course, is where the link must be made with a wider framework of spatial policies. Obviously, there must be co-ordination with national investment planning and with other levels of spatial policy. There must also be closer links than in the past with the development of other areas of politics. In the inner-city case the link with policies directed at the financial sector, and at pension funds in particular, is obvious. Inner-city policies based in the inner city must be just a part of a broader politics of location.

It is important these issues are addressed. If they are not, the AES could be as divisive as were previous spatial policies. If they *are* addressed, new areas of political expression will be opened up, potentially linking industrial and community politics.

*This essay first appeared in* Socialism in a Cold Climate, *edited by John Griffith, Unwin Paperbacks, 1983.*

## Note

1 This section draws on an article by the authors entitled 'Going to town on the jobs crisis', *New Socialist,* No. 4, 1982.

# 2

# The Shape of Things to Come

## 1983

### The changing composition of the workforce

The British labour-force is not what it was twenty years ago. The immediate disaster of Thatcherism has thrown into high relief major changes in its composition. Employment in manufacturing has collapsed since the 1979 election. Skilled manual jobs are being cut back drastically. There has even been a drop in the total workforce. It has felt like devastation, and it has been. But the intensity of the effect of Tory policies should not blind us to the fact that underlying them are longer run processes of change. The working class, and the labour force more generally, are undergoing structural changes in composition.

They are profound changes, profound enough to mean that some of the old ways of thinking and working are no longer adequate or appropriate. The labour movement too, if it is to keep ahead of events, must restructure itself, recognise the shifts, address new questions.

But it is not only the social composition of the labour force which is changing. Its geography is also being transformed. The urban and regional structure of the Britain of tomorrow (even after, that is, some recovery from Thatcher) will be different from what we have come to know, and to know how to work within. Regional divisions are being broken down. To be sure, the old north-south divide is being reinforced in terms of voting patterns, but it is not the same old north-south divide of the 1930s. Further, the pattern in which most working class jobs, particularly in manufacturing, were gathered in the towns and cities is crumbling. 'Rural areas' are no longer places without major nonagricultural employment.

This changing geography compounds the challenge facing the labour movement. The changing location of industry breaks down established relations between workplaces, and between workplaces and communities. And the new locations are different. The factory or office is situated in a different context, to which previous forms of organisation may be inappropriate. Geographical change can, in other words, alter the wider social context of the politics of the workplace at the same time as the social composition of the workforce itself is changing. And, indeed, the two processes are related. The geographical re-organisation of British capital has been fundamental to all its attempts over the last twenty years or so to become more competitive, hold down wages, restructure itself out of crisis. Geographical restructuring has already been important to capital, and it should be important to labour.

**Figure 1**: *The changing balance between manual and non-manual workers*

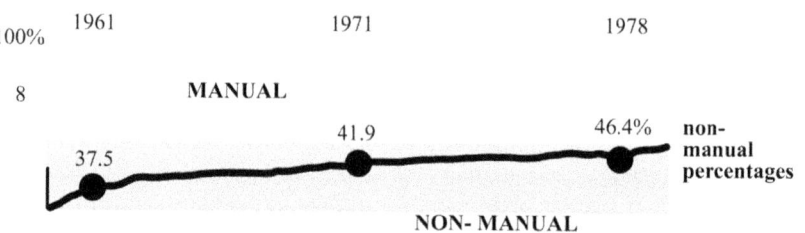

Source: calculated from Warwick University Manpower (*sic*) *Research Group*.[1]

**Table 1**: *Occupational changes 1961-1978*
(% of workforce)

|  | 1961 | 1971 |
|---|---|---|
| Administrators, managers | 6.6 | 7.8 |
| Professionals | 6.6 | 8.1 |
| Engineers & technicians | 3.5 | 4.2 |
| Clerical workers | 14.0 | 15.0 |
| Craft workers | 19.7 | 17.6 |
| Skilled operatives | 3.2 | 3.1 |
| Other operatives | 22.9 | 20.4 |
| Personal services | 8.9 | 10.5 |
| Other | 14.6 | 13.4 |
|  | **100** | **100** |

Source: Karwick Man-Power Research Group

**Figure 2**: *Women in the Workforce*

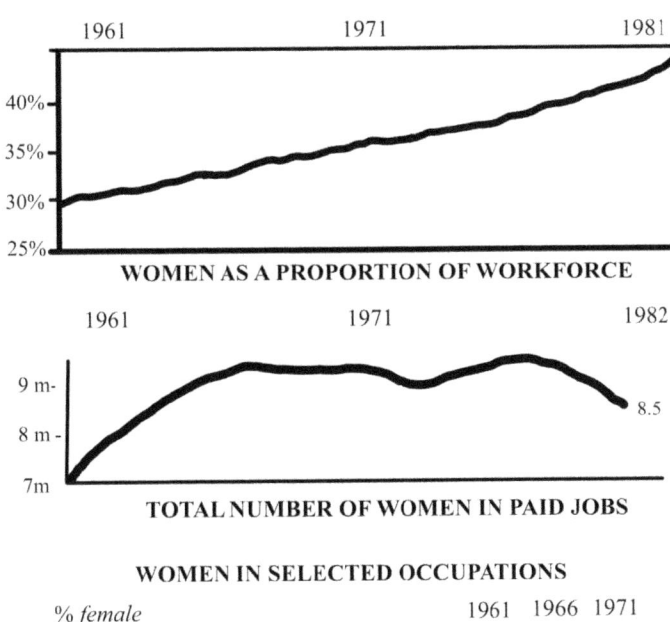

WOMEN IN SELECTED OCCUPATIONS

| % female | 1961 | 1966 | 1971 |
|---|---|---|---|
| White collar workers | 44.5 | 46.5 | 46.2 |
|  | 26.0 | 29.0 | 28.6 |

Source: ACE data; Censuses of Population

## The national level

At the national level there have been significant changes in balance between different elements of the workforce. Figure 1 shows one of the divisions which has long been central to labour movement organisation that between manual and non-manual workers. Manual workers, from having made up over 60 per cent of the working population in 1961 are now down to only about 50 per cent. This change in the shape of the labour force has been going on throughout the postwar period — manual workers having declined by about 5 per cent as a proportion of the total workforce in each postwar decade. To some extent what these figures reflect is the loss of jobs in manufacturing. This too is now a well-established phenomenon. The number of jobs in manufacturing in 1961 was 8.2 million. Since then it has fallen by a quarter and, from 36 per cent in 1961, manufacturing now makes up only 28 per cent of jobs in the economy.

These major shifts are mirrored in the changing occupational structure of the workforce. Within the generally expanding non-manual groups, it has been the higher-status jobs which have been growing fastest as a proportion of the total workforce. And this growth has been accompanied by shifts in the internal composition of each group. The particularly rapid rise in importance of professionals, for example, has been due especially to public sector expansion (we are talking here of the last twenty years!) in health and education. Similarly that wide spectrum of occupations referred to in the table as 'engineers and technicians' has seen engineering-based professionals, draftspeople and so forth, dwindling in importance, while the computer whizz-kid and the research scientist increase in both numbers and status. The managers and administrators have expanded in all parts of the economy: public sector and private, manufacturing and services. In contrast, the increase in the number of clerical workers is not so marked – each clerical worker is evidently now supporting more professionals. The declining groups reflect the obverse of these processes. And here, too, there are significant shifts in the internal composition of each category – the generally declining 'other operatives' group, for instance, includes a growing army of assembly workers.

### Participation of women

Perhaps best known and most important is the increased participation of women in the paid workforce. Figure 2 gives some details. The rise in the number of women in the labour force has not in fact been steady (the figure for 1982 is actually below that for 1964). But the increase in the proportion of the workforce which is female has been far more consistent. This obviously reflects what is happening to male employment – the recent dramatic collapse of jobs for men resulting in a rise in the importance of women in the workforce even though their own numbers were shrinking too.

But these are all national changes. They are substantial enough as they stand, but they also hide a lot else which has been going on.

For these national changes are highly differentiated from one part of the country to another and very different kinds of class changes and shifts in social composition are under way in different regions. A new geography is in the making.

Behind this new geography lie a number of interlocking processes. Each of them is related to long-term shifts in the economy as a whole and to the changing place of Britain in the international system. They can, roughly, be divided into two groups: elements of the geography of decline on the one hand and the emergence of new patterns on the other.

## The geography of decline

The pattern of employment decline in Britain today is actually the result of *two* different patterns, the one superimposed upon the other. On the one hand there is the long term decline of a range of 'old basic' sectors; on the other hand there is the newer, though by now also well-established, loss of employment in manufacturing. These two waves of decline hail originally from different periods, each reflecting the previous dominance of different international divisions of labour, and different structures of the British economy. Each, too, has its own particular geography.

## The 1930s revisited

First, there is the long term decline of jobs for men in the old basic industries of the Development Areas – South Wales, Central Scotland, the North East of England. The loss of jobs in industries such as coal mining and shipbuilding, which once formed the economic core of these areas, has been going on for much of this century. It was the collapse of these pillars of Empire which lay behind the regional concentrations of unemployment and the appalling poverty in these areas in the 1930s. (Unemployment rates in the South East were relatively low). And it was the sudden and rapid loss of jobs in these industries (particularly shipbuilding) which heralded for British industry the end of the long postwar boom and, with that, the re-emergence of 'the regional problem'. Since then the loss of jobs has varied in pace and been modulated by economic climate and political strategy. The contraction of this central element of the working class, then, is long term, and it has had and continues to have a very definite geographical pattern. It is the decline of employment in these industries which is at the heart of the 'traditional' form of the British regional problem.

But that well-known pattern is now being overlaid by another, equally dramatic, pattern of decline.

## Deindustrialisation

Deindustrialisation – reflected in the loss of jobs in manufacturing – has hit the headlines under Margaret Thatcher. But it, too, is a longer term phenomenon. The absolute *number* of jobs in manufacturing has been shrinking in the UK for nearly twenty-five years now – ever since the mid 1960s. And manufacturing's *share* of total employment has been declining for far longer.

Deindustrialisation is certainly of a different order under this government. It has accelerated, and it has spread to virtually all manufacturing sectors. Moreover, it is not just employment, it is also output which is now falling. In the late 1960s job loss in manufacturing took place in a context of rapidly rising productivity and technological change (it was the age of the white heat and productivity agreements). Today far more of it is due simply to the closure of capacity. So there is no question but that what is happening now is of a different order. But the decline of jobs in manufacturing is not itself a new phenomenon.

Now, the geography of the decline of manufacturing is very different from that of the decline of the old basic sectors. For one thing, it is more general – it is not confined to two or three regions of the country. But it does have a definite geographical pattern. The first areas to be hit by deindustrialisation were the cities. Greater London has seen the most spectacular falls. Every five years from 1961 to 1976 200,000 manufacturing jobs were lost from the city's economy. By the end of last year the number of manufacturing jobs in the GLC area was only two-fifths of what it had been in 1961.

A large proportion of the overall decline of jobs in urban areas has in fact been due simply to this decline of manufacturing industry. There has been a relative 'shift' of employment from bigger cities towards smaller towns and more rural areas. But the term 'shift' (the term most frequently used) can give the impression that the whole thing took place through actual geographical movement. It didn't. Much of it has been a process of differential growth and decline. A large part of the loss of manufacturing jobs in major urban areas has taken place through straightforward closure, with no new investment elsewhere – or certainly not in the UK.

## Decline of the cities

The loss of manufacturing jobs in the cities has not, for the most part, been because they had a high proportion of jobs in industries which were declining fastest nationally. It was not, in other words, a result of the cities' industrial structure – as it was the industrial structure of South Wales and the North East which lay behind the collapse of their employment in the 1930s. The cities suffered most because, *within* particular industries, they tended to have the oldest factories and the oldest production techniques. Most of all they had the lowest levels of labour productivity.

There were other reasons, too. In a number of cases we studied in the late 1960s, management argued that it was easier to close a plant in a large and complex labour market than in a smaller town – the job losses are absorbed, the unemployment diluted, and less 'blame' gets pinned on the individual company.[2] It was also the case that workers in the cities had often won higher wages and, in manufacturing industries, were better organised than those in more out-of-town locations. Whether explicitly motivated or not, the decline of manufacturing industry in the cities has certainly taken with it some of the old bastions of trade union strength.

But it is not *only* the cities which have been hit. As deindustrialisation has accelerated, it has spread both to more and more industries and to more and more places. The regions which have been worst affected have been those with the greatest reliance on manufacturing. The economies of the engineering-based regions, in particular the West Midlands and the North West, have been shattered. Manufacturing employment in the North West has been falling since the early 1960s, gradually picking up speed to lose 20 per cent between 1966 and 1976. In the West Midlands manufacturing jobs carried on increasing until the early 1970s. But in the four years from 1978 to 1982 each of those two regions lost over 200,000 jobs, a further 20 per cent of the manufacturing workforce in each case.

## The changing map of unemployment

So two contrasting patterns of job loss, stemming initially from very different eras, have in recent years been superimposed upon each other. The result is that the map of unemployment is now very different from the one we have been used to since the 1930s. Some elements have acquired an apparent permanence – the unemployment rate in Northern Ireland is now almost 20 per cent. But the rates in the North West and the West Midlands are now above that of Scotland. Only the South East stands out as significantly better than the national average. And that itself conceals enormous differences. Within each region, the inner cities of the major conurbations have rates of unemployment far above the national average. In London most inner-area boroughs have more in common with inner-cities elsewhere than with the outer-metropolitan area.

## The shape of the new: geographical restructuring

But it is not all decline. The employment which remains is also being restructured geographically. And the sectors which are growing (at least over the longer term) have very different geographical patterns from the ones they are replacing. The way industry makes use of the British space is being reorganised. This process has been particularly marked since the mid 1960s when pressures of increasing international competition and a shifting world order began to enforce a restructuring of British industry. That restructuring has changed a number of times in both its form and its pace in the years since then. But its net result has been to produce a major shift in the social geography of the workforce. The geography of each element of that workforce is being reorganised. And this is happening at the same time, remember, as the balance between these different elements is also shifting (Table 1).

The changing balance of corporate structures in the economy is reflected most obviously in the changing geography of management. This is discussed next. Having established that framework, it is then easier to examine the internal reorganisation of the rest of the workforce, concentrating here on the categories of production and clerical workers, and scientists and technicians.

## The geography of management

Look first, because it is the simplest, at the changing geography of management. At the heart of this change is the increasing size of individual companies and the growing dominance of the top few hundred firms. As firms have grown there has been a tendency for their head offices and upper echelons of administrative, marketing, financial and legal staff, etc, to be split off spatially from production, and increasingly the tendency is for them to be concentrated in London and the south east of England. As Table 1 showed, this stratum of managerial and associated groups has been expanding as a proportion of the national population, and it should be stressed that employment in this kind of white collar work has been growing in all regions.

But as it has grown it has also become more highly differentiated, both functionally and socially; management hierarchies have lengthened. And hand in hand with this increasing social differentiation has gone increasing geographical differentiation. The lengthening managerial hierarchies, with their associated hierarchies of functions and social status, have been stretched out over space. And the geographical pattern has taken on a very definite form – the higher level functions, the ultimate control over production, over the relations of economic ownership and possession, and the upper echelons of social strata with which such functions are associated – are increasingly concentrated in the bottom right-hand corner of the country. In 1977, 350 of the top 500 UK companies had their headquarters, and therefore all their top management, in London and the South East. In contrast, the lower the level of management, the nearer to actual production it tends to be geographically. And while HQs concentrate in the South East, the corollary is that other regions are increasingly becoming 'branch-plant' economies.

## Decentralisation of production and clerical jobs

In contrast to what has happened to management, and contrary to a long and dearly-held thesis on the Left, the concentration and centralisation of capital in ownership terms has *not* led to the geographical concentration of jobs in *production*. Indeed at precisely the same time as the concentration (both spatial and a-spatial) of ownership and control has been going on, the location of production itself has become more decentralised, both within individual regions, outwards from cities, and from the south-east and midlands of England to the regions of the north and west.

Some of this relative shift has been associated with changes in the technology of production. In a whole range of industries the kind of technological change which has been going on over the last twenty years or so has been associated with a changing demand for labour. Industries such as telecommunications, parts of electrical engineering, and electronics, are the most obvious examples. In such industries, both changes in the product (e.g., in telecommunications from electro-mechanical to semi-electronic switching gear) and changes in the production process towards more highly mechanised techniques or techniques involving major assembly stages have gone along with a shift in the kind of labour employed. The archetypal shift is from male manual workers classified as skilled to female assemblers classified as unskilled or semi-skilled.

Such changes in the social composition of the labour force are often accompanied by geographical recomposition. They have 'freed' industry from its traditional sources of labour in the old centres of manufacturing skills and have been part and parcel of a significant decentralisation to pastures, and labour forces, new. The existing workforce has been abandoned and new and different labour employed in areas with no tradition in the industry, or indeed any industry at all. The social recomposition of the labour force, changes in the technology of production, and changes in location are in such cases integral to each other.

## The service sector

Technical change has been one significant force behind the decentralisation of production, but it has not been the only one. There has also been a significant outward movement of manufacturing jobs, particularly jobs traditionally done by women, but where there has been little technological change in production. Here the driving force has been to find cheaper sources of labour. The clothing industry is a good example. In the 1960s it was caught in a vice. It was under competition from low-cost imports. But its own usual supply of women workers in urban areas (particularly London) was threatened by the expansion of the service sector. Big firms in the industry solved the dilemma by changing location. New sources of labour, more vulnerable and with fewer alternative sources of employment, were sought out. The new source of labour was older, married women, the new locations were smaller towns, trading estates and sometimes quite isolated locations in the peripheral regions of the country – the rural areas such as the South West and old heavy-industry areas such as the coalfields.

Nor has it just been manufacturing which has decentralised. Not many years later the service sector adopted the same strategy, and new geographical patterns of employment were developed there too. Both clerical wages and office rents decline once you get further than about sixty miles from London, and from the 1970s departments of the central state and large private sector firms began decentralising the more routine elements of clerical work. Clerical workers are an increasingly important part of the labour force (see Table 1), and this decentralisation is therefore a significant element of its changing geography. Longbenton in the North East is a classic example – 6,000 clerical workers process you through the DHSS here. Driving licenses are issued by nearly 4,000 similar workers in Swansea. In some areas, such as the North East, this has represented an increase in jobs available to women where there had been precious little before. In other cases the service industry arrived to compete with others, in the East Midlands, for example, chasing the shoe industry (with many of the same pressures on it as in clothing) even further north.

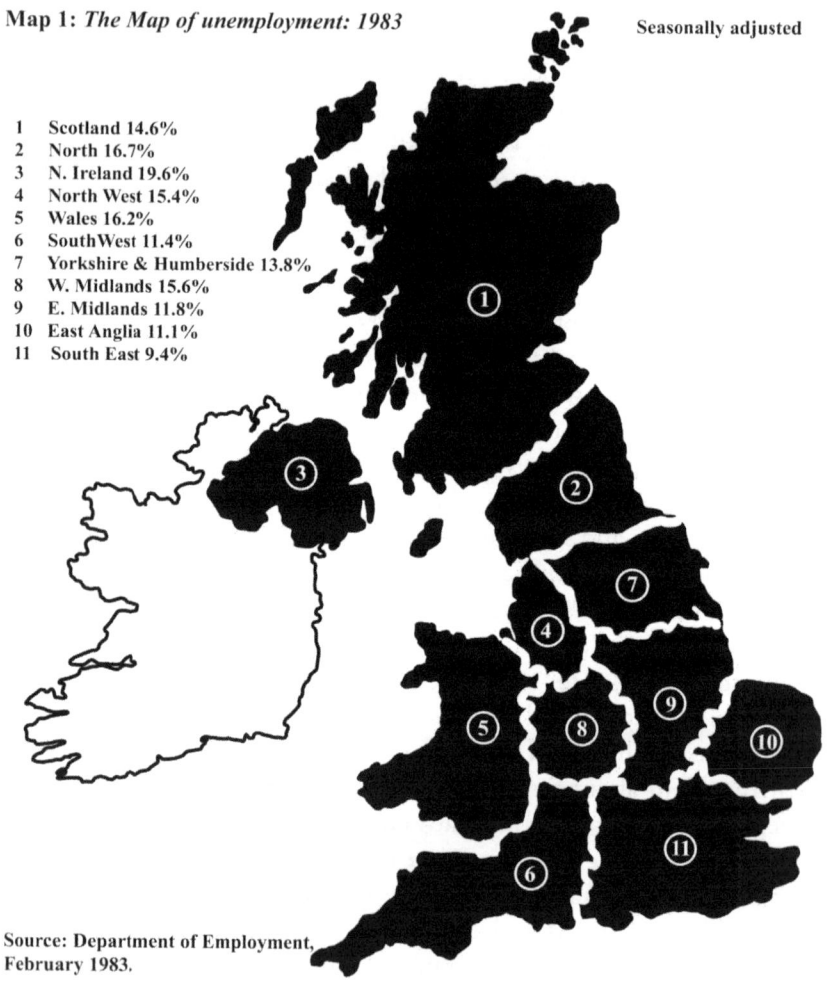

Map 1: *The Map of unemployment: 1983*       Seasonally adjusted

1   Scotland 14.6%
2   North 16.7%
3   N. Ireland 19.6%
4   North West 15.4%
5   Wales 16.2%
6   SouthWest 11.4%
7   Yorkshire & Humberside 13.8%
8   W. Midlands 15.6%
9   E. Midlands 11.8%
10  East Anglia 11.1%
11  South East 9.4%

Source: Department of Employment, February 1983.

## Scientists and technicians

While these changes have been affecting workers directly involved in production, other things have been going on at the other end of the social spectrum. An increasing proportion of the workforce is engaged in research and development and related activities, either in the research establishments of major corporations in a wide variety of industries, or in independent 'business-services' of various sorts (software consultancies, for example), or in the newly-developing hi-tech sectors. To some extent the growth of this element of the workforce is bound up with the same technological changes which produced the deskilled and decentralised production jobs. They are the necessary counterpoint to that production labour force in a long process of the separation of conception from execution.

And their geographical distribution, too, is very different. As with managerial hierarchies, so with the technical division of labour – the separation-out of a whole series of distinct functions, each related to a particular social status, has enabled also their geographical separation. The further you are from production in a functional sense the further you can be distanced geographically. The industrial technologists of a generation and more ago had a far more intimate relationship to the actual process of production than do, except in the prototype stage, the emerging technologists of today. And big companies have taken advantage of that fact, separating out geographically the different parts of the organisation into hierarchical geographical structures.

## The British sunbelt

The upper echelons of these technocratic strata have increasingly concentrated in a new 'region' of the country – the British sunbelt as it is called, that swathe of tamed rurality which stretches between Bristol, Southampton and round and up to Cambridge. The outer-outer metroplitan area. In startling contrast to the tedious assembly and clerical jobs which have for years been the main new source of employment outside this belt, and particularly in the old coal and steel areas, these jobs are almost all for graduates, and almost all for men.

And it is not just big companies. It is in this stretch of country that the new – and still small – breed of entrepreneur/scientist is gathered. Indeed it is only in this part of the country that 'the small-firm sector' lives up to its image of entrepreneurship and dynamism. What are biotechnology and software consultancies here tend in other areas to be sweatshops and scrap-metal dealers.

**Map 2:** *The Shape of things to come*

**'The sunbelt'**
All elements of the workforce, but particularly
0 New high-tech industries     <*
0 R and D of major corporations    I
9 HQs of major corporations    )

(London, not itself in the sunbelt, has
0 HQs of major corporations   -J
• The City    ^J~
% Head offices of central government.)

**'The Rest'**
production and clerical jobs
branch-plant economies —
absence of HQs
absence of R and D
declining importance of major cites

But why this part of the country? Certainly there are some plausible economic reasons; but there are social reasons too, and it is arguable that they may be at least equally important. The attraction of the area originally was a combination of accessibility to London and nearness to defence establishments. The latter provided both jobs for technicians and contracts for the growing electronics industry. But since then the place has taken off in another way. The research scientists, the technologists, those working in business services, make up the stratum of the labour force most able to choose where to live, and assume that jobs will follow. And they do. And jobs do follow. The region *itself* now has a status, a cachet, attached to it. The highly interlinked and individualistic nature of the labour market for these groups reinforces the tendency to clustering, making it difficult for other areas to compete. (And if they do try they have to do it by projecting the same image – semi-rurality, detached housing, 'good' schools.) A whole new style is being created in living, and working, outside the city.

## A new geography

Were all these trends to continue, the social geography of the British workforce would be transformed. Map 2 is a caricature, but it helps highlight the magnitude of the changes under way.

Compare it with fifty years ago. The old regional specialisms (cotton, coal, cars) have gone. The main regional contrast, in this future, is between control and conception on the one hand and execution on the other, between the sunbelt and the rest.

Of course in fact the picture is more complicated than this. Much of the old geography remains. The West Midlands, the North West, the big cities and the heavy industrial areas of the North and West, still retain much of their old economic structure. The development of the new geography (as opposed to the accelerated decline of the old) has in fact slowed down over the late 1970s, and has been interrupted by Thatcherism. The expansion of technicians and professionals, and their concentration into the sunbelt, was at its height in the late 1960s and early 1970s. So was the growth of jobs in out-of-town and smaller-town locations. Many jobs for women, in the new decentralised branch plants, have disappeared in the last few years. But the shift towards a new geography is a long term one, and is likely to re-emerge.

## The importance of local diversity

The fact that the social recomposition of the workforce also involves geographical reorganisation has a number of implications. Most importantly, it means that completely different kinds of social change can be going on in different localities. Not everywhere mirrors the national pattern – in all likelihood very few places do. The classic picture of the dwindling and disintegration of the heart of the traditional labour movement is found most clearly in the old heavy-industry and coalfield areas (for instance South Wales). In these areas, certainly, there is the fragmentation of a previous, relatively coherent, economic structure based around a few industries, and a few unions. Here too jobs for women are expanding fast and jobs for men contracting, there is a proliferation of industries and employers, often with little connection to each other, and an expansion of white collar strata.

But it is not everywhere like this. In some more rural areas the numerical importance and the structural coherence of the working class is actually *increasing* over the medium term as a result of the geographical decentralisation of industry. Cornwall is an example. Here, new employment has come into an area where the previous economic and social structure was based around self-employment and small-scale employment in agriculture and tourism. Straightforward wage-labour has been a very much less important element here than in other regions. Today that picture is changing. The traditional petty bourgeoisie is declining fast, and while a stratum of managers and professionals is certainly expanding, so too is the working class.

So the directions of social recomposition can be quite different from one area to the next. 'National' changes can take highly variegated forms across the country. The decline of the old is not always happening in the same place as the rise of the new. And what that means is that different problems are being faced, different battles fought out, in different places.

## The process of change

And it is important to remember that recomposition is a *process*. What has to be recognised politically is not just some end-state looking very different from what we've been used to, but also a process of social change which may often be difficult and painful. The actual process of change is itself an important determinant of the social and political response.

And this process of change varies locally. Where an area is coming from can be just as important as where it is going to for understanding the political climate. What are apparently similar numerical changes can have very different implications depending on the regional setting. The impact of rising unemployment, for instance, can vary dramatically depending on the wider social context, and on the historical experience of those in the area.

People in the West Midlands are newly coping with not being the boom centre of the land. To some extent epitomised by the car workers, it has gone from cocky aggressivity to agreeing to new work practices. There is a real shock of sudden vulnerability and eroding status and relative, as well as real, wages. This shock of the new is in total contrast to the weary and deeply resentful return, yet again, to high unemployment, the status of disaster area, you feel in South Wales, the north-east of England or even Merseyside. In London and the South East, the lengthy decline of the East End is apparently more like that of the older regions, but here the context is so different. From Docklands you can see the City and if you venture into town you are faced, still, with well-heeled white collar workers and the denizens of the stockbroker belt.

## The geography of gender relations

Nor is it just changes in class relations which vary across the country. There is a geography of gender-relations, too. Particularly over the last twenty years, women have been increasingly participating in the waged-labour force in all regions, but the increases have been biggest in the peripheral regions (South West, Wales, Scotland and the North East), both urban and rural, to which jobs have been decentralised. And once again, the numbers don't tell the whole story. The impact of an increase in women's participation in paid employment depends on the prevailing system of gender relations. And this varies a lot between one part of the country and another.

Possibly the extreme cases are the old heavy industry Development Areas, especially the coalfields. The 'decline' of these regions should be assessed not just from the point of view that they were heavily working class areas, and highly unionised, but also from the point of view that they were extremely *male*. As far as paid employment is concerned, the opportunities for women have been extremely limited in these regions throughout the century. This has in part been related to the nature of employment for men, and the status attached to it. The demands put on (female) domestic labour by male work down the mine are enormous. Shiftwork, too, makes it more difficult for both partners to be employed outside the home. The ideology of a sexual division of labour between breadwinner and home-keeper has probably been more firmly entrenched in these areas than anywhere else in the country.

And the associated attitudes spread beyond the domestic sphere. In clubs, in politics, in unions, women have been excluded from all but a very minor role, perhaps especially in postwar years. Attitudes existed which would be unthinkable in Lancashire, say, or London. The now-mourned homogeneity of the labour movement in these regions was based around a rigid sexual division of labour. And the shift in the sexual balance of the paid labour force has sorely disrupted this established set of practices and relations. So much so, indeed, that the late 1960s and 1970s saw calls, from male trade unionists, academics and politicians alike, for more jobs specifically for men and, in some cases, less jobs for women – a House of Commons memorandum pleaded that the established sexual balance of employment should not be too severely disrupted.

It is interesting to speculate on the degree to which this highly patriarchial past has been one of the conditions for the threat currently posed to it. Certainly, given the previous reliance on female domestic labour, the decline of male employment was an important condition for the formation of the women of these areas into a 'reserve of labour'. They were, moreover, a particularly attractive one, from industry's point of view. More than almost anywhere else in the country they lacked previous experience of employment in capitalist wage relations. They were real 'green labour'. And their previous exclusion from public life seemed to make them ideal. To the extent that it was complicit in the rigidity of the sexual division of labour in these regions, and in the exclusion of women from so many social activities, the old traditional heart of the (male) labour movement may well itself have been party to the creation of the new super-cheap labour forces industry was searching out in the 1960s and 1970s. Certainly, the geography of gender relations has been an important element in British industry's attempts to reorganise geographically; to restructure itself out of crisis.

## Local politics and national politics

In the 1960s and 1970s much of the importance of 'local polities' was seen to be in linking the local to the national, the particularities of a local area to the wider underlying mechanisms of a capitalist society. Failure to make that link was often seen as failure of the exercise as a whole. That job is still there, still needs to be done. But it did perhaps lead to a tendency to see *only* the 'wider capitalist system' at work in every local situation. The local particularities were seen as something to be cleared away to reveal what was *really* happening. But part of the importance of local politics is precisely in learning how that 'capitalist system' gets worked out in people's lives in the detailed specificity of a vast variety of local situations. 'What is really happening' *is* actually very varied. Unity between those situations isn't constructed only by proclaiming that each and every local change is underlain by capitalism: only, in other words, by asserting 'the general'. It also needs, for a solid foundation, a recognition and understanding of the reality and conditions of diversity, and of the actual processes which link the local particularities.

Geographical diversity matters politically in other ways, too. Above all it can be divisive. It is not just that 'national' changes are reflected in a geographically differentiated form, but that geographical diversity can be used as a weapon in a wider politics. The way this happens can vary, has varied, widely. In the 1960s, that combination of technological change and locational change which was mentioned earlier often set workers in one area against those in another, in the context of an individual company. More recently, as that process has slowed down, and high unemployment has spread to more and more places, 'inter-area competition' has become a weapon in the hands of both individual companies and the state. The Nissan episode, with over 100 local authorities competing against each other, has been the most glaring example of the former.

More generally, areas compete with each other by advertising the non-militancy of their labour. Regions are blamed for their own decline. The reputation for militancy of Merseyside workers is the most obvious case. In 1978 there was an attempt to draw up a local social contract; in 1979, just after the election, Prior visited the area to announce that if there were no strikes there for two years, some investment might be forthcoming. Only recently, a report on East Kilbride assured would-be investors that the situation was nothing like as bad as they might have thought – an investigation had shown that the workers there were hardly militant at all! And so the vulnerabilities of particular areas are used in a wider battle between capital and labour.

## The politics of recomposition

The joint social and geographical restructuring of the labour force is, then, producing very different conditions for political organisation and representation from those we have come to know and love. It is easy to feel that all is lost. Indeed a quick survey of socialist thoughts upon the subject of the presently-emerging geography of the working class would indicate a depressing assessment of its potential as a base for organisation.

Certainly we have been witness to the erosion of well-established and familiar bases. To the long decline of the industrial unions of the old periphery has now been added the subduing of the strength of the West Midlands. In many areas the accustomed social infrastructure of organisation has been torn apart by industrial decline. At the intra-regional scale, New Towns are well known for the passivity, in general, of their labour forces. The *process* of geographical recomposition is itself a problem. Much of the strength of the labour movement is constructed around local histories, and their dislocation can produce a sense of placelessness in the strong meaning of that word.

But on its own that negative assessment misses a lot. It is not just decline that is going on; it is recomposition. And there have been such recompositions before. The interwar years saw a massive social and spatial restructuring of employment. It was then that the basic industries plunged into decline; and the new sectors which grew up were completely different. They were at the other end of the country – in the Midlands and South East. They demanded different skills, implied a different social structure. And the unions which organised in them (TGWU, NUGMW) were different, too. This is *not* to imply that each and every change should be accepted, nor, certainly, that the present form of spatial recomposition is politically inevitable. It is merely to point out that what we have now was once itself new and untried; the organisational frameworks which are now so familiar themselves had once to be built.

Moreover, much of what is now thought of as new has not been absent before; it has simply been ignored. The past which it is commonly thought we are leaving has been inaccurately mythologised. Take this 'new' entry of women into manual jobs – women now represent about 30 per cent of all manual workers, which is about the same as in 1911! If any thing it has been the intervening years which have been the exception. Again, manufacturing employment has *never* been numerically dominant in the economy. And some of the strongest points of the labour movement have always been outside manufacturing – coal mining is the most obvious example.

So there is a need to readjust our stylised image of the past. And, anyway, we should not just be seeking the restoration of the old and well-tried. After all, it wasn't a spectacular success. We cannot re-create the old labour movement of the coalfields, for instance, and it, too, had its share of disadvantages and its own vulnerabilities.

But there *have* been major changes. And they do require a response. Is the outlook, then, as grim as most assessments would have it? Is no response possible?

One counter to the bleakest scenarios of the future is that they are, curiously, very geographically determinist. It is argued, for instance, that the great cities, with their variety of enterprises and industries, and with their anonymity, provided ideal places for union organisation, and that that is now gone. In one sense it is true. But that union organisation had to be constructed, and the form which it took corresponded to, took advantage of, the setting. That was how that particular 'geography', the urban form, was used to advantage. But by no means all the old centres of trade union strength had those characteristics. Some of the strongest bases were in small, single-industry settlements colliery villages for example.

There are now different situations, demanding different strategies and forms of organisation. The 'new geography' may look pretty unprepossessing at first sight, but there are possibilities. The problems of organising in multi-regional companies are clear, but such companies do open up new potential contact between areas. It is a difficult potential to grasp, but then it wasn't so simple to build unity on the coalfields either. The growth in numbers, unionisation and militancy of public sector workers offers opportunities at local level for linking employment with community issues, and possibilities at national level for coordinated action entailing a presence in every locality, which no other industry provides.

The problem is that the movement always seems to be on the receiving end of such processes: never to hold the initiative. The impetus for industrial restructuring has come in an immediate sense from capital. And much of it is a response to, and an attempt to break, established elements of labour movement organisation. Certainly this has been true spatially. The decline of the cities has had as one element a relative shift away from better organised workers. At the other end of the process the decentralisation of production has certainly seen managements seeking out potentially vulnerable and difficult-to-organise workforces. But the fact that that was part of the rationale does not guarantee success. At each end of the process there is now a fight back. The cities are far from dead politically, however much they might be losing jobs. The fact of decline, together with their changing social structure, has been a basis for some of them to become the seedbeds of a new kind of politics, based around new coalitions, and attempting a restructuring more on labour's terms. And it is not just the big cities. The examples of Plessey-Bathgate, of Lee Jeans and Lovable, give notice that capital might just have been mistaken in its assumption that the women workers of 'the regions' would not get organised.

So the situation is *not* all gloom and doom. There are already attempts to respond, to take back some of the initiative. But for that to be possible in a wider way does demand that we recognise the extent and the depth of the structural changes which are going on. It is certainly not that old bases, either socially or geographically, should be abandoned. But it is urgent to recognise both that they themselves are changing and that new bases must be constructed – both amongst the expanding elements of the workforce and in new parts of the country.

*This essay first appeared in* Marxism Today *in April 1983.*

## Notes

1. Thanks to Nick Miles for help in getting together the data for these figures.
2. Doreen Massey and Richard Meegan, 'The Geography of Industrial Reorganisation', *Progress in Planning*, Vol. 10, No. 3, Pergamon: Oxford, 1979.

# 3

# Heartlands of Defeat

## 1987

The election of 1983 was not an aberration. The patterns that were evident then are stronger now. What happened in this election, fundamentally, was that Labour strengthened its position in its traditional bases, but failed to break out of them. The Conservatives also consolidated their hold where they were already strong. The difference is that they have power, and they have a strategy for attacking Labour's citadels, especially in the inner cities. Labour is out of power, and as yet has no strategy for addressing those elements of Thatcherland – the bulk of the working class in the towns of the outer South East for instance – which we should have on our side.

That Labour further strengthened its position within its traditional strongholds can be seen, first, by looking at social patterns of voting. In all the groups where Labour was already the strongest party, it consolidated its position even more. Such groups are Labour's social base: semi-skilled and unskilled workers, council tenants, the unemployed, northern men, and trade unionists (see Table 1). In all of these groups the party achieved increases in its share of the vote way above the national average. There *are* some new additions over the picture in 1983, and interestingly they are all among women. Among women aged eighteen to twenty-four, among women in the north of Great Britain, and women trade unionists, Labour was not the strongest party in 1983. In 1987 it is.

A similar picture emerges if we look at groups where Labour did relatively well in 1983, getting 2 per cent more than its national share. As well as the groups already mentioned, this category includes all men, skilled workers, the relatively young, and midlands men (see Table 1). In most of these groups too, Labour did better than average in this election. Interestingly, *all* of the groups where this was *not* true were male.

In these social strongholds, Labour strengthened its position more among women than among men, though women had started from a less strong position. What this means is, and this seems to be true overall, that the gender gap is closing. So there has been a strengthening of the 1983 base especially by drawing in more women.

But the base has not been extended. There are *no* new groups, in 1987, showing ahead of the national average by more than 2 per cent. A number of groups did increase their vote for Labour considerably more than the national average. These were women (up 6 per cent), women in the age group twenty-five to thirty-four (up 8 per cent, while the male vote in that age group went down slightly), women between fifty-five and sixty-four (up 6 per cent) and over sixty-five (8 per cent), men over sixty-five (5 per cent), and therefore pensioners as a group (up 6 per cent), and working class home-owners (up 7 per cent). But none of these groups shot way ahead of Labour's national average.

If we look in more detail *within* social groups, a similar pattern emerges. In the middle class (Table 2), Labour is the weakest party in every group. The Tories have an enormous lead not only among private-sector but also among public-sector middle-class voters. Labour's highest share is among the university-educated group and it was here that it increased its vote. In total contrast, the *Guardian* also reported a poll of the 'self-made' middle class, those who have received no form of further education. They voted Tory by a massive 74 per cent as did the majority (57 per cent) of those with some form of further education, but short of a degree. It gives another slant to cuts in higher education.

Finally, and most importantly, look at the working class. Here Labour's vote did strengthen solidly amongst working class council tenants *and* working class owner-occupiers (see Table 1). Indeed all the polls show the Tory lead being cut back quite sharply among this latter group. So there are some signs of movement. Labour increased its vote only slightly among the growing white-collar clerical group. It achieved an average increase among the (declining) group of skilled workers, though the Conservatives are still the most popular party with this group. It was among unskilled and semiskilled workers, slightly expanded as a proportion of the electorate since 1983, and where Labour was already strongest, that it achieved its biggest increase.

## Table 1 Profile of the Electorate

| % of 1987 Total Voters | | The 1983 Vote | | | The 1987 Vote | | |
|---|---|---|---|---|---|---|---|
| | | Con | Lab | All | Con | Lab | All |
| 100 | Total | 44 | 28 | 26 | 43 | 32 | 23 |
| 49 | Men | 42 | 30 | 25 | 43 | 32 | 23 |
| 51 | Women | 46 | 26 | 27 | 43 | 32 | 23 |
| 14 | 18-24 | 42 | 33 | 22 | 33 | 40 | 21 |
| 19 | 25-34 | 40 | 29 | 29 | 39 | 33 | 25 |
| 33 | 35-54 | 44 | 27 | 27 | 45 | 29 | 24 |
| 34 | 55+ | 47 | 27 | 24 | 46 | 31 | 21 |
| 23 | Pensioner | 51 | 25 | 23 | 47 | 31 | 21 |
| 19 | AB -prof/managerial | 60 | 10 | 28 | 57 | 14 | 26 |
| 24 | C1-white coller | 51 | 20 | 27 | 51 | 21 | 26 |
| 27 | C2-skilled workers | 40 | 32 | 26 | 40 | 36 | 22 |
| 30 | DE-semi-skilled/unskilled | 33 | 41 | 24 | 30 | 48 | 20 |
| 67 | Owner occupier | 52 | 19 | 28 | 50 | 23 | 25 |
| 23 | Council tenants | 26 | 47 | 24 | 22 | 56 | 19 |
| 7 | Private tenants | 41 | 33 | 23 | 39 | 37 | 21 |
| 7 | Men 18-24 | 41 | 35 | 21 | 42 | 37 | 19 |
| 7 | Women 18-24 | 42 | 31 | 25 | 31 | 42 | 24 |
| 9 | Men 25-34 | 37 | 34 | 28 | 41 | 33 | 24 |
| 10 | Women 25-34 | 42 | 25 | 30 | 37 | 33 | 27 |
| 16 | Men 35-54 | 42 | 29 | 27 | 42 | 32 | 24 |
| 17 | Women 35-54 | 46 | 24 | 28 | 47 | 27 | 25 |
| 17 | Men 55+ | 45 | 28 | 25 | 45 | 31 | 23 |
| 17 | Women 55+ | 49 | 26 | 24 | 46 | 32 | 20 |
| 9 | Men 65+ | 50 | 25 | 23 | 47 | 30 | 22 |
| 9 | Women 65+ | 51 | 25 | 23 | 46 | 33 | 20 |
| 4 | Unemployed men | 25 | 49 | 24 | 21 | 56 | 20 |
| 3 | Unemployed women | 32 | 41 | 24 | 23 | 54 | 19 |
| 17 | North men | 35 | 39 | 24 | 34 | 42 | 20 |
| 19 | North women | 40 | 33 | 25 | 33 | 41 | 22 |
| 13 | Midland men | 43 | 31 | 23 | 46 | 34 | 19 |
| 13 | Midland women | 46 | 27 | 24 | 45 | 29 | 24 |
| 19 | South men | 48 | 23 | 28 | 49 | 22 | 28 |
| 20 | South women | 51 | 19 | 30 | 51 | 24 | 24 |
| | Home owners | | | | | | |
| 36 | Middle class | 58 | 12 | 29 | 57 | 15 | 26 |
| 31 | Working class | 46 | 25 | 27 | 43 | 32 | 23 |
| | Council tenants | | | | | | |
| 2 | Middle class | 32 | 39 | 25 | 28 | 41 | 24 |
| 21 | Working class | 25 | 49 | 24 | 21 | 58 | 18 |
| | Trade unions | | | | | | |
| 23 | Members | 31 | 39 | 29 | 30 | 42 | 26 |
| 15 | Men | 29 | 41 | 28 | 31 | 42 | 25 |
| 8 | Women | 34 | 34 | 31 | 29 | 41 | 27 |

The statistics above are taken from an aggregate number analysis of 23,396 voters in Great Britain interviewed by Mori during the election, weighted to the actual outcome.
Source: *Sunday Times*, 14 June 1987.

## Table 2 The New Divisions in the Middle Classes

| | University Educated | | Public Sector | | Private Sector | |
|---|---|---|---|---|---|---|
| | 1987 | 1983-87 | 1987 | 1983-87 | 1987 | 1983-87 |
| Con | 34 | -9 | 44 | -4 | 65 | +1 |
| Lab | 29 | +3 | 24 | — | 13 | — |
| Lib/SDP | 36 | +4 | 32 | +4 | 22 | -1 |
| Swing From: | | | | | | |
| Con to Lab | | 6 | | 2 | | -½ |
| Lib/SDP to Lab | | -½ | | -2 | | ½ |
| Lib/SDP to Con | | -6½ | | -4 | | 1 |

Source: *The Guardian*, 15 June 1987

Basically, however you look at it, Labour did best this time where it was already strong. It improved its position on 1983. But there are important reservations. First, this improvement since 1983 has often not been enough to reverse the longer-term trend away from Labour in these bases. Labour's share even of semi-skilled and unskilled voters is still lower than in 1974 (though that was before the SDP). Second, many of the groups in which Labour consolidated its position this time are declining as a proportion of the electorate.

But looking at national figures is not enough. Since the 1950s there has been a growth of local variation in voting patterns in Great Britain, with the Conservatives doing particularly well in the South and in rural areas, and Labour in the North and in urban areas. There has been a growing polarisation both between regions and between urban and rural areas. This time again, these old geographical divides have been further consolidated.

In general, both Labour and Conservatives did best where they were already strongest (see Map 2). Indeed the Tories actually *gained* in some southern regions – something which did not happen in 1983. So at a regional level the political polarisation of Great Britain has been increased. Hardly had a few results come in before the north-south divide became a central theme of political comment. Some of that commentary was belied by the numbers. In particular, the success in Scotland seems to have been overplayed. It is in the north of England, not Scotland, that Labour has its highest share of the vote. And it was in Wales, not Scotland, that Labour's share increased most. What *was* spectacular in Scotland was the loss by the Tories. Yet even here we must not get carried away by what the papers say. Looked at soberly, in the cold light of subsequent days, the Tory vote in Scotland is still higher (and that in spite of there being four parties), than the Labour vote in East Anglia, the South East and the South West.

Indeed, at this other end of the country Labour failed to win in any of the towns of the outer South East, and in particular the new and expanding towns, which it had targeted. These are manufacturing towns. Some of them have a higher percentage of manufacturing in their employment now than many an industrially-devastated town of the North. Basildon, Stevenage, Harlow – all of them are more manufacturing-based today than is Sheffield. Many of these towns also have high unemployment rates. Yet Labour won none of them. In most of them there has been a swing *to* the Conservatives. However the picture for Labour was not appalling. The swings to the Tories were mainly from the Alliance (mainly SDP), not Labour, and in almost all cases Labour did increase its share of the vote. Labour also holds a good number of the local authorities of these towns. Yet it failed to win the constituencies.

So the overall picture still holds: of Labour regaining its strengths in its traditional regions but failing to build bases outside; of the Tories, even in a year when their overall share went down slightly, gaining in the South. The Alliance lost everywhere, although in relation to 1983, Liberal candidates outperformed SDP candidates in all regions save East Anglia and the South East.

The Midlands remain a battleground. The West Midlands was a triumph for Thatcher in 1979, when she captured a significant share of the votes of skilled male trade unionists in the region. In 1987 she failed to advance much on that, but neither did Labour reestablish itself. The Tories are well ahead in a manufacturing region with a strong base of skilled workers and which has been devastated by de-industrialisation. The East Midlands are more a mixture of north and south, and have been a clear target of Thatcherism, with fast-rising homeownership, an economy which in parts shows signs of prosperity, and of course the effects of the Miners' Strike. The Tories were already stronger here than to the west, and they increased their vote further this time. The political divide between north and south is shifting north.

But it is not just regional polarization between north and south that is deepening, but also between urban industrial areas and more rural parts of the country. There are pockets of the North – particularly the North West which Labour has not captured. But the Tories now have *no* seats in the major urban areas of Manchester, Liverpool, Glasgow, Newcastle, Bradford and Leicester, only one in Sheffield, and two in each of Leeds and Edinburgh. And in all these places Labour did well. In Liverpool its performance was spectacular. Within the city, Labour's lowest increase in share was over $7^r$ (Riverside) and its highest was over $13^c c$ (Mossley Hill). David Alton's Liberal majority was slashed, Terry Fields doubled his, Eric Heffer soared ahead. Even in the wider conurbation the picture was the same. Cammel Laird worker Lol Duffy ran Linda Chalker a very close second in

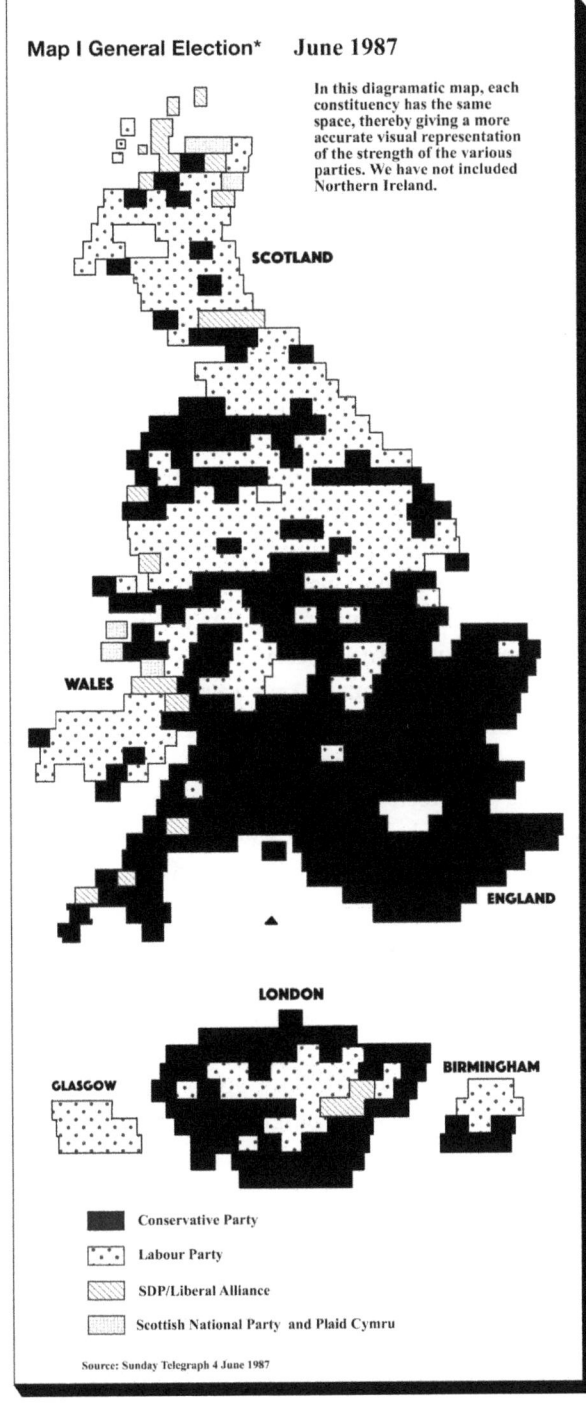

Wallasey. As Fazey commented in the *Financial Times*, 'Merseyside as a whole shifted emphatically leftwards, even in the Wirral'.

The consolidation of this geographical concentration of party support can also be seen by looking at seats where there is a majority of over 20,000. Labour and Conservatives have twenty-eight of these each. In Labour's group the swing to Labour was in every case massive. It was also in all but two cases at the expense of the Alliance; indeed much of Labour's greater strength in 1987 in its traditional groups and areas has come from the Alliance not the Tories. In this case the exceptions were Ogmore (a swing from Plaid Cymru) and all the Liverpool seats, where all the gains were from the Tories. In the Tory seats with a majority over 20,000 the swings were far lower and much more mixed.

Finally, both Labour and Conservative have forty-six seats where they hold more than 60 per cent of the vote. In all but three of Labour's forty-six its share continued to rise even more than, and often massively more than its national average increase of 4 per cent. The three exceptions were in Birmingham (Small Heath and Spark-brook) and Manchester Central. In the Tory group of forty-six there was a less spectacular concentration but in only seven did their share slip more than their national fall of 1 per cent.

This kind of concentration of votes into particular regions has a whole series of effects for Labour. It means that Labour voters are underrepresented in terms of seats. The government is finding it hard to staff its Scottish and Welsh offices. There is dark talk from Scotland of 'Doomsday Scenarios' and the constant question, 'do the Conservatives have the moral authority to govern Scotland'. Most positively, this geographical concentration has been an important condition for the local solidarisms, traditions, and kinds of strength, which are invaluable; which are the basis of a lot of what the labour movement has been built on.

One worrying effect of the geographical polarisation, however, is the real threat now of a divide between North and South within the Labour Party. The newspapers all dwelt on 'the London effect', and blamed it on what they have chosen to call the 'loony Left'. There have been lurid accounts of plans within the party to neuter the so-called London effect, and to crush the hard Left.

So 'left' is conflated within London, all are branded loony, and the hunt is on. Let us hope that none of this is true. Such divisions are right now being used by Margaret Thatcher in launching her attack on local councils and inner cities everywhere.

We should look at these arguments carefully. First, the Left in general, especially individual candidates, did rather well. There is no evidence here for saying that radicalism (or 'extremism') lost Labour the election. But second, is there a London effect and if so what is it? The Greater London area *did* provide the Tories with their biggest increase in share of the vote, higher than any other region (see Map 2). Yet London was *not* the region where Labour did worst. The party performed even less well in all the regions of the South, all the regions surrounding the metropolis.

Nevertheless, the London performance was not good. But the swings in different parts of the city were extremely varied, and there are clearly very different social processes going on beneath them. First there is the group of constituencies afflicted by the invasion of yuppies … Fulham, Battersea and Putney (now called West and South Chelsea by estate agents), Bow and Poplar and Newham South with the influx of bright young things into Docklands, and even Hackney, so conveniently close to the City. All these areas have seen recent rapid increases in professional-managerial groups, helped on by the local council in Wandsworth which has sold off council estates to developers. This is a different kind of population shift from the gentrification of, say, Islington in the 1970s. In the 1970s it was much more likely to be public-sector professionals, today they are from the private sector finance and services above all. And as we have already seen the private- sector middle-class is far more likely to vote Tory.

So that is one group of London constituencies. Other factors are in play elsewhere.

But there *are* places where it seems that 'the Left' does provide the explanation. Candidates in Ealing North and Walthamstow had to fight the election against a background of massive rates increases. Bernie Grant seems to have suffered from the campaign of vilification against him, and possibly from racism. And who knows what role anti-feminist and anti-gay feelings played in Ken Livingstone's reduced majority.

But what is one to say to that? In Ealing, the Labour council inherited dreadful services from the Tories. And the rates penalty means that over half the current rate income will go to the Treasury. Yet even now Ealing has one of the lowest rates in London.

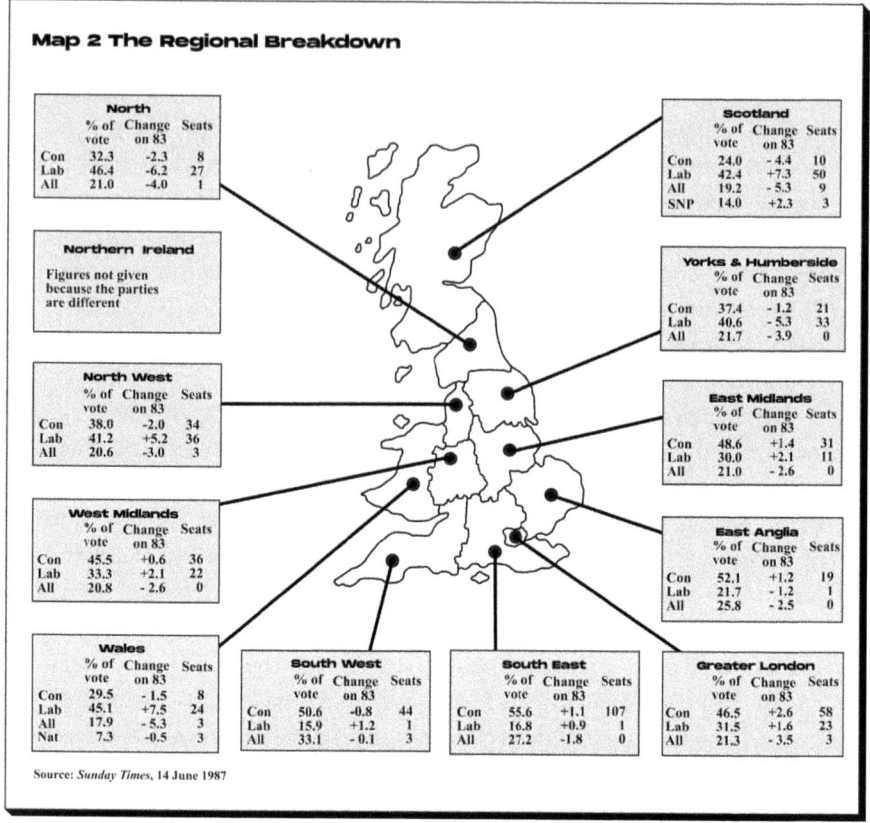

And if there was a vote against Grant and Livingstone we must ask why the effect of the GLC's anti-racist and anti-sexist policies has waned so quickly. The implication is that more work should be done on these issues; not that we should go into reverse.

One thing we have to recognise is that political cultures, and the labour movement, and what will work to make a labour movement popular and successful, varies between different parts of the country. It may be true that some of the issues discussed in London are harder to introduce in parts of 'the North'. It is equally true that northern forms of solidarism cannot be simply imported into the South. So slogans like 'Scotland shows the way to do it' *(The Observer)* are wrong. The Scottish way, the northern way, the Liverpool way even, none of them are going to pull in the punters in Billericay.

And like it or not it is in the South and the Midlands that the frontiers of Labour support have to be extended. The problem seems to be this. Labour has emerged from this election stronger and more consolidated in a base which is electorally too small to win from. The first difficulty this leads to is that this base could be taken too much for granted. It mustn't be. It is about to come under intensified economic and political attack.

The second point is that on almost every dimension Labour has reinforced its position as the party of the 'have-nots'. It is right to point to the chasms that currently exist in British society, and Labour did so in the campaign. But the party must also avoid being only the party that cares, if all that means is redistribution. Redistribution is important, but it is not enough. We also have to say more about *why* those inequalities are produced, and have policies to challenge them at source. In the election, Labour was uncertain in its economic policy, and with reason. To be consistent and convincing to a wider audience, that policy will have to be *more* radical, not less.

The divide in this election was not a class divide. More, it was about immediate self-interest. The evidence is that the best predictor of how individuals would vote was whether they thought the economy had got better or worse, and what they perceived as happening to their living-standards. In other words, people of all classes who are doing well out of Thatcherism, or even who think they may, voted Tory. This cuts across the deeper social divisions. The temptation to buy your council house is far greater in the South where prices are rocketing, than in the North. So, with over three million unemployed and manufacturing output still lower than in 1979, the Conservatives won the economic argument. Enough people feel they are doing OK.

That is the issue which faces us now. How are we going to address these groups? How are we to extend beyond Labour's traditional bases? This issue should now be at the centre of our debate. It is not going to be solved, indeed its solution will be hindered, by recriminations and knee-jerk reactions against incorrect targets like 'the left', however characterised. There are better, more positive, and more important things to do.

This article has not tried to tackle Northern Ireland because it is a special case.

*This essay first appeared in* Marxism Today *in July 1987.*

# 4

# A New Class of Geography

## 1988

Neither the inner city problem nor the north-south divide is new, nor are they simply due to Mrs Thatcher, nor to events during this government's period of office. If one had to point to one basis for the north-south divide, for instance, it would be the concentration in London of control over the British economy and society. And while it is certainly true that this has increased in recent years, it is of much older provenance.

But there have been important recent changes. Under this government the north-south divide has worsened. The changing shape of the economic and social structure has been bound up with a changing social geography. It is that social geography which is the subject of this article. In particular what is clear is that the unequal geography of Thatcherism is closely tied in with this government's championing of the cause of certain already-privileged groups. These groups are the basis of the higher levels of *average* prosperity in the outer areas of the south and east of the country.

Yet there are further changes only now on the horizon. The whole nature of inner cities may be being transformed (and with it the nature of the so-called inner city problem); and even elements of the north-south divide are being re-worked. In the past, political debate over inner cities and 'the north' has often centred on the reasons for decline. These new changes mean that it is more important now to challenge the model of growth.

But first; why anyway does 'geographical inequality' matter? The fundamental divides in this society are social – they are the divides of class, and of race and of gender. Under the Tories since 1979 inequality of many sorts has increased dramatically. There is talk of the Brazilianisation of Britain, of the shoe-shine economy, of the two-thirds: one-third society, of the super-rich and of an underclass.

With all this, why should we be worried if this glaring and increasing inequality in society as a whole is organised geographically so that some *'places'* are poorer than others?

Take the north-south divide as an example. The existence of this geographical inequality affects in a number of ways the working of the whole economy and society.

The most obvious effects are on the labour market. Mrs Thatcher is constantly calling for greater labour market 'flexibility'. Yet the north-south divide introduces a huge rigidity. Even were we to accept that people should have to leave their own areas in search of work, or that established communities should die as other places provide more profitable sites for investment ... even were we to accept all this, it is a commonplace that people today cannot get on their bikes and pedal from north to south.

Most of all, the differential in housing costs makes it impossible. We therefore have the grotesque situation of the coexistence of high unemployment and serious labour shortages. In recent weeks the business pages of newspapers, together with monitors such as Incomes Data Services (IDS), have reported labour scarcities in parts of the south east for a wide range of skills, including construction workers, retail workers, butchers, workers in banking and finance, secretaries, certain engineering skills and a wide range of public sector employees from nurses to teachers and local authority workers.

Much of this has to be taken with a pinch of salt. Employers complain of shortages when what they really mean is they cannot get workers as cheaply as they'd like to. But there is no doubt that there are real shortages too. And they result on the one hand from the national cutbacks in training in recent years and on the other hand from the unequal geography of Britain's economy. Often the skills exist in the economy as a whole, and were those jobs to be located in the north there would be little trouble filling them.

A number of solutions are being resorted to, each of which has its effects. In some cases the jobs lie empty. There has been a spate of reports recently of output being held down by the unavailability of labour. Nothing could be more ridiculous with the levels of unemployment we have nationally. It sharpens even further the point which is frequently made about the waste of human resources implied by unemployment.

In other cases, complicated geographical systems of wage-supplements have been introduced. The London allowance is now just one element in a complex system of wage differentials, within firms and sectors, between the south east and the rest of the country, and within the south east itself. In the introduction to its first *Labour Market Supplement,* on London and the south east, IDS writes: 'In a range of sectors, companies are alternately playing leapfrog and follow-the-leader with London allowances and special payments in an effort to keep retention and recruitment problems under control – no longer to provide cost compensation'. In the short term this may look good to the workers in the particular labour markets involved, though even in their cases the higher wages may get eaten into as they fuel the spiral even more and the cost of living in the south east rises even further. But for the country as a whole it is a nonsense. One set of people with particular skills is seeing its wages rise rapidly while another set of people, with the same skills but living in another part of the country, stays on the dole. Geographical inequality in this case means that income inequality worsens still further.

In yet other cases people do move from north to south to fill the jobs, but being unable to pay the housing costs in the south they work only on a weekly or short-contract basis. This is now an increasingly common phenomenon among skilled manual workers, particularly in sectors such as construction. While working they live in temporary accommodation, sometimes even in caravans. At weekends, or at the end of the contract, they go back home. The disruptive effects on personal and social life are obvious.

At the other end of the social spectrum there is evidence of rigidity in managerial and professional career structures. Given that there are many who do not wish to move to London or the south east, the concentration of 'top jobs' in those regions means that organisations (both private and public sector) are effectively restricting the range of talent they can draw on, as well as restricting the career opportunities of those based outside London.

The north-south divide is costly in other ways, too. While infrastructure is under-used or allowed to fall into decay in the north (the Town and Country Planning Association's document *North-South* points to the under-use of motorways in the north, for instance), the concentration of growth in 'new' semi-'rural' areas of the south east requires investment in new infrastructure to open up these new regions. And that is *public* expenditure. We are writing off already-paid-for investments in the north and paying for more in the south – and *all* of us pay.

What is at issue here is the distinction between public costs and benefits and private costs and benefits. The British economy at the moment is managing to incur both the social and economic costs of decline (in the cities and in the north) and the social and economic costs of congestion (in parts of the outer south east). The increasing battles over the future of the green belt are one manifestation of this. When companies close or leave a community they do not have to include in their calculations all the costs of their decision. Exactly the same is true of private decisions about *new* investment. For the private investor a green-field site may well be the most profitable. But if we were somehow able to do a social audit on the current geography of the British economy, I am sure the balance sheet would not look good.

There are many other ways in which the north-south divide has effects. I have barely touched on the subject here. The point, however, is that rather than just describing its existence and saying how awful it is, we should also be arguing why it matters. The geography of a society has important effects on the way the society works.

Moreover these effects are more than economic and social. The government is using the south – or their version of selected parts of it – against the north. If only other areas could act like this they too could have jobs and growth. So ministers tell the Scottish they need to be more entrepreneurial. Peter Hall, inventor of enterprise zones, writes almost as if 'areas' were subjects in their own right: 'Economic success lies with the country and the region and the city that innovate, that keep one step ahead of the action'.[1] Talking to Teesside Development Council (one of the government's new urban development corporations), a spokesperson mused in the *Financial Times* on its 'entrepreneurship' and 'enterprise' role: 'this secondary role of the TDC is possibly more important than its main one. All it achieves will be dead within a year or two unless we can change the culture. We have got to stimulate a new outlook in the young' (*FT* Feb 26, 1988), and Hamilton-Fazey, the reporter, continued in the same vein: 'Meanwhile the figures for youth business start-ups suggest that the majority will continue to be dependent and expect work to be found for them'. Note that 'dependent' and 'expecting work to be found' for you now apparently means not starting your own business.

It is not just that the outer south east votes for Mrs Thatcher; it is also being held up as the region which most conforms to her ideology.

And in some ways it does. This is the part of the country where levels of unionisation are lowest, and where the percentage of people owning shares is highest. The work-life of the professional strata, which form a more important part of the social structure here than anywhere else in the country, is in the greedy, fast-moving Thatcherite mould. Their labour markets are competitive and individualistic. Fuelled in part by labour shortages (and therefore again specific to this region), turnover is high.

And there is the other side of the Thatcherite imagery, too. The more recent colonisation of this region has been led by the middle class, seeking out the image of a gentrified existence in this manicured, supposedly-rural setting, amid all the imagery of a socially-settled village past in a landscape of church spires and cricket pitches which has so often been held up to typify 'England'. Thus they establish their claim to have 'arrived'.

And this is the important point. The growing relative prosperity of these parts of the outer south east is very much a reflection of long term changes in the social structure, and of this government's championing of the cause of particular groups, both through its economic strategy and through its social policy of redistribution from poor to rich.

Last year in *The Independent,* William Rees-Mogg, unexpectedly declaring himself partial to an occasional bit of class analysis, wrote: 'The new class is the electronic class, whose work is individualistic, often incentive-rewarded, personal rather than impersonal, and related to communications which span the world. It is a far, far, better way of life'. And, he concluded: 'Mrs Thatcher has had eight years in power not by luck, but, in marxist terms, because she has given leadership to the emergent class which is itself being raised to power by real changes in the economy. She was their leader. She still is.'

A glance at the statistics shows' immediately that this group, broadly defined, is indeed the fastest-growing segment of the population in paid work. Moreover, it overwhelmingly clusters in the outer areas of the south east, and in those parts of neighbouring regions, especially East Anglia and the south west, which border on the south east. The only other group to have grown at anything like the same rate is managers and administrators (see table); and they too are heavily concentrated into the south eastern corner of the country (see map). Moreover, in their case the centralisation of headquarters and finance in that region means that it is the upper echelons of the stratum which are most congregated there.

But these groups and the regions they have colonised have not prospered because of a flowering of local entrepreneurship. The government's current urging of the north to follow the example of these regions and rediscover their entrepreneurial spirit flies in the face of the evidence. More than anything else the recent surge in growth and prosperity of these regions has been a result of government policy, state expenditure, and class power.

It has been the result of government policy in numerous ways. At the broadest level it is one of the many results of this government's prioritising of the City over manufacturing. In London over 20 per cent of the employed labour force now works in banking, insurance and finance (in 1981 the figure was 15.9 per cent); and even in the south east region outside London more than one in every ten workers in that sector (11.3 per cent compared with 7.2 per cent in 1981). Other government policies reinforce this emphasis. In particular, restrictive monetary policies have further stimulated the finance sectors of the south while they have put the squeeze on regions where manufacturing is a more important element in the local economy.

The general shift from manufacturing to services is of course not new. But what has changed is the *type* of services which have been growing. From the mid 1960s to the mid 1970s it was public sector and consumer services (health, education etc,) which were more important. Since then – and especially as a result of this government's policy – it has been private sector services (not just banking, but also tourism, professional services etc). And one, among many, of the major differences between public and private sector services is their geography. Public sector consumer services are one of the most evenly-distributed sectors, geographically, in the economy, and they provide one of the few sources of professional employment for women in many areas. In total contrast, private sector services, and especially business services, are overwhelmingly concentrated in 'the south'.

The growth of the outer south east has also been aided by public expenditure. It is often said that the M4 corridor and such areas have prospered without regional aid. In fact, they have had massive regional aid, only by another name. They have had massive expenditure on transport infrastructure. Perhaps most famously, it is in these regions that the majority of government research establishments are located, and these gave an important initial stimulus to the growth there of 'high tech' industries. Recent research has also shown a similar bias in a favoured element of government expenditure – defence equipment.

But it is also class power which has kept the growth of these groups so concentrated in the south and east. The professional and technical groups which are now such an important part of the social structure of the outer south east are not for the most part locals; they migrated there. And it is now well and widely documented that what these strata, and in many cases the companies they work in, want most of all is to be as far away as possible, literally to distance themselves, from dereliction, poverty and decline. And the strength of these groups in the labour market enables them to live where they want to.

All of this together means that it is the combined effect of government policy and the social power of an elite which is currently costing us so dear in terms of the north-south divide. The fact that their incomes have been increasing so rapidly in relative terms only exacerbates the regional divide.

This last point is underlined by analysis of the distribution of incomes between groups and between regions. Moreover the results show that geography and class are reinforcing each other.

Average regional incomes have become more unequal since 1979.

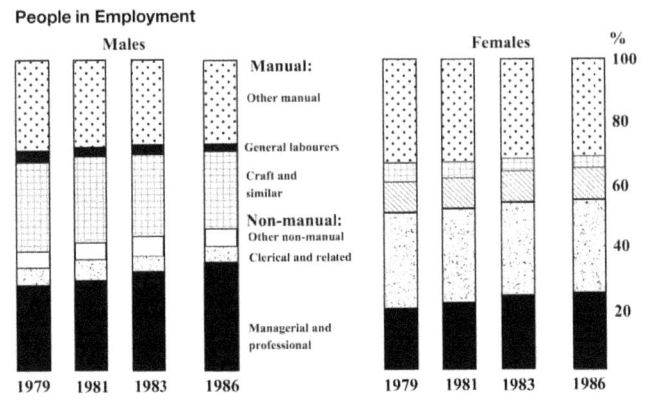

The table shows people in the employment by sex and occupation. It clearly indicates the growth in the 'managerial and professional' category among men and women.

Source: *Labour Force Surveys, Department of Employment*

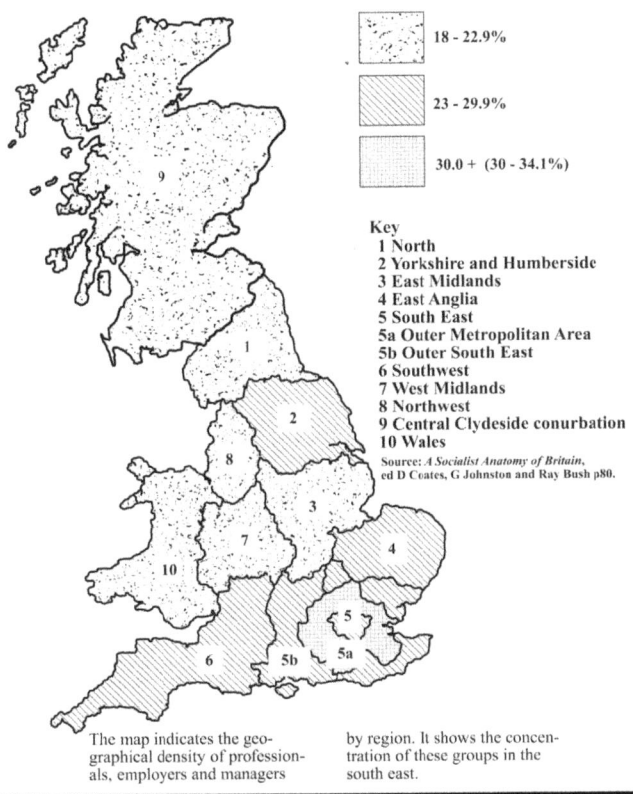

The map indicates the geographical density of professionals, employers and managers by region. It shows the concentration of these groups in the south east.

And the gap is now, much more than in 1979, a question of the south east versus the rest. To give an idea of the magnitude of this, *only* the south east in 1987 had average gross weekly earnings above the average for Great Britain. *All* other regions were below it.

In part these changes are because of the continuing concentration of higher-paid groups into the south east, at the same time as those groups have become relatively better-off. But it is also because of changes in the regional pattern of earnings *within* groups.

First of all, earnings for non-manual workers vary more between regions than do earnings for manual workers. So while wages are highest in the south east for all groups, the differential is greatest for non-manual workers. And it is greatest of all for non-manual men.

Second, for all groups of full-time workers (female/male; manual/non-manual) there is greater inter-regional variation in the earnings of the highly paid than in the earnings of the low paid. That is, the wages in the bottom 10 per cent of earners in the different regions are more similar across regions than are the wages of the top 10 per cent. Moreover, that disparity is greatest of all among male, non-manual workers. And it has increased substantially since 1979. A lot, then, can be laid at the door of highly-paid, non-manual men in the south east of England.

Third, there is evidence that some of the same conclusions apply at a smaller geographical scale; that is, variations within regions and between conurbations, for instance.

All this has a number of important implications.

First, there is a tendency to greater degrees of income inequality (measured here by the gap between the top and bottom 10 per cent of earners) in many areas of *greater average* prosperity. This is particularly true of the south east; the gap between the top 10 per cent and bottom 10 per cent is far higher in the south east than in any other region. What is more, since 1979 that gap has increased more in the south east than in any other region. It is thus quite correct to speak of a 'south-south' divide.[2] The richest region, in average terms, is the most unequal, and is getting worse.

Second, there are very considerable regional variations within the highest-paid groups. There are growing indications of the emergence of different 'types' of middle-class strata in different parts of the country. There is evidence, too, of separate northern and southern career patterns; what has been referred to as 'double-circuitry' the existence of a northern and a southern circuit. If you're in the south you daren't leave; if you're in the north you either don't want to leave or you'd like to but can't afford to get on the southern circuit.

Third, there are very considerable variations between north and south, and within regions, in the way in which poverty is experienced. While upper incomes vary a lot between regions, lower incomes vary much less. And the dole does not vary at all. But the higher level of top incomes in the south east helps fuel the cost of living. For lower-income earners in the south east, and for the unwaged, the problem of finding housing for instance, and the cost of it, is far higher than elsewhere.

Thus, the growing social inequality in Thatcher's Britain is not just reflected in, but is also moulded by, its unequal geography.

And yet, there are now some signs that 'growth', in one form or another, may be beginning to move out of its existing homelands into areas which have up till now been categorised as declining.

To the extent that this is happening, though, it will be founded on the same bases as in the outer south east – public subsidy to private capital and the in-migration of the privileged.

The first of these new changes is what appears to be a rediscovery of the inner city. It is small scale and confined to highly-selected areas but there is evidence of it not only in London, where it is well-established, but in other cities too. There are (at least) two elements to this phenomenon. On the one hand there is the return of certain upper-income groups. On 20 March, *The Observer's* property pages went to Poplar in London: 'What you could really be looking at though ... are council houses' ... some of them ... 'are not too bad at all'. The going rate was around £82,000. In the same week Wimpey Homes was given a £3.3 million urban regeneration grant towards a £10.8 million quality housing project in central Manchester. 'It will conserve three five-storey Victorian buildings and two four-storey blocks will be built in a similar style to provide 211 apartments. The buildings will surround two landscaped courtyards. There will be a wine bar, a health club and residents' parking. Mr Trippier (the inner cities minister) said the project would help make central Manchester a better place to live, work and invest.' *(Financial Times,* March 15, 1988).

Similar examples could be cited from a number of cities, especially if there are canals or docks available to be developed. Although the numbers (other than in London) may be small, the potential effects on the economy and society of our cities should not be underestimated. It means that the geography of poverty in our cities is changing. On the one hand, poverty is being pushed outwards. Some of the most deprived areas are now outside the inner city, particularly on the so-called outer-estates. On the other hand it means that within the inner city there is an increasing polarisation between rich and poor. It is most marked in London, and other cities will perhaps never experience it so sharply, but the evidence is clear.

London, today, has the highest level of average weekly earnings in the country, and the largest concentration of unemployment in the industrialised world. It has the highest house prices and the highest levels of homelessness. Amongst its employed population it has the highest level of inequality in earnings, and the sharpest rate of increase in inequality.

But it is not just some elements of the upper-income groups which are rediscovering the inner city. It is also certain elements of capital. Once again it is only in small and highly-selected areas, but it is happening. Property developers are vying over likely-looking sites; in March, eleven of the largest civil engineering and property groups formed a joint operation to invest in basic infrastructure for sites of commercial development in inner cities; even large derelict sites (some of them) are being eyed for possible development potential.

A number of points should be noted here. First, much of this will need, and will get, subsidy (often today called 'leverage'). It is the same story again, of major so-called 'free market' developments needing state handouts to get going. The Docklands in London have received hundreds of millions; the areas in northern cities will need far more, especially if anything serious is to be done about inner city revival. They will get far less, but it will be enough to produce property development on a few well-chosen sites.

Second, once again it is not 'local entrepreneurship'. Indeed it is often not even local capital. These developments in northern cities are likely to be overwhelmingly dominated by outside capital. They thus stand to increase the 'branch-plant' status of northern cities. It is a potential function of UDCs to create new fields of profitable investment for big capital. And on occasions there have been signs of resistance to the invasion, on the part of local capital.

Third, Mrs Thatcher with her inner city policy is thus seizing a moment. The combination of a bit of gentrification and a bit of property development is just what she needs to break down what she sees as the dangerous oppositional bases in the cities and claim economic success for her inner city policy. Cities are potentially at a moment of change. She is making sure it happens on her terms and for 'her' people. Urban development corporations create greenfield sites free of any troublesome local influence. The new document *Action For Cities* is not a policy document to deal with poverty and unemployment. It is an investment brochure.

The other recent change is the beginning of a movement north; and this is even more just a hint rather than an established process. But the image of the north seems to have been reworked a bit of late. There is less mention of satanic mills. More, the talk (in the south) is of how *wonderful* the countryside is, and the quality of life it is possible to have, and of how low house prices are. The recent study, *Northern Lights,* picked out the top ten northern towns (Knutsford, Beverley, Lytham St Annes, Morpeth ...) using criteria such as *Good Food Guide* restaurants, *Michelin Guide* hotels, number of antique shops, presence of golf course, proportion of social classes one and two and the number of households with more than one car. A recent *Financial Times* survey on Cheshire headlined it: 'The nearest thing to the south'.

Now, to the extent that all this will promote real economic growth it cannot just be rejected, though the form of the growth it implies can be questioned. But it raises two issues. First, what happens to the great northern cities in all this? This movement is not to the areas of decline in the north, the areas which need new investment; it is an extension northwards of the search for rurality. And second, much of it is not about economic development at all. Commuterland is spreading by the week up British Rail's InterCity lines. Much of the current reconstruction of the image of the north is about turning some of its more rural areas into overspill dormitories for people whose jobs remain in the south.

So what do we say? Two main arguments have been put here. First, that the current levels of urban and regional inequality matter;

they have effects. Second, however, that they have been produced by wider changes in the economy and society, including government policy and the social power of certain groups. That means that urban and regional issues cannot be treated as separate from wider economic and social policies. Mrs Thatcher is using her inner city policy to demonstrate that monetarism works, even in these areas. A serious reply would be at the same level. Some of the most difficult conundrums we face at the moment are not about decline but about the form of new development and investment. In the end, it is this government's model of growth, and its class politics, which are at issue.

*This essay first appeared in* Marxism Today *in May 1988.*

## Notes

1 Ed P. Hall and A. Markusen (eds), *Silicon Landscapes*, HarperCollins, 1985, p5.
2 See the documents from SEEDS (The South East Economic Development Strategy).

# 5

# Vocabularies of the Economy

## 2013

At an art exhibition last summer I engaged in a very interesting conversation with one of the young people employed by the gallery. As she turned to walk off I saw she had on the back of her t-shirt 'Customer Liaison'. I felt flat. Our whole conversation seemed somehow reduced, my experience of it belittled into one of commercial transaction; my relation to the gallery and to this engaging person had become one of market exchange. The very language positioned us, the gallery, and our relationship, in a very particular way.

We know about this practice, and its potential effects, in many arenas. On trains and buses, and sometimes in hospitals and universities too, we have become customers, not passengers, readers, patients or students. In all these cases a specific activity and relationship is erased by a general relationship of buying and selling that is given precedence over it.

The language we use has effects in moulding identities and characterising social relationships. It is crucial to the formation of the ideological scaffolding of the hegemonic common sense. Discourse matters. Moreover it changes, and it can – through political work – be changed. We have been *enjoined* to become consumers rather than workers, customers where once we were passengers. (And indeed the process is never complete. Although the young person in the gallery had no choice but to wear this t-shirt, our conversation was nonetheless authentic and engaged, even to the extent of overflowing our assigned roles – maybe even resisting them.) The point is that attempts to mould our identities through language and naming take political work, and may be contested. In the 1950s the adjective 'public' (worker, sector, sphere) designated something to be respected and relied upon. It had, if only vaguely, something to do with our collectivity. It took a labour of persistent denigration of 'the public' to turn things around. And that labour has been crucial to the ability to pursue the economic strategies we are currently enduring. 'Equality' too was once a term to be used with unquestioned positivity; under New Labour the very word became unsayable. And so on.

The vocabulary we use, to talk about the economy in particular, has been crucial to the establishment of neoliberal hegemony.

There is a whole world view – and economic theory – behind that meeting in the gallery. It is one in which the majority of us are primarily consumers, whose prime duty (and source of power and pleasure) is to make choices.

The so-called truth underpinning this change of descriptions – which has been brought about in everyday life through managerial instruction and the thoroughgoing renaming of institutional practices in their allowed forms of writing, address and speech – is that, in the end, individual interests are the only reality that matters; that those interests are purely monetary; and that so-called values are only a means of pursuing selfish ends by other means. And behind this in turn, the theoretical justification of this now nearly-dominant system is the idea of a world of independent agents whose choices, made for their own advantage, paradoxically benefit all. Moreover, for this to 'work' no individual agent can have sufficient power to determine what happens to the whole.

That the world is not like that is evident. There are monopolies and vastly differential powers. There is far more to life than individual self interest. Markets in practice need vast apparatuses of regulation, propping-up and policing – a 'bureaucracy' indeed. Moreover, this privileging of self interest, market relations and choice in each sphere of economic and social life leads inexorably to increased inequality. And this now glaring inequality (globally as well as intranationally) is protected from political contest by another shift in our vocabulary. Every liberal democratic society needs to negotiate some kind of articulation between the liberal tradition and the democratic tradition. In our present society that articulation is quite specific: 'liberty' has come to be defined simply as self interest and freedom from restraint by the state, and that reduced form of liberty has become so much the dominant term that the resultant inequalities have eviscerated democracy, and the vocabulary of equality has been obscured from view. Much has been written elsewhere about all these things.

Our argument here is that this vocabulary of customer, consumer, choice, markets and self interest moulds both our conception of ourselves and our understanding of and relationship to the world. These 'descriptions' of roles, exchanges and relationships in terms of a presumption that individual choice and self interest does and should prevail are in fact not simply descriptions but a powerful means by which new subjectivities are constructed and enforced. Gramsci's understanding of the significance of 'common sense', Althusser's theory of ideological state apparatuses and the 'interpellation' of subjects, and Foucault's descriptions of discourses as aspects of 'governmentality' are theoretical resources through which these phenomena can be recognised and understood.

The new dominant ideology is inculcated through social practices, as well as through prevailing names and descriptions. The mandatory exercise of 'free choice' – of a GP, of a hospital to which to be referred, of schools for one's children, of a form of treatment – is, whatever its particular value, also a lesson in social identity, affirming on each occasion that one is above all a consumer, functioning in a market.

By such means we are enrolled, such self-identification being just as strong as our material entanglement in debt, pensions, mortgages and the like. It is an internalisation of 'the system' that can potentially corrode our ability to imagine that things could be otherwise.

This question of identity and identification, moreover, goes beyond our individual subjectivities. *Everything* begins to be imagined in this way. The very towns and cities we live in are branded in order to contend against each other, including internationally, in a world in which the only relationships are ones of competition.

So, the vocabularies which have reclassified roles, identities and relationships – of people, places and institutions – and the practices which enact them embody and enforce the ideology of neoliberalism, and thus a new capitalist hegemony. Another set of vocabularies provides the terms through which the system describes itself and its functions. These frame the categories – for example of production, consumption, land, labour, capital, wealth – through which the 'economy' (as a supposedly distinct and autonomous sphere of life) is understood. These definitions constitute another element of 'common sense' – about the way the economic world 'naturally' is and must remain.

### The names of the system

What are the key terms in this system of definitions, and how do they work? Here it is useful to think about bundles of ideas.

There is, for instance, a bundle around *wealth, output, growth* and *work*. The economic system is assumed to be about what we call wealth-creation, and the achievement of 'growth'. Growth is measured by the increase in 'gross national product', which is an aggregated sum of everything produced in the economy, whether made within the private or public sectors. It is usually cited as a percentage rate of change, often on an annual basis. The dominant conception is that it is the well-being of individuals and society alike (in so far as these are clearly distinguished as values or entities) that is denoted by these terms. Apart from the ongoing debate about anomalies in how these things are measured, there has also been, thanks to the achievements of social democracy, some recognition that increases in aggregate wealth are by themselves an insufficient measure of well-being, given that the fruits of growth are not distributed equally. But social democrats have traditionally confined their ambitions to altering the balance of distributions – between what is called the private and the public, the market and the state systems – while not seriously questioning the dominant architecture of the system.

We argue that this dominant architecture now needs to be called in question. The whole vocabulary we use to talk about the economy, while presented as a description of the natural and the eternal, is in fact a political construction that needs contesting.

Let us focus for a moment on the example of *growth*, currently deemed to be the entire aim of our economy. To produce growth and then (maybe) to redistribute some of it has been a goal shared by neoliberalism and social democracy. But this approach must now be questioned. Why?

In the first place, there is what might be seen as a technical problem – at least for the social democratic argument that growth allows mitigation of inequality through redistribution. In the case of the British economy and probably more widely, there is in the immediate future likely to be insufficient growth to enable the degree of redistribution desired by a progressive agenda (or at least not without major political confrontation). A return to the redistributive model of social democracy of decades past is therefore impossible. This model, in its crudest formulation, entailed providing the conditions for the market sector to produce growth and to accept that this would result in inequality (though it should also be noted that different models of growth produce different degrees of inequality – the model we have in the UK at the moment being acutely inegalitarian). The role of the state was then, through taxation, the provision of public services and so on, to redistribute some portion of this growth in order to help repair the inequality resulting from its production.

This is anyway a bizarre arrangement. It institutes a curious sequentialism – first produce a problem, then try to solve it. (Why produce the problem – inequality – in the first place?) This does nothing to question the inequality-producing mechanisms of market-exchange (though of course some restraints have been introduced). Indeed, this arrangement has meant that the main lines of struggle are focused on distributional issues, rather than the nature of the system. Moreover, the very success of even this restricted distributional struggle was one of the reasons for the breakdown of the arrangement. As we pointed out in our framing statement for the Kilburn Manifesto, the gains made by labour under social democracy proved intolerable to capital and a backlash was launched.[1] Even mere redistribution could only be allowed to go so far. And one crucial element in that neoliberal backlash was the dislodging of the common sense which underpinned these aspects of the social democratic approach – in particular the commitment to (a measure of) equality and the important role of the state and public intervention – and indeed the very notion of the public- in achieving this. Changing our economic language was crucial in shifting our world-view.

The fact that the neoliberal successor to this social democratic model has now run into its own crises provides an opportunity for a new imagining. As already said, rates of growth are likely to be insufficient to reinstate the previous arrangements. Moreover the whole ideological and political – and discursive – climate has changed so much that a return to the previous model would be difficult to pull off. It would in fact be no greater a task to argue for a new model altogether – one in which the workings of the economy did not in the first place produce a level of inequality that demanded subsequent correction.[2] Certainly it would involve a more thoroughgoing, and popular, critique of market forces as producers of inequality. It would also mean arguing again for the vocabulary, and politics, of equality. Some new vocabulary is indeed already emerging – though not the most easy on the ear or on popular imaginings – 'predistribution'. The word may be awkward, but if it is pointing to the need to design a system of production which, in its own very workings, is not productive of intolerable levels of inequality, then it is on the right track.

A second reason why our current notion of wealth, and our commitment to its growth, must be questioned – certainly in the global North – is to do with our relation to the planet. The environmental damage – in particular but not only through climate change – brought about by the pursuit of growth threatens to cause a catastrophe of which we are already witnessing intimations. This is a global issue in which relatively rich, though unequal, societies such as the United Kingdom have international responsibilities. The UK on occasion prides itself on its relative greenness. But to the extent that there has been any improvement it has resulted from the closure of coal mines (not pursued for environmental reasons!) and – even more – from the outsourcing of our manufacturing. If, as we argued in our framing statement, one stimulus to globalisation was capital's desire to escape the demands of 'First World' labour, then one of its results has been a shift in the geography of the production of pollution to the global South. China, among others, now produces goods that would once have been made in the UK, and which we still need (or anyway want). But the dominant voices criticise China for its pollution; and official statistics do not even count the energy used, and the environmental damage done, by the transport across the world to our shores of everything from machinery to pet food to Christmas decorations. Meanwhile there exists an export trade in the toxic wastes that we do produce to countries so impoverished they are prepared to deal with it for us.

Of course much of the change in the global South derives from the increasing industrialisation and wealth of a few of its constituent countries. Yet it is argued that in no foreseeable technology could the planet cope with everyone living at the standards now common in the global North. Who then must change?

Moreover, environmental destruction and the catastrophes consequent upon climate change will not fall evenly across the world. Probably such ills will fall most quickly, and most heavily, on more impoverished places, which in any case have fewer resources with which to offset such damage. The prospect is a nightmare of potential famines, forced migrations, social disorganisation and wars.

Finally, there is perhaps an even deeper question. We now know that increased wealth, when it is measured in the standard monetary terms of today, has few actual consequences for people's feelings of well-being, once there is a sufficiency to meet basic needs. In pursuing 'growth' in these terms, as a means to realise people's life-goals and desires, economies pursue a chimera since, while growth may occur, all the evidence is that our levels of satisfaction with our lives remain obstinately static. Indeed, insofar as the dominant model of growth leads to increased inequalities, as it does, we now know also that it is a prime generator of ill health, crime, and social suffering, compared with what might be the case in a more equal and fair society. There is increasing unease with a concept of wealth, and of gross national product, measured only in monetary terms. It was widely questioned in particular at that moment of the implosion into financial crisis, when all the talk was of disaster brought about by competitive greed. Even David Cameron mused that there was more to life than GDP. That moment has been lost, but deeper dissatisfactions surely rumble on. And they cannot be addressed by adding something warm and cuddly on to the GDP; the problem is structural. Can we redefine wealth to include riches that go beyond the individual and the monetary? Might we not ask the question, in the end, 'What is an economy *for*?'. What do we want it to provide?

We could take this line of questioning, and its provocation to re-imagining, in many directions – and we hope that readers will participate in doing so.

'*Work*' is another area within this cluster of ideas around wealth-creation and growth that is in need of new words and new imaginations. There are many aspects to this. For instance, and most obviously, there is the question of what counts as work. Where only transactions for money are recognised as belonging to 'the economy', the vast amount of unpaid labour – as conducted for instance in families and local areas – goes uncounted. This is a major gender issue too. Childcare provided in exchange for a wage counts towards the national income, while childcare provided by parents or neighbours or grandparents does not. In its Industrial Strategy of the 1980s the Greater London Council found that a substantial proportion of the labour performed in the capital was unpaid – and this was labour that was necessary for the social reproduction of the city. This is a question of recognition, of the way we think of the economy as a part of society, and of valuing what it takes for a society to be reproduced.

Moreover, beyond even this, we would like to question that familiar instrumental categorisation of the economy as a space in which people reluctantly undertake unwelcome and unpleasing 'work', in return for material rewards which they can then consume. Indeed, this view of 'work', to be traded off against 'leisure', is required by the neoclassical economic theory that currently holds sway (as though paid work and leisure is all of our days, so that the other – unpaid – things that we have, and want, to do in life thus once again disappear from view). But it is a view that misunderstands where pleasure and fulfilment in human lives are in reality found. Work is usually, and certainly should be, not a liability and a sacrifice, but a central source of meaning and fulfilment in human lives. This is widely recognised in the anguish felt when work is absent, for example when, as in many countries today, up to half the population of young people can find no employment. And it is seen in the higher rates of sickness and mortality which are associated statistically with retirement from work. This is in part because it is through work that people develop and express their capabilities as human beings. And also because work is a principal way in which people maintain connections with their worlds, both in immediate ways (through relations with co-workers or those for whose well-being work is done) and in more abstract but nevertheless meaningful terms, such as in making a contribution to the good of others, which then gives moral sense to the benefits which are obtained in return. Work, as earlier generations of socialists once understood, has – or could have – moral and creative (or aesthetic) values at its core. It is misunderstood by the dominant discourse, in which it is assigned merely self-regarding and possessive purposes. A rethinking of this could lead us to address more creatively both the social relations of work and the division of labour (a better sharing of the tedious work, and of the skills) within society.

A second bundle of terms that deserves further attention is that clustered around *investment, expenditure* and *speculation*. It should be noted immediately, for this is crucial to what follows, that these terms carry with them implicit moral connotations. Investment implies an action, even a sacrifice, undertaken for a better future, while speculation (here in the financial rather than intellectual sense) immediately arouses a sense of mistrust. And while investment evokes a future positive outcome, expenditure seems merely an outgoing, a cost, a burden.

*Investment* and *expenditure* are distinguished from each other according to a strict economic rationale, a distinction required by the way in which the national accounts are set up. But this distinction is cross-cut in popular parlance and ordinary political debate by another understanding. Together they produce rich soil for the construction of political attitudes. Thus, in the national accounts, investment is money laid out for physical things such as buildings and infrastructure, while expenditure is money used to pay – for instance – for the wages of people operating the services for which the investment provides the physical possibility. So building a new school is investment, paying the teachers, the administrators and the dinner ladies is expenditure. (Pause for a moment, and ponder the gender implications of this distinction.)

This distinction, moreover, is often cross-cut with another – that between public and private. On this understanding, money advanced by a private firm to further its profit-making intentions is seen as a worthwhile investment, while money advanced by the state, whether for infrastructure or for employment in schools or the health service, is seen as only increasing the deficit, because it is paid for out of taxation.

The political effect of the combining of these definitions is devastating. Thus, for instance, while building new houses or railways through taxation may be seen as investment by the first distinction, paying for doctors, social-service workers, teachers, nurses, street-cleaners, dinner ladies – when this is done by the public purse – is seen on both definitions as merely a cost. Paying for them through taxation, therefore, emphatically carries the connotation of being simply a burden. But if we return to that question 'what is an economy *for*?', and if we answer that it has something to do with the reproduction of a society, then this vocabulary is misleading (to say the least). Education is equally then an investment, generating the capacities on which a society depends. Likewise, the provision of health and social services more generally is one of the most valuable and essential forms of production and investment there can be.

And crucial to maintaining these things within the public sector (thus taking on the second distinction, between public and private) is challenging the persistent characterisation of taxation as a negative thing. 'Everyone hates paying taxes don't they?' But people lay out money in the market sector seemingly without a second thought, including for things they could perfectly well get through the state, and it seems not to incur such opprobrium. Private transactions – OK; taxation for social investment and services – almost universally resented. What is in contention here is social solidarity; the knee-jerk language reflects – and reinforces – the prioritisation of individual choice over collectivity, over the very notion of (the construction of) a society. Words and oft-repeated phrases carry, and reinforce, understandings that go well beyond them.

These questionings of our vocabularies are perhaps obvious. But we need to *argue* them. The existing vocabulary is one of the roots of the elite's ability to maintain the horrible straitjacket we are in.

Moreover, there is one distinction we should be making a lot more strongly: that between *investment* and *speculation*. Or, perhaps more properly put, between value creation and value extraction. The term 'investment' is widely used in the media for both activities. So when businesses put money into plant and machinery, or research or staff development, it is called investment. And when finance is put into buying something that already exists (an asset) – commodity futures, fine wines, already-existing property ... – that is also called, conventionally, investment. But in the first type of case the money goes into a process of value creation; in the second there is no such process – the 'investor' just holds the asset in the hope that the price will rise, and then will sell it at a profit. This is, on other occasions, called speculation. It is not the creation of value but the extraction of value from the pool that already exists. Its effect, therefore, is not the expansion of the pool but its redistribution, towards (if prices rise) those who purchase the assets.

The above is a very rough and ready distinction, and the difference is anyway not absolute, but the broad contrast is important for us to address at this moment because much of what lies behind the recent decades of neoliberalism, in addition to the predation of the public sector by the private, is this buying and selling of already-existing assets, and indeed the creation of new ones in which to speculate – derivatives and various forms of the commodification of risk, carbon futures.

Again we can take this further. For the obfuscation of the difference between value creation and value extraction helps obscure another one: that between *earned* and *unearned income*. As Andrew Sayer wryly observes, 'Interestingly, [this is a distinction that] has fallen out of use just when unearned income has expanded'.[3] Unearned income derives, not from participation in the production of goods and services (value creation) but from controlling an already-existing asset. And it is the latter that has formed the economic basis of the rise, under neoliberalism, of the super-rich. It has not been as a result of participation in production that they have gained their wealth. (The idea that the City is a centre of wealth-creation is thus bizarre – it is more a centre of a system of wealth-extraction that spans the world.) In this sense much of the new economic elite is parasitic, extracting value from the rest of society. They are 'rentiers' – here too we need to reclaim and revitalise our vocabulary. And many in the upper-middle strata of rich societies have been drawn into this as well – through house-price rises (unearned, and in the UK greatly exacerbating not only general inequality but also the north-south divide), and through pensions (invested in secondary share-markets). And so material interest melds with misleading economic vocabulary to further the transformation of common sense, to fortify a financialised ideology, and to pacify many into at least acquiescence if not enthusiasm.

The results of all of this have included a massive redistribution from poor to rich, a significant contribution to a rise in food prices and malnutrition around the world, property booms, the underpinning of a new financial imperialism and, of course, instability and crash, with their repercussions around the world, as the speculative bubbles burst. Moreover this extraction of value has reduced the ability of the rest of the economy to pursue value creation. And we should note that the City of London, seen as the centrepiece of the UK economy, was a prime mover in all of this.

These are important economic, and political, distinctions. The rise in the significance of the trading of assets has been central to the financialisation of national and global economies. It relates too to that erasure of activities other than those of exchange – whether that be creating goods and services, being passengers on a train, or visiting an art gallery. All that is necessary in this (their) world is to buy and to sell. The naturalisation of this, through financialisation, as the essential nature of economic activity, has thus been a crucial element in the establishing of a new common sense. Indeed, as Mariana Mazzucato has argued, 'the battle against the excesses of the financial sector will remain lost without a theory able to distinguish when profits move from being a result of value creation, to [being] ... a result of value extraction'.[4]

## The (supposed) naturalness of markets

Underpinning the apparent common sense of these elements of our economic vocabulary (and there are many more) is the understanding that markets are natural: that as either external to society or inherent in 'human nature', they are a pre-given force. The assumption is all around us. There is the language that is used to describe the financial markets as they roam Europe attacking country after country – an external force, a wild beast maybe, certainly not the product of particular social strata and their economic and political interests. There is the understanding of 'human nature' and of the long histories of human societies as 'naturally' – as part of their very nature – given to market trading (and that therefore markets are the best way of organising societies) – an understanding beautifully demolished by Karl Polanyi in *The Great Transformation* as long ago as 1944, but still living on as an effective underpinning of political discourse. There is that shrug of resignation and powerlessness by ordinary folk as something happens that they do not like: 'Well, it's the market I suppose, isn't it?'. A 'thing' one cannot gainsay. There is the idea that we 'intervene' (social action) into the economy (equated with the market and seen as an external nature). There is, within the academy itself, the pretension on the part of neoclassical economics to be a natural, or physical, science, rather than a social science. The degree to which these ideas, this ideological scaffolding, currently infuse the hegemonic common sense is astonishing. The assumption that markets are natural is so deeply rooted in the structure of thought, certainly here in Europe, that even the fact that it *is* an assumption seems to have been lost to view. This is real hegemony.

And it has effects. It removes 'the economic' from the sphere of political and ideological contestation. It turns it into a matter for experts and technocrats. It removes the economy from democratic control.

This assumption of the naturalness of markets is crucial to the insistence that There Is No Alternative. It is one of the ghastly ironies of the present neoliberal age that we are told (as we saw at the outset of this argument) that much of our power and our pleasure, and our very self-identification, lies in our ability to choose (and we are indeed bombarded every day by 'choices', many of them meaningless, others we wish we didn't have to make), while at the level that really matters – what kind of society we'd like to live in, what kind of future we'd like to build – we are told, implacably, that, give or take a few minor variations, there is no alternative – no choice at all.

At the international level too the same kind of language is deployed, aiming for the same effects. Thus, that common-sense sequence of 'underdeveloped – developing – developed' places 'developing' countries behind 'developed' ones, in some kind of historical queue, rather than as co-existing in their differences. It thereby – and not coincidentally – obscures the many ways in which the 'developed' countries restrict the potential of the so-called developing (the power-relations within neoliberal globalisation for instance) and implies that there is only one possible historical path, which all must follow.

We are not arguing that there is no place for markets in a reformed economy. What we are challenging is the special status our current imaginings endow them with. We should be thinking of 'the economy' not in terms of natural force and intervention but in terms of a whole variety of social relations that need some kind of coordination. Each form of social relation has its own characteristics and implications, and thus appropriateness to different parts of the economy and society. Above all, we need to bring 'the economic' back into society and into political contention, and not just as debates about economic policy, but questioning also the very way we *think about* the economy in the first place. Without doing this we shall find ourselves always arguing on the political terrain of existing economic policy. For something new to be imagined, let alone to be born, our current economic 'common sense' needs to be challenged root and branch.

*This essay first appeared in* Soundings, *54, Summer 2013.*

## Notes

1. See Stuart Hall, Doreen Massey and Michael Rustin, 'After neoliberalism: analysing the present', *Soundings*, 53, Spring 2013. See also www.lwbooks.co.uk/journals/soundings/manifesto.html.
2. Subsequent instalments of the Manifesto will develop thoughts about economic strategy.
3. A. Sayer, 'Facing the challenge of the return of the rich', in W. Atkinson, S. Roberts and M. Savage (eds), *Class inequality in austerity Britain*, Palgrave Macmillan, 2012.
4. Mariana Mazzucato, 'From bubble to bubble', *Guardian*, 16 January 2013.

# The New Urban Left and the Miners' Strike

6

# The Great Male Moving Right Show

with Lynne Segal and Hilary Wainright

1984

The left's current passion for slinging mud at itself is starting to have an effect. On the one hand, admiration for Thatcher and the belief that she has touched basic undercurrents within British society has allowed the debate to shift on to her terms. On the other, pessimism has been a condition of moving rightwards. Eric Hobsbawm and others have drawn strategic implications from all this.

For instance, socialist economist Bob Rowthorn used his one half-hour of television time to attack not the right, but the left. And Stuart Hall *(New Socialist,* May/June 1983) accused the left as a whole of a lack of vision. It was his particular contribution – one of the more thoughtful pieces of criticism – that stimulated this article.

Such critics propose an anti-Thatcher alliance constructed in such a way as to accommodate the centre and centre-right. It is Hobsbawm's version of this strategy (as expressed in *Marxism Today,* October 1983) – the most recent and fullest statement, and one clearly influential with Neil Kinnock – which this article addresses. Our discussion focuses on the Labour Party, but the issues are, of course, of much wider relevance across the left generally. It is ironic how many of the starting points we share – yet we believe they lead to different conclusions. We believe that it is necessary to make 'alliances' – alliances are central to the strategy we are suggesting – but alliances with whom? On whose terms?

Hobsbawm would like Labour to become 'once again' the focus for all those who want democracy. We agree. But when *was it* such a focus? And who is now making all the running on that front? It is the new local authority initiatives and the left, not the right, of the Labour Party which are most concerned with the issue of democracy. It is the left that is leading the fight for democracy in the unions.

Hobsbawm wants the Labour Party to appeal to women, *all* women, 'across class lines', But the old right of the Labour Party, or the Communist Party, can hardly claim to have taken women seriously. Once again, within the Labour Party, it is the independent left which has been in the forefront, insofar as any attempt has been made to construct a feminist politics.

Hobsbawm says that we must 'take account of quite reasonable demands of bodies of people who are not satisfied that at present they are adequately met by Labour'. We agree. But he is talking about 'home-owners, people who are dissatisfied with their children's schooling, or worried about law and order.' We agree there are real issues here. But is it not significant that he makes no mention of single-parent families, blacks or homeless people alongside the homeowners?

Then he writes that it is necessary to appeal to all workers, not just some of them. We agree. He says, 'the strength of the labour movement has always been that it could represent *all* parts of the working class – and did not discriminate against any'. To us as women this came, to say the least, as something of a revelation!

The reason for enumerating these points is that they help reveal what underlies the strategy of alliance. It means, in fact, The Alliance moving right. It seems to assume that the rest – the homeless, the blacks, the unilateralists – will vote Labour (which seems for this strategy to be the only important measure of socialism) because there is nowhere else for them to go. Yet we know that many of them did not vote at all on 9 June 1983 – and with good reason.

It is not that we don't want to attract such people to our ranks – we do. But such a strategy offers no re-thinking of what socialism can mean in today's world, and no new vision. It merely picks up bits of policies here and there which seem to have gone down well when used by others, and tacks them on to a complacency about the 'old labour movement'. There is no going back to the problem – decent housing, for instance – and trying to create new solutions. It is not reformulation: it is capitulation.

What the Hobsbawm strategy essentially does is attack all the work of the left in the unions and the Labour Party. People did not vote Labour in 1983, Hobsbawm writes, 'because they felt the party did not represent their interests and aspirations adequately or effectively'. Quite. But that was not a product of the early 1980s, as Hobsbawm deliberately implies. The Labour Party has had many years in power over the last two decades. *For twenty years* it has not been representing the aspirations of what ought to be its constituency. What was different in 1983 was that there was a choice of party. Hobsbawm ignores this record, just as he paints a glowing picture of the labour movement as he pretends it was.

In contrast to all this, we argue that what is being built now, on the left, at the grass roots, is far more of a real coalition than anything proposed by Hobsbawm and company. It is not enough; but it is innovative and socialist. Not only does Hobsbawm's strategy ignore these initiatives: it *depends* on ignoring them. In that sense the overwhelming pessimism of earlier analyses laid the basis for the strategic move to the right.

## Gloom and doom

There are, of course, massive criticisms which must be made of the recent performance in Britain of 'the left' broadly defined, and of the Labour Party in particular. There is a lack of vision, an overwhelming defensiveness, a refusal to be bold, and a refusal to confront the scale and nature of Labour's defeat. It is important to recognise the seriousness of the problem which the left faces and the deficiencies which it must counter. But this article seeks to balance the current tendency to wallow in defeat, because it is the job of socialists not just to write Olympian articles about the unmitigated disaster of it all and call from on high for alternatives, but to set about developing the initiatives from which a socialist vision is already being fashioned.

The victory of Thatcherism has been devastating, but it is neither complete nor invulnerable. Nor is it simply that there are just pockets of resistance left, where the present and the past continue to be defended: there are also places where something new is being built. We are concerned to help make these initiatives more widely known, and more central, to discussions of strategy. The examples that follow suggest ways in which Thatcherism can be attacked. They are characterised by two things in particular. First, they attempt to change the terms of the political debate as it exists. And secondly, they base this attempt on the growing points in the 'grass roots' resistance to Thatcherism.

Changing the terms of the debate is essential because so much of Thatcher's attack succeeded precisely because there *was* so much to criticise. Nationalised industries *are* unresponsive to both worker and consumer. On a day-to-day level, many people experience the welfare state as oppressive, impenetrable and hostile (not that Thatcher's state is any less so, of course).

We don't want the old, social democratic state back, either. If the public sector is to be defended, whether it be the National Health Service or local authorities, we have to think through from scratch again what it is about the public nature of provision which ought to be attractive and beneficial – a publicly available resource to be drawn upon, rather than the heavy hand of the state. This is a major task, but the challenge is being taken up.

In the second place, the importance of political demands from the base should be evident. Real contact with and experience of alternatives *has* to be central to any strategy for the left. This is not just because we need to combat that view of socialism as the grim legacy of the Wilson years. It is also necessary because it is the way we will reach people. It is the level at which the real impact of Thatcherism is being felt; and it is also one way to beat the media – to take a different route. Moreover it is at the base – in the factories, offices, hospitals and communities – that at least a part of the power and the skills to bring about socialism must be built.

The debate on how to develop a positive response to Thatcherism begins with the experience of local authorities, particularly those in the major cities. The issues raised around the provision of services are decisive for socialism, and certainly Thatcher has been quick to recognise this arena as crucial.

The Labour Party has important bases in many of Britain's big cities. Thatcher attacks such local authorities not simply because they are big spenders (why perform statistical acrobatics to avoid penalising high spending Tory councils?) but because *they have the potential to show that there is an alternative.* The basis for the defence of local authorities *must not* simply be 'defensive'. And for once the left – or a section of it – is changing the terms of the debate. Campaigns to defend local authorities are being built around new forms of local democracy and, increasingly, in terms of an emerging socialist alternative, which several of their new initiatives illustrate.

The GLC and Sheffield in particular are trying to develop this alternative in two ways. First they are undertaking activities over which they have (for the time being) direct power as both policy-maker and employer – for example transport. Second, and equally important, they are going well beyond the traditional role of local government to strengthen and support trade union initiatives both in the public sector and in private industry.

These developments contain the potential for a powerful and novel alliance between the political power, however precarious, of socialists in local government, and the extra-parliamentary power of trade union and community campaigns. Our second category of examples, therefore, covers new ideas and experiments going on in industry and in the public sector beyond local government.

## Resistance by the local state

The first thing to understand is that the working class did not vote for the dismantling of state services. Thatcher was forced continually to lie about her commitment to the NHS before the 1983 election. People *are* unhappy with existing services, but they are not prepared to see them abolished altogether.

This is probably the principal area in which arguments for a socialist society can still be heard. Such arguments reject the strategy behind Tory policies of privatisation – commercial rather than collective responsibility for meeting people's needs. They are now coming most strongly from left-wing Labour councils and from certain metropolitan authorities, such as South Yorkshire, the West Midlands and the GLC – which is why these are the areas of local government that Thatcher is determined to cripple.

Further cuts in central government support to municipalities, and legal limits on local rate increases, are going to make confrontation inevitable. What is important is that in the defence of local government it is the issue of *democracy* and *accountability* which is central.

Further national interference in local government both prevents accountability of any sort and removes all possibilities for democratic control. Yet we are all aware that it is the very structures of local government which prevent any popular participation in how they are run. Everyone is kept in ignorance of how, when, and what services we will get in relation to what we need. (Though we are always made to feel that for what little we receive we must be truly grateful.)

Some socialist councillors are now arguing that they can only build support to defend local government if they can provide the services which people want. Not all the old structures are worth defending. It is for this reason that councils like Islington, Hackney, Brent and Camden, for instance, have pushed ahead with local decentralisation plans, attempting through public meetings and discussions to increase local participation in planning their use of resources.

This is also why the GLC and Sheffield Council, for instance, are developing an approach to economic planning based on coordinating and encouraging initiatives from working-class and community organisations.

In Walsall, where decentralisation was first initiated by a left Labour council elected in 1983, thirty-three neighbourhood offices were set up with housing departments and repair teams more localised and accessible than before. These offices proved so popular that an anti-Labour coalition, which came to dominate the Council in spring 1982, has been unable to dismantle them. But decentralisation is not just about making councils more accessible. What is important about decentralising local services is the attempt to demystify and democratise them.

This unearths enormous problems. At the moment, even elected councillors have very little power in determining municipal policies. Administration is firmly in the hands of non-elected senior officers, unused to consulting anyone – including councillors. Any attempt at genuine democratisation would have to tackle these top layers of the rigidly hierarchical local bureaucracy, with working groups of councillors determined to influence local policy.

Then there is the danger that decentralisation and consultation could serve – like participation schemes in the past – merely to monitor and control discontent rather than to build people's confidence and determination to fight for and defend the services they want. They will strengthen resistance only if the independence of groups outside the council is fostered and encouraged. Despite the fact that this is part of the thinking behind the creation of women's committees, ethnic minority and police monitoring groups in some left Labour councils, it has to be continually reasserted. Council funding for women's and gay centres, trade union, community and resource centres is a manifestation of this trend.

Despite the enormous problems and constraints, there are examples of how to challenge and change the hierarchical and undemocratic assumptions of existing social provision. It is not just a question of making bureaucrats and 'experts' more approachable and accountable to those they serve, it is enabling users and workers in state services to gain the confidence and creativity to run things differently – to run things themselves.

At the Centre for the Disabled in King Henry's Walk, Islington, the hostel works on the principle that it is the disabled who should run it. The Centre takes disabled people out of hospitals and other institutions, and provides helpers who work with them individually with the ultimate aim of equipping them to move into sheltered accommodation in nearby flats. Not surprisingly, it is residents from this hostel who fought for and won the Dial-a-Ride transport service for the disabled which now operates in Islington, Camden and other London boroughs.

What is clear to us is that the confidence to live creatively, resist and change, is inseparable from the push towards real democracy. Such local experiments provide the basis for a much wider debate about the institutions of political democracy.

And it is not just services that can be changed for the better. In certain local authority employment strategies there has also been some fundamental re-thinking – as in the question of paid and unpaid labour. The GLC has endorsed demands to treat domestic work as an essential part of the economy. This is of great significance for women. For, though women have won more autonomy and independence than formerly, their economic and domestic disadvantages remain. In fact, they get worse: Britain is still unable to provide anything like adequate care for its young, old, sick and dependent people – not to mention for its male workers – except at the expense of women.

Yet up to now the Labour Party, almost as much as the Tories, has encouraged private rather than social responsibility for meeting people's personal needs – regardless of the strain on individual women. The GLC endorsement means it will assist funding for projects which aim to remove the isolation of domestic work. One example is the Norwood Children's Centre, which aims to combine provision for laundry, cheap food and child care.

Other examples are services which make the link between home and work. Crèches in workplaces, nurseries, daycare and drop-in centres for the elderly and disabled can provide socially useful jobs, as well as tackling women's inequality, and provide living examples of socialist rather than individualistic values. These are not just of local significance. They have fundamental implications for planning economic strategy at national level.

Such initiatives have not come out of the blue, of course. Inside the Labour Party, they are the product of the long haul of a new breed of socialists; outside, they come from the equally important influence of feminists and independent socialists. They will always have to be fought for, against traditional labourism, which wants only to disown them.

The Labour Party and the labour movement have to be continuously pushed and pulled along, from inside and out, before they learn how to act on anyone's behalf who is not a male waged worker. The Labour Party has always been patriarchal, paternalistic and invariably suspicious of any movements outside Parliament and the trade union leadership. This is not the tradition which can re-build a socialist movement strong and confident enough to resist the current Tory attack.

The defence of services will only be possible through alliances between councillors, trade unionists and campaigning groups. In the case of the metropolitan authorities, these alliances will be necessary to defend the councils' very existence. Where local authority funds support trade union and community initiatives, there are bonds of common material interest in the survival of the council – as well as a shared political commitment. Conflicts of interest are inevitable. But we have plenty of examples of successful co-operation. In Hackney, tenants' groups work with the direct labour organisation to improve repairs. In Kentish Town, the health centre has set up a consumer group. In Haringey, the Women's Project is carrying out a survey of local needs and feeding the results back to the council.

NUPE in London has drawn up a comprehensive strategy for fighting privatisation and defending services.[1] It stresses the need to build unity between workers and users, and to increase workers' and users' control to improve services. Local surveys and studies are important. *Brighton on the Rocks*,[2] for instance, monitors the tragic cost of council spending cuts and the failure to provide for elementary social need. The authors point the way towards an alternative plan for Brighton, based around democratic welfare and useful production. The proposals of initiatives like these, and the collective action they can inspire, contain enormous hope for the spreading of socialist values.

## Union campaigns

In the unions, too – a long way from Congress House – there are activists extending the scope of trade union demands in ways which could help to construct a popular alternative.

Most of the examples we describe involve a Labour local authority, although the impetus has in each case come from trade unionists. The local authority connection is partly a result of our own bias. But the very fact that trade unions turn to local councils for support indicates the political character of trade union initiatives, and the limitations of trade union action on its own – especially when it concerns jobs.

The participation of local councils explicitly on the side of labour, comes from a political understanding that the forces they are up against – the big corporations, the government, and the recession – can undermine the employment initiatives of even the largest local authority, unless these initiatives have a strong trade union base.

Such initiatives come from a minority. The Michael Edwardes/ Margaret Thatcher tactic of raising the political and material stakes of every threatened industrial dispute has had contradictory consequences. It has certainly caused fear and demoralisation amongst the majority of trade union members, but in the minority has prompted a more strategic reaction.

The initiatives of this minority include campaigns against privatisation (which are gaining increasing support amongst the majority); making contact and exchanging information across national boundaries within multinational companies; establishing co-operatives out of struggles to resist closure; and pushing forward the social uses of new technology.

The significance is not merely that they indicate a more sophisticated rank and file trade unionism in the work place. As these initiatives develop, they could become a vital part of a convincing socialist economic strategy.

There are three reasons for this. First, the initiatives can illustrate and develop an alternative to market economics. The campaign of the Telecom unions against privatisation, for example, challenges traditional arguments about productivity and profitability. In the past, these unions have tended to accept management's approach to efficiency and productivity based on commercial criteria. The unions could confine their number of jobs within that economic framework. But now these are the arguments used to justify privatisation: the present campaign pushes to the fore the case for a telecommunications system which is a public service, run to meet social needs whether or not those needs are profitable.

Similarly, several co-operatives supported by local authorities have begun to illustrate how industry, too, could be organised on the basis of social need. In Sheffield, a group of engineering workers formed a co-operative after the defeat of a long struggle to keep their factory, Snow's, open as a machine tool company, part of the Elliott Consortium. Now they are making dehumidifiers for council houses. These engineers have worked on the design of the dehumidifiers with local tenants and have received financial aid from the council.

In a small way, the ability of the public sector to put to good use what the market has wasted, illustrates the case for a planned economy. All these initiatives can do is *illustrate* the argument. But the work of developing an economic strategy must build on such illustrations.

Secondly, many of the cases of a political trade union response show that it is the white collar workers – commonly assumed to have no interest in such matters – who are actually in the forefront of applying socialist ideas to technological change.

In ICL, for example, white collar trade union representatives from different factories started meeting regularly in the late 1970s to devise strategies for defending their jobs. Now they are discussing how to design software that will be useful to trade union and community organisations. A first step, they believe, is to educate the labour movement in how it can turn computers to its advantage; how software could be designed for its benefit. As part of this education the ICL combine is now working on a pilot project of software for a computer to be used by trade union and community resource centres.

Finally, most of these initiatives have the effect of pointing out ways of implementing socialist industrial policies. This is important for the present debate about the causes and lessons of electoral defeat. The unpopularity of the left is not so much a consequence of popular *disagreement* with left ideals, as feeling that they are pie in the sky, because there is no way they can be put into practice.

Take the problem of multinationals. A group of workers threatened by management policies in any one factory can be paralysed by the very thought of the global power and resources they are up against. Yet there are several examples of trade unionists beginning to build the contacts and share the information which can overcome this sense of powerlessness. In Kodak, local authorities and trade unionists in France and England have begun to achieve an international co-ordination which will at least help resistance to get off the ground, even though it is unlikely to ensure its success.

## From local initiative to national strategy

These are some of the ways that new ideas are being generated even in the midst of Labour's defeat. They are only a beginning. They are far from perfect. But the point is that they exist and it is important to take account of them.

Panoramic views of the left which ignore such initiatives first of all denigrate the energy and imagination of many people. Secondly

– and this is perhaps the most immediate danger – a sweeping dismissal of the left as a movement devoid of positive ideas, imagination or hope for the future implies that there is nothing left to defend. The fallacy of this is illustrated by Thatcher herself, who certainly recognises that there is much left to attack. It is important that the experiments which are under way are defended in the most imaginative terms possible. Thirdly, the promulgation of mass pessimism helps reconcile people to defeat. It even helps to bring it on.

But there is also a wider reason than these. Recognition of these kinds of initiatives poses a direct challenge to the proposals and strategies currently emerging from a section of the labour movement – the Great Male Moving Right Show. The shifts by Hobsbawm and company do *not* mean that we on the left should go on the defensive, immobilised in old strategies. We do need a new vision. What we have argued here is that some people are trying to get on with creating it.

We must put all our effort into strengthening, popularising and advocating these initiatives. We must use every possible access to the media and invest more resources in our own forms of communication. We can spread the word until it becomes a national challenge. In defeating Thatcher, we have to build a new type of socialism.

*This essay first appeared in* New Socialist, *No. 15, January/Feburary 1984.*

## Notes

1 See Dexter Whitfield, *Making it Public*, Pluto Press, 1983.
2 *Brighton on the Rocks: monetarism and the local state*, Queenspark Books, Brighton, 1983. There are many other examples – from the Merseyside Socialist Research Group, Centerprise (London E8), the Strong Words Collective (Durham), the Coventry Workshop.

# 7

# Beyond the Coalfields: The Work of the Miners' Support Groups

with Hilary Wainright

1985

The Miners' Strike seems to epitomise those aspects of the labour movement and class politics that certain interpreters have found 'old fashioned', sectional and, by implication, bankrupt. Male manual workers, the old working class with a vengeance, fighting to save jobs in what is officially described as a declining industry, state-owned and located in isolated declining regions. And yet around this struggle a massive support movement has grown up – almost unreported – with as broad a social and geographical base as any post-war radical political movement.

**The coalfields**

The social structure of the mining communities reflects the industry which is their livelihood: lack of white-collar jobs, their proletarian nature, the overwhelming dominance of male, manual labour. The regions are distinctive in other ways too. They are predominantly white; they are socially conservative; traditional sexual divisions of labour – woman as home-maker, man as bread-winner – have been deeply ingrained and only recently begun to break down.

Their politics have been workplace-based. They are the fiefdoms of one of the most important unions in labour movement history, symbolising – at least for men – the old strengths of a solidarity born of mutual dependence at work, and the reliance of a whole community on a single industry. The themes of discipline and collectivism run deep and strong in the political atmosphere. These are regions owned, regulated, fed and watered by the central state. The industry is nationalised, high proportions of the inhabitants live on state subsidies, and for an alternative to work in the pit they appeal to state regional policy. They have voted Labour for years, through thick and (mainly) thin. And the local state, for ages too, has been in the hands of the Labour Party right wing. They are the heartlands of labourism. What this means is that the strike is taking place in some of the most self-enclosed and socially homogenous regions of the country. And indeed that geography is part of the rationale and the character of the strike. The one-to-one relationship between community and coal, at least for male employment, has been one of the bases of its solidarity. Levels of militancy have been in part related to dependence on the industry (this, it should be noted in passing, is a nice boomerang of that 1950s 'anti-regional policy' of keeping alternative employment for men out of the coalfields). And that dependence on a single industry has also been one of the bases for the struggle going beyond the workplace, to become an issue of community survival. Again there is some kind of relationship: it is the coalfields most affected by the reconstruction of the 1950s and 1960s, for instance by new workers moving in from other areas, and therefore the more recently constituted communities, which have been least solid in the strike. Geographical coherence therefore has been an element of strength but its corollary – geographical separation – has, potentially been an isolating factor.

Put these social and geographical characteristics together and the strike could easily be seen as an old politics, slogging away in its own redoubts, far away from where 'the rest of us' live. And indeed, several commentators on the left (as well as the right) have seen it in those terms. The last gasp of the old labour movement, in its decaying heartlands, isolated, sectional, macho, and with little resonance beyond its regions, its unions, and – of course – what they call the 'hard left'.

## Support from elsewhere

What has actually happened has been quite different. One of the most stunning aspects of the strike has been that in many ways it has not remained locked within those characterisations. With trade-union leadership at sixes and sevens, their creaking structures, and their lack of credibility, unable to lead any response, and with party political leadership embarrassed by the whole affair – in spite of, maybe because of, all this heavy-footed inertia – there has sprung up a completely different way of organising support, indeed an expansion of what the concept of support means. 'The grass roots', people of all sorts, previously politically active and not, have just got on with it. Often in the most unexpected ways and places, support networks have been organised, fundraising events launched, and distribution systems established.

## The cities

Some of the strongest support has come from Labour's other base – and Thatcher's other opposition – the big cities. What the cities share with the coalfields – apart from Labour MPs – is industrial decline and the feeling that they have been singled out for attack. The Prime Minister knows the geographical bases of her enemies. In the cities, in addition to economic devastation, the assault comes in the form of rate-capping and the proposed abolition of the GLC and the Metropolitan Counties.

In other ways, however, the cities and the coalfield regions are very different from each other. In the cities there is generally a great mix of industries, including services, and a variety of jobs. Many of those in work are on low pay, in casual occupations, working in small firms, and in many areas levels of unionisation are low. There is a different kind of physical dereliction. In the middle of all this lives an enormously diverse population; in many cities ethnic minorities, gay and lesbian communities, women's groups and 'alternative' networks of many kinds form an important element. The trade-union movement is also different from that in the coalfields. Here its very industrial variety has been the basis for a tradition of local links and networks. Public sector and white-collar unions are especially important.

All this in recent years has begun to spawn a politics quite distinct from coalfield labourism. It is often anarchistic, socially adventurous, with a commitment to politics outside the work-place as well as within. It is the radical, as opposed to the labourist, end of the labour movement – if you like; a different kind of trade unionism in uneasy combination with an alliance of the dispossessed.

And yet, in spite of these contrasts, the support from the cities has been massive. On Merseyside there are fourteen support groups, which between them have sent off £1 million so far (a *million* pounds – from a city itself in desperate poverty), and that's not including work-place collections, and new groups are still being formed. There are normally fifty to sixty miners out in the city centre. From Birmingham support goes to South Wales, and also to other more local coalfields. From London it has gone to Kent, South Wales, Staffordshire and the North East; individual boroughs and support groups of various sorts have twinning arrangements with pits in many different coalfields. There are people with buckets, collections of food, on high streets everywhere, an anarchy of support groups and what appear to be a number of different attempts to form umbrella organisations.

The Garston Miners' Support Group in Liverpool typifies the close links which are beginning to be formed between city and coalfield. 'Each week', notes John Bohanna, one of the group, 'at least some of the group go knocking on people's doors asking for food for the striking miners. Equally, each week some of the group go asking for money in the local pubs. Raffles and two huge jumbled sales have taken place during the summer. The raffles concentrated in work places and any sympathetic individual the group could encourage support from. The group had transported car-loads of food to North Wales striking miners' families and has provided van-loads for the striking miners' families in the Lancashire Pits. It has also developed links with Bolsover families.' The latest high point in the groups' work was organizing a party for 150 kids in Bolsover. It was a bit like transporting a prefabricated house and a prefabricated party (almost) complete with balloons, presents, sandwiches, ice cream, jelly and Father Christmas, 120 miles. John Bohanna takes over the story: 'Never in the history of partying can the efficiency of that group be equalled in its work-rate and determination to provide all that a children's party should have. We found pleasure in seeing many fathers of the children along with mothers at the party. A miner taking photographs was heard to remark – "Orgreave was safer than this". It gave an opportunity to embrace our (small) physical display of solidarity with our verbal concern and wishes to the adults. Leaving the little town of Bolsover we saw parents and children lining the pavement and waving their thanks. But we had thanks to give them for allowing us into their lives.' The 'two ends of the labour movement' are linking up.

The nature of the support from the cities reflects the characteristics of the conurbations, and grows out of a constellation of very varied connections people have made. Movingly, impressive support has come from those who are themselves experiencing industrial dereliction. Liverpool 8 (Toxteth) was one of the first places on Merseyside to spawn a support group: 'it grew up literally overnight at the end of April'. The support group in Kirkby, a 1950s outer-city council area shattered by economic collapse, has achieved a fifty per cent response to its door-to-door collections. In London, people in the areas around the Royal Docks have set up the Durham-Docklands Miners' Support Group. On an early visit they took £750 with them to the North East. As they handed over the cheque to the Durham Women's group 'there were tears in their eyes – and ours'. The secretary of the Docklands Group recalls: 'It was the derelict villages that shook me. You could see how much they depended on the pit. The villages without a pit were dead. New factories had once been built but they've been closed long since. We know from the experience of what happened to us what will happen to them.' The Docklands, like the coalfields, was a community dependent on a single dominant economic focus. The slogan of the Durham-Docklands Miners' Support Group is: 'Don't let the mines go the same way as the docks'.

Support comes, too, from the trade unions in the cities. In Liverpool although some of the work-place collections seem to have been slower to build up momentum there are now contributions from most factories. The body plant at Ford, Halewood gets about £1,000 every fortnight and the PTA plant between £900 and £1,300 every week. The collections are for different, specific needs each time, so people know how they are helping. In London a vast variety of branches, chapels and workplace communities have regular collections, have adopted pits, and organise special appeals and events. Support has been especially strong in Fleet Street, Inner London local authorities, the Civil Service, hospitals and schools.

Perhaps the most notable of all has been the support from marginalised and oppressed groups. The Labour Party women's section is central to the organization of support in Merseyside. Afro-Caribbean groups, Cypriot groups, the Asian community and Turkish people have contributed and organized support. As early as May two coachloads of miners and their families came from Kent to the Multi-racial Carnival in Brent. And unemployed people have been prominent in the work of many groups. On Merseyside it's unemployed people who keep the co-ordinating centre going for the support groups. And centres for the unemployed are often the physical base for the support organizations. In Southampton, Cardiff, Manchester, York, Glasgow and Edinburgh there are 'Lesbians and Gays Support the Miners' groups. In London by December over £3,000 had been raised through regular collections at lesbian and gay clubs. All these social groups have been important sources of support for the strike in all parts of the country, but in the cities they also form a crucial element in the recent emergence of a new radical urban politics.

Fringe culture has been drawn in as well. There are gigs, collections at fringe theatres (such as the Half Moon) and at clubs (such as Islington's Wrong Horse), benefit discos and day-long benefit variety shows (e.g. at the Tricycle) with films, food, comedy and music. In Liverpool at a concert – for two to three thousand people – local bands played free and several friendly sound companies lent equipment cheap.

And finally the left-wing local authorities themselves play a part, though necessarily circumscribed by red (i.e. blue) tape. Both City and County Councils are part of Merseyside's Trade Union Labour Party Campaign Committee, a central part of the support activity. In London Ken Livingstone chairs the 'Mineworkers' Defence Committee' set up to co-ordinate support from the different political groups, and in Camden and Islington women from Kent were given mayoral receptions. The GLC's evidence to the Sizewell enquiry is part of the wider case for coal and more recently the Council has produced *London In the Dark*, a pamphlet on the possibilities and impact of coal shortages and power cuts in London. And developing plans for combined heat and power systems (for instance in Newcastle, Sheffield, London, Edinburgh and Glasgow) will make more efficient use of energy. Local state politics and policies can be part of constructing a long term national energy plan. The cities may not produce much coal (though there is a joke going around about Islington Main Colliery, due to all the strike-related activity in that borough), but they are major consumers of it.

## Thatcherland

Most unexpected of all has been the support which has come from the outer-metropolitan and more rural stretches of south and east England. Electorally this has been Thatcher's strongest base, with the Alliance coming second. It is not an area without its problems. Here too older manufacturing industry is in decline (the railways at Swindon for example), and unskilled school leavers have little to look forward to other than unemployment or a job at a routine, repetitive end of a service industry (insurance perhaps), or one of the much vaunted high-tech growth industries. But the dominant image at least is affluence, confidence, prosperity. Unemployment is below the national average, both jobs and people are moving into the area, and there are high proportions of the new middle class and their social accoutrements – the gin-and-Jaguar belt.

Much has been made in recent political speeches about the increasing gap between North and South. It is a political and ideological divide as well as an economic one. And yet, during this strike, thousands of people from such unlikely sounding places as Borehamwood (Cecil Parkinson's seat) and Rottingdean not only contributed to the Christmas Appeal for the miners and their families, but also wrote letters saying why, expressing their support, and urging the miners to go on. St Albans and Wivenhoe have become renowned, through media coverage, for their organisations, activity and generosity. It would be wrong to pretend that this stretch of the country had suddenly turned radical. The very high proportion of Christmas letters which came from Thatcher country may well have been precisely a result of the relative lack of more organised campaigning in such areas. Contributors to the Appeal expressed a strong desire to dissociate themselves from the popular image of satisfied southerners: 'Even in rural Somerset there is support and admiration for *our* miners' stated one.

In some letters there is a real sense of embarrassment at geographical privilege: 'Many of us in the prosperous south are appalled at the treatment miners are receiving, my small contribution is perhaps the only positive action my family can take' wrote a contributor from New Milton, Hampshire.

At times the letters create an impression of people outside the mining communities almost *willing* the miners to win, and not only for the sake of the mining communities. The appeal seemed to have opened up an opportunity for people to express themselves, to become involved. For instance, one contributors wrote: 'Please tell the miners and their families we are with them and not to give in'.

But support has not been confined to donating money and writing letters. There has also been, even in these parts of the country, the development of active support groups with direct involvement in the strike. Two examples may help to illustrate what is happening.

Cambridge is one of the hearts of high-tech land. It is set in a basically Tory area, but the town has a hung council and Labour local control (which has had its advantages – such as getting a licence for collecting). The university has always resisted the development of manufacturing industry, so there is no major manual trade-union base. Its Labour Party is large – the result, perhaps, of the social nature of the town – for the bulk of the membership comes from the white-collar and intellectual sections, those who live in the terraced houses of the centre, rather than from the small outer-council estates, though the latter do vote solidly Labour.

The social group involved in what is now a major and sophisticated support network reflect that 'sunbelt' Cambridge image. The most important elements are intellectuals and white-collar strata in general, together with people active in issue-politics, particularly feminism and the nuclear question. But the organisational contribution of unemployed people has also been very important. The initiative for the support group came from the trades council but its political composition includes members from just about every left party or group and many non-aligned – it is a 'very important political development locally in itself'. The weekly meetings have between fifteen and fifty people attending.

Cambridge has twinned with Blidworth and Rainworth, two pit villages in Nottinghamshire where only a minority came out on strike. The choice was based on a mixture of personal contact (through a left political group) and the belief that life for strikers might be harder here than in more 'solid' areas. And in support of those strikers, Cambridge has had gigs, ceilidhs, house meetings, college collections, jumble sales, an art sale, and numerous other things. The main sources of money are private donations, the Labour Party levy from members and awards, and – above all – the big Saturday street collections in town. All told, Cambridge Miners' Support group sends off £600 a week to Blidworth and Rainworth (and they also give some support to Gwent, but there isn't the space to tell everything here). Each village gets about £150 in cash and £150 in food, regularly, every week.

Milton Keynes is a very different bit of the British sunbelt. Not ancient academic spires, but Britain's biggest new town. Like most new towns Milton Keynes shares one thing with Cambridge – the lack of a major tradition of manual-labour trade unionism. When they began the support group the organisers reflected on this and were cautious about how much support they would raise – 'It's a strange place Milton Keynes, it's not like an old labour movement area. It's not like Liverpool and places ... it's bred into them in Liverpool'. In the event, a major organisation has been established, drawing together all kinds of local groups and individuals including 'lots of people completely new to politics'. Milton Keynes Miners' Support Group began through the trades council and is based in the Unemployed Workers' Centre. Between 150 and 200 people are associated with it, not all coming to meetings, but available to provide meals, accommodation and help. People are there as individuals, but very important links have been established with the Afro-Caribbean Club, the Sikh Society, the large local Peace Group and the Ecology Party. In contrast to Cambridge, the political parties have not been significant here. The constituency Labour Party seems to have been very reticent 'but individual branches have been great' (another case yet further down the structure, of the 'lowest orders' not waiting for the higher echelons to move but just getting on with it).

Milton Keynes today supports South Derbyshire and contributes to Cannock, Staffs. From the initial work-place collections, activities have now branched out to become wide-ranging. As elsewhere there have been numerous visits to the coalfield, 'bus-loads of people ... to see what's going on', and a special fund, started with amazing foresight on September 1, for Christmas. Each pit got £800 and all 380-odd children got a present. A number of local shops came up with quite spectacular donations of food, clothes and toys. More regularly, there are weekly or twice-weekly collections in Milton Keynes, Bletchley, Newport Pagnall and the Open University. All houses in Milton Keynes are being leafleted with requests and then visited each day for collections – 'we get food, clothes, and some abuse'. In total this activity brings in between £800 and £1,000 per week in support of the strike. 'Milton Keynes must have sent getting in for £30,000 already'.

All this activity, in the cities, in Thatcherland and throughout the country has been far more than simply giving aid to some distant struggle. It has had an integral relation to the strike. A typical comment, this one in fact from Liverpool, runs 'there is a constant flow of information about the strike ... people feel really involved in the strike ... it doesn't feel like charity. When miners arrive they are immediately put to work. They feel involved in the organisation, part of the same movement, rather than the recipients of charity'. And in Milton Keynes there is a keen awareness that although one of the areas it supports has only a small minority out on strike, aid there is vital for the strike as a whole – 'those few strikers are vital. Keeping them able to stay out stops the NCB being able to say any area is back completely'. So all this organization and support is essential, and the people involved see that; they have a strategic sense of what they are involved in.

## Explanations

What has led such diverse groups of people to feel that this strike, however geographically and socially distant, concerns and involves them? There is no single explanation but there are several common themes. They crop up in letters sending donations, in conversations during street collections, in discussions about why a particular group is giving an unexpected amount of support.

## Resonance

A recurring theme is the resonance – sometimes based on sympathy, sometimes on respect, on fond memories or past friendships and family connections – which the miners have with people of every region and nearly every social group. The letters to the national Christmas Appeal express this resonance most vividly.

Many letters recall experiences of the generosity of the miners and their families. A retired social worker writes: 'I worked in the coalfields for seventeen years. I know how quickly miners responded to the appeals for help from those who were less fortunate than themselves. They most certainly do not deserve the abuse that flows from those who know so little about them'. Two pensioners from Herne Bay remember: 'the wonderful friendship shown to us in Derbyshire. For me it was as a lonely soldier during the war, training amongst strange people and far from home. For my wife it meant being offered a refuge for two very young children. We never forgot how our buckets of coal came to us after that'. The strike brought back other memories of the war: 'I am old enough to remember how much the miners responded to all that was asked of them during the war and feel indignant that this be forgotten in hard times now'. Shades of the Earl of Stockton. There were contributions 'with thanks for comradeship of those miners I knew as a Bevin Boy forty years ago', from people who worked on the 'Save the Miners' Fund in London in 1926' and 'on behalf of my late husband, born and bred in Tonypandy – whose family experienced the troops in 1911'.

## A common cause against Thatcher

The pent-up hostility expressed towards Thatcher is overwhelming, whatever people's views on the strike itself. 'Anti-Scargill, anti-all violence but above all *anti-Thatcher*. Good luck' says one Home Counties' contributor to the Christmas Appeal. 'Thank God for the NUM, at least one union has the guts to stand up to her' writes a contributor from Hastings, expressing a view of many who feel that the NUM is taking on a common enemy. 'As a civil servant', another man wrote starkly, 'I feel that your cause is ours, if you fail we all fail'.

Street collectors found a similar sense of common cause. During a first collection in Milton Keynes an unemployed man with a family gave £10 after cashing his giro. 'You can't afford to give that much surely?' said the collector. 'I can't afford not to', was the response.

Support groups from all over report that the people most deprived and battered by Thatcher's policies give with greatest generosity. We've just seen that in Liverpool support is strongest in Toxteth and Kirkby and that in London's Docklands the experience has been similar. One of the organisers describes the response to their weekly collection: 'Pensioners nearly always give, so do the Asian and Afro-Caribbean Community and young people. The well-dressed people give less. We didn't do as well as I expected from them'.

In Toxteth, Brixton, Chapeltown in Leeds and other inner-city areas where blacks are in a majority, an understanding of what it is like to live under police occupation lies behind the strong feelings of support. Memories of police aggression are also a factor behind the support of one of the most well paid and traditionally sectional trade-union groups in the country: the Fleet Street Chapels of the NGA. Most of these chapels raise £1-2 per member per week and there are regular exchange visits. Coach loads of NGA members travel up to Bold in St Helens and Birch Coppice in Staffordshire and pit villages in Durham and Northumberland. 'It's Warrington that's produced this response', says Mike Power, Father of an NGA chapel at the Daily Mail, 'the Warrington picket line on the night of November 31st 1983 has changed the NGA. There's a real feeling of solidarity with the miners especially because of the police.' On 31 November NGA members, including five hundred from Fleet Street, were on the picket line and experienced police violence for themselves.

The reasons for NGA support are typical of the wider pattern of labour movement support, especially in the cities. Where workers have already had their own clashes with the government, whether they've won or lost, whether they have traditionally been left or moderate, there is a groundswell of sympathy and considerable contact between pit villages and work-place support groups. Civil servants for instance were among the most numerous of those who identified themselves in contributing to the national Christmas Appeal. They included a trade unionist from GCHQ who had refused to resign from the union. He sent £250. In London campaigning groups in schools that came into being to defend the Inner London Education Authority have in many cases become the basis of miners' support groups.

The sense of a common threat is one factor behind the support of women's groups for the strike. A Midlands Women's Aid Centre for instance, wrote with a cheque for the Christmas Appeal: 'We too are suffering at the hands of the Tory Government. Next year our Urban Aid grant will be halved, the following year none at all. We fully support your struggle'.

## Finding Allies

But the wholehearted and enthusiastic involvement of all kinds of women's groups, Labour Party women's sections, women's peace groups, and childcare campaigns, in the industrial action of a notoriously male-chauvinist union is not based just on anti-Thatcherism. Their involvement has been inspired by the power and confidence of the women in the mining communities.

The response of the Enfield women's peace group in London sums it up: 'We were inspired by the women. We wanted to show them that they weren't alone, that we need each other. Our links with the women in Cannock have helped to overcome our isolation and sense of powerlessness'. The involvement of the women had helped people outside the coalfields to understand the community issues at stake.

The people who set up the Durham-Docklands support group illustrate this. Eddie Corbett explains: 'Before I met the women (from Durham) I'd felt sympathetic to the miners but I didn't really want to be involved. I saw them collecting outside tube stations and thought of them just as trade unionists. After hearing the women and their stories of hardship and the police I understood it was families and communities at stake.' It was then that he and the others made the connection between their fight for democratic control over their community against a non-elected government quango, the London Docklands Development Corporation and the miners' defence of their communities against the government-appointed NCB. 'They are fighting the same regime, the same undemocratic process as we are.'

Other groups which have made positive links include the environmental movement, the peace movement and the anti-nuclear movement. In Milton Keynes for instance the Ecology Party is very active. They quickly saw the links between the strike, the nuclear issue, the open-cast mining which they are against for environmental reasons. In the same town the large peace group, which itself involves a broad coalition, has put over the miners' case in several meetings. 'Mines not Missiles' is now a common theme at rallies organized by CND and miners' support groups. Miners' support meetings increasingly reflect these and other links and the speakers most in demand are those who make the connections. Tony Benn has done nearly 300 miners' support meetings, most of them packed to overflowing, since the Chesterfield by-election. From the figures we have, he must have addressed over 200,000 people. Platforms often include speakers from other campaigns and these multi-purpose platforms are not only speaking to the converted. People new to political activity, though often involved in local community issues, have been turning up and getting involved. At a rally of 900 in Liverpool, 300 new people signed up to become involved and twenty-five per cent of these are now active in their local support group.

## Political catalysts

These are some elements, then, of an explanation for the extraordinarily widespread support which exists for the miners, behind the media picture of an isolated and sectorial strike. But an adequate explanation must include the driving forces behind the initial formation of the larger support groups. In most cases, town or city-wide support groups have been initiated by trades councils or local Labour Parties, with socialists outside the Labour Party providing important support. The impetus to create support groups was more than trade-union solidarity. Memories of the 1972 and 1974 miners' strikes provide a powerful image, a source of great expectations. When the miners take action, governments fall. At the beginning there was a strong sense of the miners' power to break Thatcher's grip. It was not that people wanted to leave it to the miners, it was rather a feeling that Thatcher would find it difficult if another front was opened up, especially in the coalfields. In the cities, campaigning alliances were already forming to fight abolition and rate-capping. There was a feeling that at last a trade-union battalion, the most militant, had gone into action. As the strike developed and the other big battalions held back, not so big now, as the women became an organised force and the strike increasingly became a strike about communities, the significance of the support groups became clearer. It seemed increasingly that their work was crucial to the miners' power and their chances of success. Personal links and the adoption of pits created a momentum of their own. A new, or at least more confident, do it yourself politics flourished out of necessity.

## Forms of organisation

That phrase 'out of necessity' comes up again and again as people explain the work of their support groups. It helps to explain the form that the support movement takes. Out of necessity, the support movement has started from existing organisations and resources. Picking up whatever in the old structures suited their urgent purpose. They grew from whatever organisations could be most rapidly geared into action, from networks of friends, to tightly organised NGA chapels. They used whatever resources were available from church halls to county halls, from the Labour Party's duplicator to the WRP's newsletter. Out of necessity the initial organisation have moved outwards to extend support.

In doing so they have often changed themselves. The NGA for instance, normally a rather exclusive organization, has helped to co-ordinate and extend a miners' support group in small offices and work-places throughout the City. Women who come together for a women's canvass in the Chesterfield by-election became the Chesterfield Women's Action Group to support the miners. In January it organised a women's march through all the nearby pit villages.

## Co-ordination

In most towns and cities there are miners' support groups that play a co-ordinating role, organizing big functions, rallies, concerts, etc. In the larger cities the co-ordinating meetings also play an important role in sorting out some of the problems which arise within groups, between groups and in relations with strike centres. As we have already said these groups have usually been initiated through the local Labour Party or trades councils. All left parties are normally involved, though the Socialist Workers Party was a latecomer to the support groups, and initially chose its own form of direct support for the strikers. Everyone comments on the unique degree of co-operation between political groups. On at least one occasion it has gone so far as discussing with each other whether or not to sell their papers during street collections and deciding against! In addition to city-wide support groups there is an immense variety of smaller community and work-place groups which spring from groups of friends, from collections by individuals and from visits from miners themselves. The Garston Miners' Support Group is a good example of a community group, though most of its members also organize regular collections at work. It started with a group of friends who had worked together on other issues.

One of its members describes its organisation: 'There are no regulations in the group. GMSG doesn't have standing orders. No bureaucracy, just straightforward action to help the section of the class that had the guts to challenge the rich. No command structure, no leaders, just a grouping of socialists that did what it could. However, there was a need for a co-ordinator that kept the energy of the group ticking over. That fell to Eileen and Mark.'

## Twinning and the distribution of food

Connections of personal friendship, political commitment, and material sustenance between the support groups and the pits are the energy supply of the support movement as much as the life-blood of the strike.

Take Cambridge for instance. They've organised holidays for miners' families; there was a massive exercise at Christmas with, amongst much else, an individually chosen present and collection of stocking-fillers for each child (over two hundred of them); there's at least one trip a week from Cambridge to Notts, and there have been long and short visits, both ways. 'We've had speakers down from them and spoken ourselves up there. We've picketed, had women pickets, worked in the kitchens, gone to the Cash and Carry, looked after the children, joined in parties, pub sessions and gigs'.

Sometimes the connections are called 'twinning' but the associations are more flexible and varied than such a one-to-one relationship implies. At the beginning of the strike there were problems when groups adopted the pit with which they first had contact – often through visiting miners. Some pits received more money than others. Such problems remain, but there is a growing bush telegraph and an acute awareness of the need to achieve an equitable distribution. The Milton Keynes Support Group for instance now supports South Derbyshire and contributes to Cannock in Staffs. But this has not always been so. The story behind it tells a lot about the sensitivity and flexibility of the 'alternative distribution systems' which have developed during the strike. Milton Keynes is in the South East Region of the TUC and its money was originally sent off along the 'normal channels' of organisation to the centre, and to Kent (also SERTUC). It soon became apparent, however, that Kent was getting a lot of support, especially from London, so it was decided to adopt pits in Leicestershire. This lasted for about six months until Leicestershire, too, began getting more from its local towns. So Leicestershire suggested Staffordshire and South Derbyshire with whom they had close relations, and who were having a rough time. This carefully thought out allocation of aid is vital for the strike.

Many support groups, like Garston, share funds between pits. Or, like the Durham–Docklands support group, they contribute to a regional co-ordinating centre. *Socialist Worker* carries a list of strike kitchens in need. *Labour Briefing* lists pits which are not yet twinned. In the mining communities themselves the womens' support groups have become well organized. They have had to – managing hundreds of pounds each week, feeding over 300 people every day. They co-ordinate regionally and do their best to ensure that funds and provisions reach areas of need. In South Wales, there is a particularly co-ordinated multi-level system, providing channels of support (from urban and rural areas of Wales, from England and from international sources to the coalfields).

### Preaching to the unconverted

Just as the groups have improvised to find the best way of distributing the support, so they have tried all kinds of ingenious ways of collecting funds and putting across their arguments. Individuals have been buying and selling British Telecom shares and sending the proceeds to the Christmas Appeal. Greenham Women have marched from pit heads to nuclear power stations, giving out leaflets and holding meetings on the way to make the connection between the case against nuclear power and the miners' demands. The most impressive thing about this aspects of the work of the support groups is the emphasis on reaching out to the uncommitted. It is as if all the heart-searching about the left being stuck in a ghetto, shop-floor leaders being out of touch with their members and so on, has produced an almost evangelical commitment to win support on the street, in the pubs, on the shop floor and in door to door collections. In Kirkby for instance the support group has leafletted each house at least three times and visited at least once. Few election campaigns could better that! Its political importance is that arguments are reaching people, independently of the media.

The forms of organisation in the support movement, and in the mining communities are an extraordinary combination of traditional labour-movement structures with the open, campaigning styles of CND and the women's movement. The women in the mining communities have played perhaps a leading role in inspiring the support movement. And their relationship with the NUM nationally as well as locally sets the example for this combination. In a sense their organisation and its importance is sustaining the strike and extending support has given a new legitimacy to the demands of women outside the coalfields for real power within labour-movement organisations. A recent national meeting of Women Against Pit Closures was symbolic. There they were sitting around the board table in the reserved seats of the NUM executive. Ann Lilburn, a grandmother from Whittle, Northumberland, sat in the seat reserved for A. Scargill and Katherine Slater, a miners' wife from Barnsley in the seat for P. Heathfield. They were discussing the distribution of £1-2 million. Their treasurer, Jean McCrindle, has handled nearly £1 million this year, in her spare time. At one point Arthur Scargill in person put his head round the door smiling benignly, but no one really noticed.

## Conclusions

Whatever the outcome of the strike, labour movement politics will never be the same again. There will no doubt be attempts to block, if not stamp out, the new initiatives that cut across so many traditional procedures and hierarchies. It will be a struggle to consolidate and develop the improvised democracy produced inside the coalfields and beyond, by the strike.

But the pressures to continue the process of change will be strong. Through the strike and the support movement many people new to political involvement have become experienced, effective speakers, expert organisers and confident socialists. A lot has been learned. Amongst these new activities a gut anti-Thatcherism has begun to be more precisely articulated to win a positive belief in another way of organising society.

This is partly the result of learning about the problems of other groups. Miners, for instance, learned through their visits to the cities of the problems of racism. As one Nottingham miner put it 'I'd never been racist, I don't think, but I'd never really understood it before.' Support groups in the rural south learnt from the solidarity and collectivism of the mining areas, from 'the steadfastness and sheer courage up there,' as one of the Cambridge group told us.

Travelling and exchange visits across the country are an important source of power. Usually it is only the leadership that has an overview of what is going on. Moreover these visits help create unity at the base, across the old structures. They have also created connections between different, previously quite separate, sections of the working class; cleaners fighting privatisation in London speaking on one platform at miners' meetings; miners from Nottingham joining the picket line at Addenbrooks Hospital in Cambridge; miners promising to join the people of Docklands in action to stop a businessman's airport. Finally, there has been a learning of an immensely practical sort; learning to manage thousands of pounds on behalf of hundreds of people; facing up to the real problems of building an alternative welfare system, a system of distribution according to need. Such experience leaves more than memory.

The support groups we have talked to in most detail already have plans for the future. In Cambridge, they want to find a way of consolidating the network into a more permanent organisation after the strike is over. In Liverpool they feel they have established a strong organisation which they will need again and won't let collapse. In Milton Keynes they are already planning a 'trade-union month' as part of an attempt to strengthen the unions there.

One of the most politically decisive experiences of many who have been part of the support movement is that they have tried the traditional hierarchies and leadership of the labour movement and found them severely wanting. The lack of political leadership has been most important. It has been the failure of some of the Labour Party's Parliamentary leaders to get across the economic and social arguments for the mining communities which has created the vacuum that the support groups are trying to fill. Even now the parliamentary leadership seems to be making little attempt to give effective national backing to the support movement or even draw media attention to its size and scope.

But instead of wasting time passing resolutions calling on the leadership to do the things that will never materialise, people in the localities have, on the whole, just got on with it. This has not only been on a local basis but also nationally. A conference attended by over 1,500 support groups was held in December at Camden Town Hall. This confidence amongst the support groups to take the initiative in their own hands, rather than simply making calls on the leadership, sets an important precedent for the future.

In much of their work many support groups illustrate in practice the kind of movement we need to build in order to achieve socialism. A commitment to change through building up democratic power at the base, in the factories and in the communities; a breaking down of the traditional, inhibiting boundary between politics and trade unionism; a sense of local strength and identity which at the same time is not parochial; a commitment to a non-sectarian but principled form of unity, in which different political tendencies are respected and work together; an emphasis on reaching out, a confidence that radical demands can be popular if they are argued for.

It would be wrong to pretend that all this has happened without problems. In all this activity there have of course been tensions; tensions between different political perspectives and groups, conflicts between the new-found strength of women and the power-bases previously established as male, suspicions of the white left on the part of some black groups. But constructing links between groups, between areas, between issues can never be achieved without tensions. There are real contradictions between the multiple issues which have become linked to the support network during the strike and no genuine democratic 'alliance' could ever be built without recognising and facing up to them. In this context the strength of the support networks is precisely that 'alliances' have been built in the course of real, day-to-day, political action. These are not 'links' established simply by writing out lists of policies, nor are they a 'common programme' negotiated between party leaders.

We are not claiming the world. But nonetheless something radically different has emerged out of a movement in support of what was seen as an 'old' struggle. Many thought this impossible. They have argued that the left must move with the times – that 'old-fashioned' class struggles are doomed to isolation, without resonance or relevance to present-day socialist policies. Behind this argument is an equation of class politics, on the one hand, and the existing institutions of the labour movement on the other. To make such an equation leads to an incorrect assessment of the political choice before us, as one between industrial muscle and the new social movements. The existing institutions of labour *are* old fashioned and sectional. But what the Miners' Strike has shown is that these institutions can be superseded and challenged without abandoning class politics. It has shown that it is not a question of *either* industrial action *or* the new social movements, nor is it one of just adding the two together. What is important is a recognition of a mutual dependence and a new openness to influence, of the one upon the other. What this strike has demonstrated is a different direction for class politics. New institutions can be built through which 'class politics' can be seen as more than simply industrial militancy plus parliamentary representation.

*In this article we have written mainly as reporters of an aspect of the strike which has been almost completely ignored outside the left press. We have interviewed people throughout the country about their support activity but have focused on four groups in particular. We would like to thank the following for their assistance although none of them are responsible for our political interpretations: Tony Benn, Kate Bennett, John and Joan Bohanna, Eddie Corbett, Bill Dewsbury, Vic Graves, Doreen Humber, Dave Hailwood, Liz Knight, Alison New, Kevin Machin, Bernard Regan, Mike Power, Liane Philips.*

*This essay first appeared in* Digging Deeper: Issues in the Miners' Strike, *edited by Huw Beynon, Verso, 1985.*

# 8

# Keep Moving On …

## with Hilary Wainwright
## 1985

The strike is over. As a strike it was defeated. But it was also part of a longer, and wider, process which is by no means over. Many times during the strike it was said that things would never be the same again. We all made promises to keep going 'afterwards'. Can we now deliver? It is vital that we do.

First, there is a wide range of immediate tasks. Most obviously, that 'alternative welfare distribution system', which was one of the most impressive achievements of the strike, still needs to be sustained. While community kitchens will be closed down or put to other uses (for old age pensioners and unemployed people), the distribution of food parcels will go on for months. The legacy of debts is enormous. It is a situation already made worse by recrimination by the NCB. In some areas where a minority of miners were on strike, returning strikers have been downgraded and face wages lower than those of a year ago.

There are also specific groups and campaigns which urgently need action. There are at present about 140 people in gaol – prisoners of the dispute. They must not be forgotten. There is a need for financial help, both to keep the prisoners' families going, and to provide money for prison visits. Further, there is the issue of individual moral support, for both prisoners and their families. Several support groups are suggesting the adoption of prisoners. Some way of coordinating this – so no one gets left out – needs to be established. Urgent action is also necessary on the issue of an amnesty.

Then there is the work of documentation. This has two aspects. The first relates to what is going on in the coalfields now. For while the NCB and the government have not won the argument at a national political level, at the level of the individual coalfield, community, and miner, they are grinding home their victory at the ending of the strike. Union men have systematically been put on the worst shifts, shift systems have been changed, closures have been threatened, people have been sacked, others regraded. The revenge being taken is vicious.

It is up to us to make what is happening public. A number of support groups are planning an information bulletin which will both collect and document information about victimisation and spell out what support is needed. In addition to Police Watch, we need an 'NCB Watch'.

## A time to write

Support groups are already turning their hands to their second aspect of documentation. This is the documentation – through writing, poetry, photography – of the strike itself and of their activities. It has often been said that the strike has created the possibility of a new form of politics, based in particular around the network of local groups and alliances. The plans to record that year's activity are an important step in building confidence and in consolidating what has been learnt. What becomes of those beginnings of 'a new politics' will depend in part on whether we ourselves recognise, and learn from, what happened and what was built.

But it is not only support of a defensive sort which will continue to be necessary. Since the NUM's industrial campaign has been defeated, for the time being, the political campaign of the NUM and all its allies will become increasingly important.

An initiative is already off the ground to bring together local authorities with an interest in coal. Late in the strike, Labour local authorities came together at the suggestion of the Barnsley employment department to form the 'Coalfields Communities Campaign'. One of its aims is to demonstrate the potential market for coal in the public sector. The thirty-five affiliated councils are committed to a coal-based energy policy for their own buildings and to combined heat and power schemes as a more efficient means of providing heat for their tenants. If they adopt a strong campaigning approach they could become a powerful force linking the needs of their ratepayers as energy consumers, with the physical and human resources of the mining communities. The campaign will be launched publicly in May. (For details contact Brian Gladstone, Employment Department, Barnsley Town Hall, Barnsley, South Yorks.)

**Dig out academics**

Initiatives like this need the input of the socialist economists and technologists scattered – sometimes buried – throughout the universities and polytechnics. There are also several organisations (the Conference of Socialist Economists, the Socialist Environment and Resources Association, the Socialist Society, etc) who try to organise the intellectual resources of the left. Yet, speaking as members of these organisations we recognise that *we* were very late in even beginning to get our collective act together. We still have not learnt how to use socialist intellectuals as a resource. But at last, a social economics, a strategy for union control over the introduction of new mining technologies, and ideas for the political marketing of coal are being publicly spelled out. (For details of meetings organised by CSE, SERA and the Socialist Society, contact Guy Austin, 9 Poland Street, London W1.)

A central part of the argument for coal is the case against the government's nuclear programme. Again, the campaigning links were not made strongly or publicly enough, especially at a national level. Part of the problem is that neither the parliamentary Labour party nor the TUC has a clear energy policy, let alone a clear commitment to reverse the government's nuclear programme. They allow conflicting trade pressures to produce a fudge. You can't build a campaign on fudge. The other problem is that, at national level, the links between the NUM and the anti-nuclear campaigns have not yet been built, though in the course of the strike local links have gradually been made. A more active campaign to halt the nuclear momentum is high on the agenda. In Northumberland, members of the Women's Support Group are joining the campaign against the Druridge Bay Power Station.

## Clarity not fudging

The strike has also raised to the level of explicit public debate a range of deeper issues which we must not allow to go away. For they are part of a wider critique of Thatcherism. The argument over coal has put in question the idea that 'profit' represents the only rationale for production. Not a new discovery for socialists, but it is important that it has been publicly questioned in (some) newspapers and (occasionally) on television. It is an issue at the heart of other major battles against this government. In inner cities, and in many other places, the most desperate needs, and the human and physical resources to meet those needs, exist side by side in the grossest social irrationality. The logic of profit cannot bring them together.

All this relates to the notion of community, and the recognition that the fight for jobs is also a conflict over wider issues, including control over local economies. The experience of the strike has in many ways deepened this consciousness of locality. It is obvious in the coalfields. But many support groups also comment on the same learning process, and the development of a commitment to continue as broad-based local action groups.

## Local social audits

Yet, precisely because it has emerged in the context of a network, this is not a parochial localism. The aim must be now to bring out the same issues again and again, in place after place. They underline the arguments against rate capping and abolition, for instance.

In the longer run, support groups might turn their attention to the future of their local economies, doing local social audits, perhaps documenting local needs and resources, maybe even producing a network of alternative plans which talk in terms of the reproduction of communities in opposition to Thatcher's external logic of profit. If it were possible, it would be an amazingly powerful, and positive, challenge to the government's economic philosophy. It is a lot to ask, but it is not impossible. A number of radical local authorities have behind them now quite a few years of alternative enterprise boards, economic policies, and support, for trade-union and other local campaigns; it is experience from which new initiatives can learn (from their mistakes as well as their successes).

The political strength of such a challenge has been immensely increased by the organisations and networks built in the course of the strike. In the coalfields and beyond a rare kind of collective politicisation has taken place among people, especially women, who have never been politically active before. A continued effort now will ensure that this process is not easily reversed, or cut short, by the defeat of the strike. After all, part of the politicisation was understanding what we and they were up against.

However, the defeat of industrial action will not, among this politicised minority, produce a turn down an exclusively parliamentary road. The experience of four Labour governments echoed by the parliamentary Labour party's performance during the strike means that the political directions in which people will be looking will be more than electoral. However, there is no single direction, no one party clearly pointing the way.

## No Labour monopoly

This politicisation is most likely to be expressed through the Labour Party. But the strike demonstrated more clearly than ever before that there is not one Labour Party, but several, with considerable autonomy from each other. On the one hand, there is the Labour Party of Neil Kinnock; on the other, the Labour Party which initiated support groups and put its resources wholeheartedly behind the miners. This second party was, and still is, part of alliances which include many who are not members of the Labour Party. The experience of working together on an issue as politically far-reaching as the Miners' Strike could create something lasting. Much has been learnt and established independently of both party and union leadership.

It is too early to tell what will last. But of one point we can be sure: the strength of what continues will be determined crucially by our ability to support the campaign of the mining communities now that the strike is over.

*This essay first appeared in* New Socialist, *No. 26, April 1985.*

# 9

# Equal Opportunities: The GLEB Experience

## 1987

The purpose of this paper is to reflect upon the experience of the Greater London Enterprise Board in its attempts during its early years of existence to introduce policies of equal opportunities into its investments. Because the aim of the paper, and of the conference, is to learn from these experiences, the focus here will be on the problems. This is not to say that there were not successes; indeed there were many, both in the specific area of equal opportunities and in social objectives more generally. Much of what will be discussed in this paper is indeed relevant to social objectives as a whole, as well as more specifically to equal opportunities. The focus, as has been said, is on the issue of equal opportunities within GLEB's investment portfolio.

When GLEB was established it was given two, rather different, objectives. The first was to create and maintain jobs within the London economy, achieving commercial viability within a period of two years on any investment. This objective is now generally referred to as the 'commercial objective'. Secondly, the aim was to improve the quality of employment within London, this to include equal opportunities. This objective is the one which came to be known as the 'social objective'. In the early years there was much unclarity about the relationship between these two objectives. The questions of how they were to be prioritised against each other, and of whether or not they were mutually contradictory, were rarely explicitly discussed. In practice therefore the two objectives maintained an uneasy and changing relationship, and on reflection much of the experience of the early years can be seen as an attempt to work out in practice how in fact the two objectives related to each other.

This ambiguity about the relationship between the two objectives led to a number of difficulties. Firstly there was some tendency to counterpose the two objectives in terms of a dichotomy between the 'realism' (i.e. the constraints of the market economy) of the commercial objective and the 'idealism', academicism or intellectualism of the social objective. Being able to read company accounts was consistently seen as 'tough', while social objectives were occasionally referred to as 'soft' and, on one now famous occasion, 'wishy washy'. There was much talk of the need for skilled personnel in relation to the commercial objective, but much less recognition of the need for skilled personnel in relation to the social objective. To some extent this represented a real situation. The social objective is much less easily quantifiable, indeed much less easily set down in any formal terms at all, than is the commercial objective. It did therefore for a long time remain more vague. However, this does not mean that it is more easy to deal with, rather that it is more difficult. Both on the board of GLEB, and more widely within the organisation, there was a lack of understanding of the intellectual and political challenge of the issues of social objectives. Secondly, another way in which the two objectives related, was that on occasions social criteria would be used simply to 'soften' the operation of the commercial objective. When this was done without there being any clear social targets, it was simply a retreat from one objective without any clear advance being made towards the other. Thirdly there was, and still tends to be, a tendency to see success and failure solely in commercial terms. It is hard, precisely because of the lack of quantifiable targets, to see social failure and success in quite the same decisive terms.

Apart from these issues which relate to the double nature of the objectives set for GLEB a range of other problems was also encountered in the operation of equal opportunities, and more widely social, objectives. There were organisational difficulties: for a long time equal opportunities policies were far too dependent for their implementation on the individual good will of particular people within the organisation. There was no adequate structure for their implementation and enforcement. There were huge difficulties of enforcement and monitoring, and of countering resistance from management in the enterprises where we were investing. There were clear cases where management was so eager to get the investment which GLEB could provide, that they were prepared to agree to anything, but without really reckoning on having to fulfil the conditions. Enforcement of equal opportunities policies was difficult enough in those situations where GLEB had control over the company in ownership terms; in cases where this was not true, enforcement was virtually impossible. The implementation of equal opportunities policies also faced conflicts of interest within the labour movement. This was particularly the case because equal opportunities policies were at first both designed and implemented through the process of Enterprise Planning. That is, the policies were to be the product of joint negotiations between GLEB, the workers in the enterprise and the management. This hit a number of difficulties. First of all, enterprise planning itself turned out to be a much longer, more difficult and tortuous process than had initially been envisaged. For that reason equal opportunities policies were slow to develop. Second, however, this very structure meant that equal opportunities policies were to be drawn up by people already working in the enterprises where GLEB had investments. Since one of the aims of GLEB investment might be to broaden the spectrum of workers involved in the enterprise, this posed immediate problems. It might involve, for instance, challenges to existing ways of working and recruitment. It might involve challenging apprenticeship systems, for example; or systems of recruitment from union lists. There were certainly some successes in dealing with these potentially very serious conflicts of interest, but such issues held up the design and implementation of equal opportunities policies in a good number of investments.

A further issue of concern about equal opportunities policies revolved around the Interim Appraisal Criteria, which GLEB had from the beginning as a means of selection of investments. These criteria included a set of premia. The premia were 'awarded' to potential investments on the basis of certain social characteristics; for instance the proportion of ethnic minorities, or women, that they employed. Scoring high on these sets of premia would imply that the amount of investment per job which an enterprise could claim would be raised. It soon became clear that there were a number of problems with the operation of these premia. In fact it seems that, at least in the early years, the maximum level of investment per job was actually rarely reached on the initial investment anyway. In other words, the operation of the premia did not significantly shift the spectrum of enterprises within GLEB's overall portfolio. Moreover, on examination, the portfolio turned out very much not to be dominated by firms employing a majority of white males. Further it soon came to be realised that while these premia might in principle be a workable method of aiding in the process of selection of investments, what was really needed was a way of selecting firms which related not so much to their existing characteristics as to the potential which they embodied for the implementation of equal opportunities strategies. There may, for instance, be more room for progress on equal opportunities in a firm initially dominated by white male skilled workers, than in one dominated by black and/or female workers.

All these issues provoked discussion, if somewhat intermittently, within GLEB. And much was learned. There came to be agreement that investments could be failed on social grounds, and agreement that equal opportunities (or at least reaching a minimum level of equal opportunities agreements) should be a separate requirement from that of enterprise planning. This would have two effects. First, equal opportunities would be removed from the long-drawn-out process of enterprise planning, in which only existing workers are involved. Secondly, some level of adherence to equal opportunities would not be a subject for negotiation; it would be a requirement prior to investment. Again, in recognition of some of the early organisational difficulties, equal opportunities, though still grossly understaffed, is as a division now centrally placed within GLEB. Finally, projects are now to have individually-tailored social plans, with properly laid out and measurable targets and dates, together with services and advice available to aid in their achievement. This should greatly increase the possibility of both monitoring and enforcement.

### Some more fundamental issues

In many ways, then, GLEB reflected upon and learned from some of its early difficulties in the design and implementation of equal opportunities objectives. It remained, however, up against some more fundamental and structural difficulties. Two of these will be discussed below.

The first of these really concerns GLEB's very formation as an institution. This has deeply affected the kind of portfolio which it has been able to build up. As the previous section indicated, there has been considerable progress on the design and implementation of equal opportunities policies at the level of the individual project. What has been more difficult, and far less clearly addressed, is the issue of how to incorporate equal opportunities policies in the design of the overall portfolio. Clearly, the selection of sectors, the operation of premia in the selection of firms (referred to above), and the operation of policies such as support for black-led businesses, are all part of this design. But a strategy for intervention in the local economy which actually *started* from GLEB's commitment to equal opportunities might produce very different criteria for selecting a portfolio from the ones which have been in operation so far. The feminist literature, to take one example, provides considerable discussion of the kinds of things which can be done; and a number of these were incorporated in the London Industrial Strategy. Even conceptualising 'the local economy' can turn out very differently if one starts, not from the sectoral divisions and definitions of work handed down to us by capital, but from what the London Industrial Strategy calls 'an economics geared to need'. Another way of putting the same thing is to talk of the conceptualisation of the economy as the reproduction of community in the fullest sense. If that is done, then, as the London Industrial Strategy points out, domestic labour becomes the most important sector of the economy in terms of time expended. Out of 280 million hours work done reproducing London every year only 100 million hours is paid for. 180 million hours – that is almost two-thirds of the work – is unpaid labour, primarily domestic. 'Yet', says the London Industrial Strategy, 'in spite of its importance the household is regarded as somehow outside the economy by traditional economists and rarely, if ever, does it make its appearance as part of an economic strategy'. The London Industrial Strategy goes on to analyse how the economy of London's households is in crisis, and concludes the section by saying 'for an economics centred around finance these issues are marginal. For an economics centred around need they should be our starting point' (LIS paragraphs 1.57-1.66).

In spite of this, GLEB, which was to be one of the main instruments for the implementation of the GLC's economic strategy, was established in such a way as to make it structurally unable to work around an economics geared to need. The stumbling block is the nature of its commercial objective: the commitment to commercial viability within the space of two years for each individual investment. Such an objective means that GLEB cannot challenge the *conception* of the economy, which is one of the most capitalist things about it; nor can it change the boundary between what is 'economic' and what is 'social'. The economic is defined in terms of that which will produce a commercial financial return. This division between economic and social was enshrined in the division between GLEB and the GLC. GLEB was to produce the economic investments, and the GLC would provide grant finance for social programmes. This meant that GLEB, as in so many other ways, was unable to change the shape of the economy. The socialisation of domestic labour, for instance, through the provision of laundries or creches, was not within its scope, precisely because they could not in the short-run be profitable sectors. It is precisely their current location outside of the 'economic' which means that the competition which they face is from unpaid, generally female, labour. For this reason, provision of such facilities – i.e. the creation of a new sector of production – is extremely expensive and will therefore need subsidising if the facilities are not to remain available only to those with high incomes. Any economic strategy which aims to go beyond the formalities of equal opportunities, to produce an anti-sexist programme of intervention, will have to think about the very shape of the economy itself, and about the division between what is currently called economic and what is currently called social. As it stands at the present, GLEB is unable to pursue an equal opportunities policy of this type.

The second structural constraint which GLEB faces in the implementation of its equal opportunities strategies, and social objectives more generally, again revolves around the nature of its commercial objective. Here the concern is with the investment in an individual enterprise. Assume that a firm has been selected for investment, has fulfilled all the criteria, and an individually-tailored social plan has been drawn up for implementation. The question remains: how will the implementation of this social plan be paid for? Almost all aspects of serious equal opportunities policies have costs attached to them, whether they be costs in terms of time, or of money. In the early days, the issue of the financing of social plans was barely considered explicitly. This was in part because of the reigning ambiguity about the relationship between the two objectives, and in part because clearly specified social plans were anyway only rarely drawn up for individual enterprises. Implicitly, it is probably fair to say that the assumption was that the firm itself would pay. In fact, even where there were clear objectives to be achieved, there was frequently neither the time nor the money within the enterprise to get serious social programmes going. In part at first this was explained by the fact that most of the firms in which GLEB was investing were financially marginal. This indeed is likely to be true of a high proportion of firms which enterprise boards fund. But the problem is not confined to such firms; the competition of the market would mean that extra costs loaded onto an enterprise are anyway going to be a problem whatever the circumstances. More recently, debate within GLEB seems to be coming round to the idea of dividing the budget allocated to any individual enterprise into two distinct parts: the first to be a clear commercial investment demanding a rate of return, and the second a grant for defined social purposes.

This formulation, although certainly much clearer than the woolly operation of the past, in its turn also raises a number of issues. First of all, and in relation to the previous discussion, it means that GLEB is, far from challenging the current given distinction between economic and social, explicitly reinforcing it. Secondly, and more practically, it will not always be possible simply to separate social costs from investment monies demanding a rate of return. Thirdly, and probably positively, this separation between investment and grant highlights even more the difficulties with the most 'obvious' criteria of GLEB's success — of numbers of jobs and cost per job. Cost per job is a criterion of success which has anyway been subject to a good deal of criticism. It is clearly important to raise when discussing the cost of an investment which creates or maintains jobs in relation to what would have been the cost of unemployment. It is more difficult to use, however, in competition with other economic initiatives, for instance enterprise zones. GLEB's commitment to creating *decent* jobs must mean that its jobs will cost more. Separating the budget into investment and social elements might allow that point to be made more forcibly. Having separately-costed social plans, moreover, will also make clear that there is some choice between numbers of jobs and quality of jobs; a commitment to better jobs will also mean that the number of investments overall will be reduced.

Fourthly, however, and more importantly, the separation of the budget into economic and social has implications for the nature of GLEB's political project. GLEB initially formulated its political aim in terms of a commitment to 'exemplary projects'. GLEB's investments would show how firms might be. There was an assumption that the kind of thing that GLEB was doing could be spread more widely throughout the economy. This was a reflection, yet again, of an implicit assumption that the commercial and social objectives could be added on to each other; and further that both of them were compatible with continuing to exist in a sea of market forces. Separating commercial and grant money is in a sense explicitly saying that projects are not now exemplary in the same way. That is, the positive characteristics cannot be expected to spread more widely amongst other firms in the economy. But this in turn has further implications. It means that the grant-funded social plans within GLEB's portfolio amount to no more than a set of social additions within those individual firms. They do not amount to an equal opportunities strategy which is expected to have implications more widely. In other words they amount to a series of improvements within firms, without those firms necessarily having been selected as the best place to introduce them. Had we started with equal opportunities as a strategy for selecting firms we might well have picked a completely different set of firms to subsidise – we might for instance have opted for expanding firms where there were more opportunities to intervene, for instance, in training and recruitment.

The fifth implication of this decision to divide investment is closely related to the fourth. If social plans are to be subsidised through grants, then they will imply, not just the control and ownership which the difficulties of enforcement have already been mentioned as requiring, but also a long term involvement with each enterprise. Properly drawn-up social plans will anyway take a long time to put into operation. And if their operation is subsidised, then it is clear that GLEB cannot simply withdraw from investments when it has turned them round commercially; what it is involved in is building up a gradually expanding portfolio of firms with progressive equal opportunities strategies. The way in which such a portfolio could be 'exemplary' is by forming a basis for wider programmes of campaigning.

This paper started by referring to GLEB's twin objectives. Thoughout the discussion an important element has been the ambiguity in the relationship between these two objectives. A common view is that the two are in simple opposition. On the one hand there is a need for commercial viability; on the other hand social improvements cost money, and are thereby a drain on the possibilities of commercial viability. This opposition is sometimes counterposed quite starkly in relation to accumulation. In this formulation the commercial objective reflects public intervention with the aim of promoting accumulation in capitalist terms, while the social objective has as its aim that of changing the relations of production. This formulation is in turn based on an analysis which would argue that, in relation to their commercial objectives, the function of enterprise boards such as GLEB is to step in where the market, or other characteristics of local capitalism, are not functioning properly. In GLEB's case there have been two particular strands to this argument: that there exists a finance gap, and that there are large areas of the London economy in decline simply because of a lack of good management. In other words, the analysis is that capitalism is working badly, and that GLEB could do better. There is no doubt some element of truth in this argument, and no doubt either that the malfunctionings of British capitalism do indeed provide a toehold for intervention on the part of agencies such as GLEB. But it can only be a toehold. The problems of unemployment in so many local areas of the British economy do not arise because of a malfunctioning of capitalism; they arise precisely as *part* of its functioning. If that is the case, however, then the relationship between the commercial and social objectives of an institution such as GLEB cannot be as postulated above. Even the creation and maintenance of employment becomes a 'social' objective. If this is so, we are once again faced – as in so many of the discussions in this seminar – with the necessity to formulate different methods of accounting from those currently in use in the private sector and the enterprise boards. Moreover this is the case not only for equal opportunities, and social objectives more widely, but for the very process of rebuilding local economies.

*This essay first appeared in* Developing Local Economic Strategies: Some Issues and Ideas, *edited by Allan Cochrane, Open University Educational Enterprises, 1987.*

# Politics of Place

# 10

# A Global Sense Of Place

## 1991

This is an era – it is often said – when things are speeding up, and spreading out. Capital is going through a new phase of internationalisation, especially in its financial parts. More people travel more frequently and for longer distances. Your clothes have probably been made in a range of countries from Latin America to South East Asia. Dinner consists of food shipped in from all over the world. And if you have a screen in your office, instead of opening a letter which – care of Her Majesty's Post Office – has taken some days to wend its way across the country, you now get interrupted by e-mail.

This view of the current age is one now frequently found in a wide range of books and journals. Much of what is written about space, place and postmodern times emphasises a new phase in what Marx once called 'the annihilation of space by time'. The process is argued, or – more usually – asserted, to have gained a new momentum, to have reached a new stage. It is a phenomenon which has been called 'time-space-compression'. And the general acceptance that something of the sort is going on is marked by the almost obligatory use in the literature of terms and phrases such as speed-up, global village, overcoming spatial barriers, the disruption of horizons, and so forth.

One of the results of this is an increasing uncertainty about what we mean by 'places' and how we relate to them. How, in the face of all this movement and intermixing, can we retain any sense of a local place and its particularity? An (idealised) notion of an era when places were (supposedly) inhabited by coherent and homogeneous communities is set against the current fragmentation and disruption. The counterposition is anyway dubious, of course; 'place' and 'community' have only rarely been coterminous. But the occasional longing for such coherence is nonetheless a sign of the geographical fragmentation, the spatial disruption, of our times. And occasionally, too, it has been part of what has given rise to defensive and reactionary responses – certain forms of nationalism, sentimentalised recovering of sanitised 'heritages', and outright antagonism to newcomers and 'outsiders'. One of the effects of such responses is that place itself, the seeking after a sense of place, has come to be seen by some as necessarily reactionary.

But is that necessarily so? Can't we re-think our sense of place? Is it not possible for a sense of place to be progressive; not self-enclosing and defensive, but outward-looking? A sense of place which is adequate to this era of time-space-compression? To begin with, there are some questions to be asked about time-space-compression itself. Who is it that experiences it, and how? Do we all benefit and suffer from it in the same way?

For instance, to what extent does the currently popular characterisation of time-space-compression represent very much a Western, coloniser's view? The sense of dislocation which some feel at the sight of a once well-known local street now lined with a succession of cultural imports – the pizzeria, the kebab house, the branch of the Middle-Eastern bank – must have been felt for centuries, though from a very different point of view, by colonised peoples all over the world as they watched the importation, maybe even used, the products of, first, European colonisation, maybe British (from new forms of transport to liver salts and custard powder), later US, as they learned to eat wheat instead of rice or corn, to drink Coca Cola, just as today we try out enchiladas.

Moreover, as well as querying the ethnocentricity of the idea of time-space-compression and its current acceleration, we also need to ask about its causes: what is it that determines our degrees of mobility, that influences the sense we have of space and place? Time-space-compression refers to movement and communication across space, to the geographical stretching-out of social relations, and to our experience of all this. The usual interpretation is that it results overwhelmingly from the actions of capital, and from its currently-increasing internationalisation. On this interpretation, then, it is time space and money which make the world go round, and us go round (or not) the world. It is capitalism and its developments which are argued to determine our understanding and our experience of space.

But surely this is insufficient. Among the many other things which clearly influence that experience, there are, for instance, race and gender. The degree to which we can move between countries, or walk about the streets at night, or venture out of hotels in foreign cities, is not just influenced by 'capital'. Survey after survey has shown how women's mobility, for instance, is restricted – in a thousand different ways, from physical violence to being ogled at or made to feel quite simply 'out of place' – not by 'capital', but by men. Or, to take a more complicated example, Birkett, reviewing books on women adventurers and travellers in the nineteenth and twentieth centuries, suggests that 'it is far, far more demanding for a woman to wander now than ever before'.[1] The reasons she gives for this argument are a complex mix of colonialism, ex-colonialism, racism, changing gender-relations, and relative wealth. A simple resort to explanation in terms of 'money' or 'capital' alone could not begin to get to grips with the issue. The current speed-up may be strongly determined by economic forces, but it is not the economy alone which determines our experience of space and place. In other words, and put simply, there is a lot more determining how we experience space than what 'capital' gets up to.

What is more, of course, that last example indicated that 'time-space-compression' has not been happening for everyone in all spheres of activity. Birkett again, this time writing of the Pacific Ocean: 'Jumbos have enabled Korean computer consultants to fly to Silicon Valley as if popping next door, and Singaporean entrepreneurs to reach Seattle in a day. The borders of the world's greatest ocean have been joined as never before. And Boeing has brought these people together. But what about those they fly over, on their islands five miles below? How has the mighty 747 brought them greater communion with those whose shores are washed by the same water? It hasn't, of course. Air travel might enable businessmen to buzz across the ocean, but the concurrent decline in shipping has only increased the isolation of many island communities... Pitcairn, like many other Pacific islands, has never felt so far from its neighbours.'[2]

In other words, and most broadly, time-space-compression needs differentiating socially. This is not just a moral or political point about inequality, although that would be sufficient reason to mention it; it is also a conceptual point.

Imagine for a moment that you are on a satellite, further out and beyond all actual satellites; you can see 'planet earth' from a distance and, rarely for someone with only peaceful intentions, you are equipped with the kind of technology which allows you to see the colours of people's eyes and the numbers on their numberplates. You can see all the movement and tune-in to all the communication that is going on. Furthest out are the satellites, then aeroplanes, the long haul between London and Tokyo and the hop from San Salvador to Guatemala City. Some of this is people moving, some of it is physical trade, some is media broadcasting. There are faxes, e-mail, film-distribution networks, financial flows and transactions. Look in closer and there are ships and trains, steam trains slogging laboriously up hills somewhere in Asia. Look in closer still and there are lorries and cars and buses, and on down further, somewhere in sub-Saharan Africa, there's a woman on foot who still spends hours a day collecting water.

Now, I want to make one simple point here, and that is about what one might call the *power-geometry* of it all; the power geometry of time-space compression. For different social groups, and different individuals, are placed in very distinct ways in relation to these flows and interconnections. This point concerns not merely the issue of who moves and who doesn't, although that is an important element of it; it is also about power in relation *to* the flows and the movement. Different social groups have distinct relationships to this anyway differentiated mobility: some people are more in charge of it than others; some initiate flows and movement, others don't; some are more on the receiving-end of it than others; some are effectively imprisoned by it.

In a sense at the end of all the spectra are those who are both doing the moving and the communicating and who are in some way in a position of control in relation to it – the jet-setters, the ones sending and receiving the faxes and the e-mail, holding the international conference calls, the ones distributing the films, controlling the news, organising the investments and the international currency transactions. These are the groups who are really in a sense in charge of time-space-compression, who can really use it and turn it to advantage, whose power and influence it very definitely increases. On its more prosaic fringes this group probably includes a fair number of

Western academics and journalists – those, in other words, who write most about it.

But there are also groups who are also doing a lot of physical moving, but who are not 'in charge' of the process in the same way at all. The refugees from El Salvador or Guatemala and the undocumented migrant workers from Michoacan in Mexico, crowding into Tijuana to make a perhaps fatal dash for it across the border into the US to grab a chance of a new life. Here the experience of movement, and indeed of a confusing plurality of cultures, is very different. And there are those from India, Pakistan, Bangladesh, the Caribbean, who come half way round the world only to get held up in an interrogation room at Heathrow.

Or – a different case again – there are those who are simply on the receiving end of time-space-compression. The pensioner in a bed-sit in any inner city in this country, eating British working-class-style fish and chips from a Chinese take-away, watching a US film on a Japanese television; and not daring to go out after dark. And anyway the public transport's been cut.

Or – one final example to illustrate a different kind of complexity – there are the people who live in the favelas of Rio, who know global football like the back of their hand, and have produced some of its players; who have contributed massively to global music, who gave us the samba and produced the lambada that everyone was dancing to last year in the clubs of Paris and London; and who have never, or hardly ever, been to downtown Rio. At one level they have been tremendous contributors to what we call time-space-compression; and at another level they are imprisoned in it.

This is, in other words, a highly complex social differentiation. There are differences in the degree of movement and communication, but also in the degree of control and of initiation. The ways in which people are placed within 'time-space-compression' are highly complicated and extremely varied.

But this in turn immediately raises questions of politics. If time-space-compression can be imagined in that more socially formed, socially evaluative and differentiated way, then there may be here the possibility of developing a politics of mobility and access. For it does seem that mobility and control over mobility both reflects and reinforces power. It is not simply a question of unequal distribution, that some people move more than others, and that some have more control than others. It is that the mobility and control of some groups can actively weaken other people. Differential mobility can weaken the leverage of the already weak. The time-space-compression of some groups can undermine the power of others.

This is well established and often noted in the relationship between capital and labour. Capital's ability to roam the world further strengthens it in relation to relatively immobile workers, enables it to play off the plant at Genk against the plant at Dagenham. It also strengthens its hand against struggling local economies the world over as they compete for the favour of some investment. The 747s that fly computer scientists across the Pacific are part of the reason for the greater isolation today of the island of Pitcairn. But also, every time someone uses a car, and thereby increases their personal mobility, they reduce both the social rationale and the financial viability of the public transport system – and thereby also potentially reduce the mobility of those who rely on that system. Every time you drive to that out-of-town shopping centre you contribute to the rising prices, even hasten the demise, of the corner shop. And the 'time-space compression' which is involved in producing and reproducing the daily lives of the comfortably-off in First World societies – not just their own travel but the resources they draw on, from all over the world, to feed their lives – may entail environmental consequences, or hit constraints, which will limit the lives of others before their own. We need to ask, in other words, whether our relative mobility and power over mobility and communication entrenches the spatial imprisonment of other groups.

But this way of thinking about time-space compression also returns us to the question of place and a sense of place. How, in the context of all these socially-varied time-space-changes do we think about 'places'? In an era when, it is argued, 'local communities' seem to be increasingly broken up, when you can go abroad and find the same shops, the same music as at home, or eat your favourite foreign-holiday food at a restaurant down the road – and when everyone has a different experience of all this – how then do we think about 'locality'? Many of those who write about time-space-compression emphasise the insecurity and unsettling impact of its effects, the feelings of vulnerability which it can produce. Some therefore go on from this to argue that, in the middle of all this flux, people desperately need a bit of peace and quiet and that a strong sense of place, of locality, can form one kind of refuge from the hubbub. So the search after the 'real' meanings of places, the unearthing of heritages and so forth, is interpreted as being, in part, a response to desire for fixity and for security of identity in the middle of all the movement and change. A 'sense of place', of rootedness, can provide – in this form and on this interpretation – stability and a source of unproblematical identity. In that guise, however, place and the spatially local are then rejected by many progressive people as almost necessarily reactionary. They are interpreted as an evasion; as a retreat from the (actually unavoidable) dynamic and change of 'real life', which is what we must seize if we are to change things for the better. On this reading, place and locality are foci for a form of romanticised escapism from the real business of the world. While 'time' is equated with movement and progress, 'space'/'place' is equated with stasis and reaction.

There are some serious inadequacies in this argument. There is the question of why it is assumed that time-space-compression will produce insecurity. There is the need to face up to – rather than simply deny – people's need for attachment of some sort, whether through place or anything else. Nonetheless, it is certainly the case that there is indeed at the moment a recrudescence of some very problematical senses of place, from reactionary nationalisms, to competitive localisms, to introverted obsessions with 'heritage'. We need, therefore, to think through what might be an adequately progressive sense of place, one which would fit in with the current global-local times and the feelings and relations they give rise to, *and* which would be useful in what are, after all, political struggles often inevitably based on place. The question is how to hold on to that notion of geographical difference, of uniqueness, even of rootedness if people want that, without it being reactionary.

There are a number of distinct ways in which the 'reactionary' notion of place described above is problematical. One is the idea that places have single, essential, identities. Another is the idea that identity of place – the sense of place – is constructed out of an introverted, inward-looking history based on delving into the past for internalised origins, translating the name from the Domesday Book. Thus Wright recounts the construction and appropriation of Stoke Newington and its past by the arriving middle class (the Domesday Book registers the place as 'Newtowne' ... 'There is land for two ploughs and a half ... There are four villanes and thirty seven cottagers with ten acres', pp227 and 231), and contrasts this version with that of other groups – the white working class and the large number of important minority communities.[3] A particular problem with this conception of place is that it seems to require the drawing of boundaries. Geographers have long been exercised by the problem of defining regions, and this question of 'definition' has almost always been reduced to the issue of drawing lines around a place. I remember some of my most painful times as a geographer have been spent unwillingly struggling to think how one could draw a boundary around somewhere like the 'East Midlands'. But that kind of boundary around an area precisely distinguishes between an inside and an outside. It can so easily be yet another way of constructing a counterposition between 'us' and 'them'.

And yet if one considers almost any real place, and certainly one not defined primarily by administrative or political boundaries, these supposed characteristics have little real purchase.

Take, for instance, a walk down Kilburn High Road, my local shopping centre. It is a pretty ordinary place, north west of the centre of London. Under the railway bridge the newspaper stand sells papers from every county of what my neighbours, many of whom come from there, still often call the Irish Free State. The postboxes down the High Road, and many an empty space on a wall, are adorned with the letters IRA. Other available spaces are plastered this week with posters for a special meeting in remembrance: Ten Years after the Hunger Strike. At the local theatre Eamon Morrissey has a one-man show; the National Club has the Wolfe Tones on, and at the Black Lion there's Finnegan's Wake. In two shops I notice this week's lottery ticket winners: in one the name is Teresa Gleeson, in the other, Chouman Hassan.

Thread your way through the often almost stationary traffic diagonally across the road from the newsstand and there's a shop which as long as I can remember has displayed saris in the window. Four life-sized models of Indian women, and reams of cloth. On the door a notice announces a forthcoming concert at Wembley Arena: Anand Miland presents Rekha, live, with Aamir Khan, Salman

Khan, Jahi Chawla and Raveena Tandon. On another ad, for the end of the month, is written 'All Hindus are cordially invited'. In another newsagents I chat with the man who keeps it, a Muslim unutterably depressed by events in the Gulf, silently chafing at having to sell *The Sun*. Overhead there is always at least one aeroplane – we seem to be on a flight-path to Heathrow and by the time they're over Kilburn you can see them clearly enough to tell the airline and wonder as you struggle with your shopping where they're coming from. Below, the reason the traffic is snarled up (another odd effect of time-space-compression!) is in part because this is one of the main entrances to and escape-routes from London, the road to Staples Corner and the beginning of the M1 to the North.

This is just the beginnings of a sketch from immediate impressions but a proper analysis could be done, of the links between Kilburn and the world. And so it could for almost any place.

Kilburn is a place for which I have a great affection; I have lived there many years. It certainly has 'a character of its own'. But it is possible to feel all this without subscribing to any of the static and defensive – and in that sense reactionary – notions of 'place' which were referred to above. First, while Kilburn may have a character of its own, it is absolutely not a seamless, coherent identity, a single sense of place which everyone shares. It could hardly be less so. People's routes through the place, their favourite haunts within it, the connections they make (physically, or by phone or post, or in memory and imagination) between here and the rest of the world vary enormously. If it is now recognised that people have multiple identities then the same point can be made in relation to places. Moreover, such multiple identities can either be a source of richness or a source of conflict, or both.

One of the problems here has been a persistent identification of place with 'community'. Yet this is a misidentification. On the one hand communities can exist without being in the same place – from networks of friends with like interests, to major religious, ethnic or political communities. On the other hand, the instances of places housing single 'communities' in the sense of coherent social groups are probably and, I would argue, have for long been quite rare. Moreover, even where they do exist this in no way implies a single sense of place. For people occupy different positions within any community. We could counterpose to the chaotic mix of Kilburn the relatively stable and homogeneous community (at least in popular imagery) of a small mining village. Homogeneous 'communities' too have internal structures. To take the most obvious example, I'm sure a woman's sense of place in a mining village – the spaces through which she normally moves, the meeting places, the connections outside – are different from a man's. Their 'senses of the place' will be different.

Moreover, not only does 'Kilburn', then, have many identities (or its full identity is a complex mix of all these) it is also, looked at in this way, absolutely *not* introverted. It is (or ought to be) impossible even to begin thinking about Kilburn High Road without bringing into play half the world and a considerable amount of British imperialist history (and this certainly goes for mining villages too). Imagining it this way provokes in you (or at least in me) a really global sense of place.

And finally, in contrasting this way of looking at places with the defensive reactionary view, I certainly could not begin to, nor would I want to, define 'Kilburn' by drawing its enclosing boundaries.

So, at this point in the argument, get back in your mind's eye on a satellite; go right out again and look back at the globe. This time, however, imagine not just all the physical movement, nor even all the often invisible communications, but also and especially all the social relations, all the links between people. Fill it in with all those different experiences of time-space-compression. For what is happening is that the geography of social relations is changing. In many cases such relations are increasingly stretched out over space. Economic, political and cultural social relations, each full of power and with internal structures of domination and subordination, stretched out over the planet at every different level, from the household to the local area to the international.

It is from that perspective that it is possible to envisage an alternative interpretation of place. In this interpretation, what gives a place its specificity is not some long internalised history but the fact that it is constructed out of a particular constellation of social relations, meeting and weaving together at a particular locus. If one moves in from the satellite towards the globe, holding all those networks of social relations and movements and communications in one's head, then each 'place' can be seen as a particular, unique, point of their intersection. It is, indeed, a *meeting* place. Instead then, of thinking of places as areas with boundaries around, they can be imagined as articulated moments in networks of social relations and understandings, but where a large proportion of those relations, experiences and understandings are constructed on a far larger scale than what we happen to define for that moment as the place itself, whether that be a street, or a region or even a continent. And this in turn allows a sense of place which is extroverted, which includes a consciousness of its links with the wider world, which integrates in a positive way the global and the local.

This is not a question of making the ritualistic connections to 'the wider system' – the people in the local meeting who bring up international capitalism every time you try to have a discussion about rubbish-collection – the point is that there are real relations with real content – economic, political, cultural – between any local place and the wider world in which it is set. In economic geography the argument has long been accepted that it is not possible to understand the 'inner city', for instance its loss of jobs, the decline of manufacturing employment there, by looking only at the inner city. Any adequate explanation has to set the inner city in its wider geographical context. Perhaps it is appropriate to think how that kind of understanding could be extended to the notion of a sense of place.

These arguments, then, highlight a number of ways in which a progressive concept of place might be developed. First of all, it is absolutely not static. If places can be conceptualised in terms of the social interactions which they tie together, then it is also the case that these interactions themselves are not motionless things, frozen in time. They are processes. One of the great one-liners in marxist exchanges has for long been 'Ah, but capital is not a thing, it's a process'. Perhaps this should be said also about places; that places are processes, too.

Second, places do not have to have boundaries in the sense of divisions which frame simple enclosures. 'Boundaries' may of course be necessary, for the purposes of certain types of studies for instance, but they are not necessary for the conceptualisation of a place itself. Definition in this sense does not have to be through simple counterposition to the outside; it can come, in part, precisely through the particularity of linkage *to* that 'outside' which is therefore itself part of what constitutes the place. This helps get away from the common association between penetrability and vulnerability. For it is this kind of association which makes invasion by newcomers so threatening.

Third, clearly places do not have single, unique 'identities'; they are full of internal conflicts. Just think, for instance, about London's Docklands, a place which is at the moment quite clearly *defined* by conflict: a conflict over what its past has been (the nature of its 'heritage'), conflict over what should be its present development, conflict over what could be its future.

Fourth, and finally, none of this denies place nor the importance of the uniqueness of place. The specificity of place is continually reproduced, but it is not a specificity which results from some long, internalised history. There are a number of sources of this specificity – the uniqueness of place.[4] There is the fact that the wider social relations in which places are set are themselves geographically differentiated. Globalisation (in the economy, or in culture, or in anything else) does not entail simply homogenisation. On the contrary, the globalisation of social relations is yet another source of (the reproduction of) geographical uneven development, and thus of the uniqueness of place. There is the specificity of place which derives from the fact that each place is the focus of a distinct *mixture* of wider and more local social relations. There is the fact that this very mixture together in one place may produce effects which would not have happened otherwise. And finally, all these relations interact with and take a further element of specificity from the accumulated history of a place, with that history itself imagined as the product of layer upon layer of different sets of linkages, both local and to the wider world.

In her portrait of Corsica, *Granite Island,* Dorothy Carrington travels the island seeking out the roots of its character.[5] All the different layers of peoples and cultures are explored; the long and tumultuous relationship with France, with Genoa and Aragon in the thirteenth, fourteenth and fifteenth centuries, back through the much earlier incorporation into the Byzantine Empire, and before that domination by the Vandals, before that being part of the Roman Empire, before that the colonisation and settlements of the Carthaginians and the Greeks ... until we find ... that even the megalith builders had come to Corsica from somewhere else.

It is a sense of place, an understanding of 'its character', which can only be constructed by linking that place to places beyond. A progressive sense of place would recognise that, without being threatened by it. What we need, it seems to me, is a global sense of the local, a global sense of place.

*This essay first appeared in* Marxism Today *in June 1991.*

## Notes

1. D. Birkett, *New Statesman And Society,* 13 June 1990, pp41-2.
2. D. Birkett, *New Statesman And Society,* 15 March 1991, p38.
3. P. Wright, *On Living In An Old Country,* Verso, 1985.
4. D. Massey, *Spatial Divisions Of Labour: Social Structures And The Geography Of Production,* Macmillan, 1984.
5. D. Carrington, *Granite Island: A Portrait Of Corsica,* Penguin, 1971.

## 11

# Places and Their Pasts

## 1995

In a telling paragraph which has given me much pause for thought, Herbert Schiller asks, in an article in *Intermedia*: 'What is national identity?' The reply he produces is that 'there is no totally satisfying definition. It is much easier to recognize its absence. A Kentucky Fried Chicken in Paris, for example, surely does not qualify as part of the French national identity. A McDonald's outlet in Kyoto hardly expresses the Japanese ethos'.[1] What he is pointing to, possibly inadvertently, is a felt dislocation between the past and the present of a place.

In daily life, in politics, in battles over development and conservation, we often operate in ways which mobilise this kind of view of place. Arriving in Paris, say, on the first day of a much-needed holiday we finally reach the kind of café we are looking for – the smell of Gauloises, the taste of good coffee and croissants – 'ah', we sigh with satisfaction, 'this is the *real* France'. (We hadn't felt this in the airport; we had avoided the hamburger joints.) On the other side of the continent, in what used to be Yugoslavia, Serbs claim whole stretches of what is today clearly multicultural country on the basis that it is – really – Serbia. Or again, in London's docklands 'the local community', itself a term with a multiplicity of interpretations, fights off new developments singing 'this land is our land' in the face of the London Docklands Development Corporation[2] but shouting also 'this is a *white* working-class area' in the teeth of a growing population which hails, at some distance, from Asia. Different as these examples are in terms of their political import and practical effect, they are calling upon a particular way of conceptualising 'place'.

One aspect of this is a deeply essentialist and internalist way of thinking about a place and its character. This Isle of Dogs is essentially white working class; this land is uniquely Serbian. Influences, 'invasions', developments, from 'outside', are to be resisted. The Kentucky Fried Chicken is American, not French; the new people in the council flats are from Bangladesh. What such constructions fail to realise, or to admit, is that places are always already hybrid. The 'real local character' of Docklands could not be as it is without the deep imbrication of that area into a nineteenth-century international division of labour and pattern of trade and all the influences which that brought. (The recent battles have not really been about the local versus the global, as much as about how this local area should be inserted into the *current* international division of labour.) The 'real France' which we breathe in at the café, and into which as Schiller says a Kentucky Fried Chicken seems such a dislocating intrusion, is itself composed of influences, contacts and connections which, over time, have settled into each other, moulded each other, produced something new ... but which we now think of as old, as established ... the essential France. The new 'intrusions' are no more from outside, nor more 'out of place', than were in their time many of the components of the currently-accepted 'character of the place'.

There are two points which I want to draw out of these illustrations. The first is that places, in fact, are always constructed out of articulations of social relations (trading connections, the unequal links of colonialism, thoughts of home) which are not only internal to that locale but which link them to elsewhere. Their 'local uniqueness' is always already a product of wider contacts; the local is always already a product in part of 'global' forces, where global in this context refers not necessarily to the planetary scale, but to the geographical beyond, the world beyond the place itself.'[3] For the purposes of the argument here, I should like to take that point as given. But there is a second point which is raised by these various illustrations. All of them indicate a feeling that there is or has been some kind of disruption between the past of these places and at least some elements of their present or their potential future. Indeed, in all these cases 'the past' is seen in some sense to embody the real character of the place. It is from this kind of thinking that we find ourselves, probably all the while knowing that the term evokes a million unfortunate implications, talking of other places as 'unspoilt' (by which we usually mean: it is as we have imagined it to have been in some distant past).

These kinds of (implicitly or explicitly) internalist and essentialist constructions of the character of places, then, not only fail to recognise the long history of interconnectedness with elsewhere (the history of the global construction of the local), they also presuppose a particular relationship between the assumed identity of a place and its history.

## The past of places

One possible response to this kind of view of place is to interpret any kind of positive affective attitude to a particular area as being inevitably imbued with nostalgia and thus, almost equally inevitably, a hindrance to a progressive politics. Thus David Harvey expresses extreme scepticism about anything which he dubs 'local' (that is to say not global, which in his terminology has more the implication of 'universal') as a basis for the construction of a radical politics. And one reason for this scepticism is the necessity of such local struggles' reliance on 'tradition' (why so-called 'global' struggles do not also have to rely on such foundations he does not say). Thus: 'the assertion of any place-bound identity has to rest at some point on the motivational power of tradition'.[4] Now, it is certainly true that many place-based struggles, and struggles about places, such as the defensive struggles in Docklands, do often fall into the traps implied by such claims. They do indeed become place-*bound* rather than place-*based* (and Harvey's use only of the former term implies that they inevitably must). And tradition may well become a hindrance to progressive change. A singular sense of the past, and its relation to, the present, become assumed, closed down as areas of contestation or debate.

Yet 'tradition' need not be thought of in this way. On the one hand, and as hinted above, it need not be place-*bound*. The pre-Kentucky-Fried-Chicken 'real France' is itself formed out of a long history of interconnections with the beyond. (Globalisation in the wider sense of the global construction of the local is by no means new. What is different about the current phase is its intensity and – perhaps even more pertinently – the fact that this time the direction of the flows is different, the First World and *its* identity are being more obviously challenged.)

On the other hand, traditions do not only exist in the past. They are actively built in the present also. The concept of tradition which sees in it only nostalgia understands it as something already completed which can now only be maintained or lost. It is something from which we feel ourselves inexorably, inevitably, distant. Talking of places as 'unspoilt' evokes just this notion. So do many aspects of place-conservation, which are all too often attempts to freeze a (particular view of a) place at a (selected) moment in time. And, to return to our opening examples, even that innocent feeling in the Parisian café of a dislocation between past and present, that somehow coffee is French but Kentucky Fried Chicken is not, is at least potentially falling into that notion of tradition as something which is almost inevitably in the past and to be lost.

Paul Gilroy's *The Black Atlantic* (1993) presents an interpretation of something which might be called tradition (he dubs it 'the changing same') but which overturns these static and bounded notions. Here, in black culture on both sides of the ocean, is a 'tradition' which is internally varied, constantly being built, moulded, added to, and which depends for this, and for its strength and vitality, not on an inward-looking self-preservation but precisely on the dynamism which comes from interconnection.

There is, moreover, a further issue arising from the fact that the past of a place is as open to a multiplicity of readings as is the present. Moreover, the claims and counterclaims about the present character of a place depend in almost all cases on particular, rival, interpretations of its past. A small example may help to illustrate this point'.[5] In 1993, there was a flurry of dispute over a proposed development in a small area in the Wye Valley on the borders of England and Wales. The proposal was to turn an existing set of buildings into a 'traditional farm' where local products, including crafts, would be sold, and where there would be a restaurant and car park. This scheme would, it was argued by its proponents, serve as a tourist attraction and bring in a source of income. The proposal aroused considerable, high-profile, opposition. The opposition, perhaps unusually in such cases, came in major part from newcomers to the area: professional people in the arts, the media, and suchlike who, presumably, had migrated here from other parts of the country. Their opposition to the development centred on the argument that it was 'inappropriate', a term which implied agreement on the nature of the place. *Their* view of the place, conditioned and manifested in their decision to move there, was clothed in quotations from Wordsworth. For them the place offered a romantic association with nature and what was termed 'seclusion': one of them called the place 'an area which for centuries has been sought for its seclusion'.[6] (One immediate line of enquiry might be to ask: seclusion from what/whom? Seclusion, presumably, from the very worlds from which the incomes which enable them to retreat to this place are drawn.) This view of the place was greeted with a mixture of anger and wry amusement by those local people who supported the scheme. For them, the place was where they had always lived and, crucially, where they made their living, largely from farming. 'Nature' was the physical basis for agricultural activity. 'Seclusion' probably just meant long distances to suppliers and markets. For them this was a place of work, and this has been its history too. As one of the proposers of the development remarked, 'they quoted Wordsworth when once the Wye Valley was highly-industrialized with iron works, charcoal works, all sorts of things. It's now a major tourist area ...'[7]

What we have here are two different interpretations of the identity of a place, each clearly based on the different socio-geographical position of the groups which promote them. Moreover, each of these contesting interpretations depends on the mobilisation of a particular reading of the area's past. (Just how different, indeed contradictory, these readings are is indicated by the fact that farming and farmers – the economic activity and the daily, yearly round of labour in the area – are completely erased in the protestors' interpretation. The latter are cited as having campaigned partially to remove farm work even from the present, with a scheme to prevent tractors and noisy machines being operated for two days each week!) And these conflicting interpretations of the past, serving to legitimate a particular understanding of the present, are put to use in a battle over what is to come. What are at issue are competing histories of the present, wielded as arguments over what should be the future.

Both of these histories of the past, moreover, are constructed so as to confirm the views and convictions of the present. It is this which enables them to warrant the building of particular futures. It is indeed a form of the 'invention of tradition' discussed by such authors as Benedict Anderson and Eric Hobsbawm; what is evident here, however, is that such invention for the purpose of establishing the nature and coherence of a place is by no means confined to the level of the nation state. It is the kind of structure of argument in play in the working-class defence of London's docklands against the building of Canary Wharf, in the white working-class defence of the same area against new, ethnic minority, neighbours, as well as in claims for a greater Serbia. It is, of course, a way of relating past and present (and implicitly or explicitly – arguments about potential futures) which has been widely and thoroughly criticised. However, I want to argue here that debates over how to think the relationship between past, present and future can help us to reinvigorate the way in which we conceptualise geographical places. Put briefly, it helps us to think of them as temporal and not just spatial: as set in time as well as space.

Places, then, on the argument so far, can be understood as articulations of social relationships some of which will be to the beyond (the global), and these global relationships as much as the internal relationships of an area will influence its character, its 'identity'. Moreover, this constitution through interconnection with other places is not something which is new (with our newly-appreciated globalisation, with foreign food on the High Street, or 'immigrants' in the neighbourhood); it has been as true of the past as it is true of today (although clearly the intensity, depth and direction of connections and influences all change over time). The identity of a place is thus not to be seen as inevitably to be destroyed by new importations. On this alternative reading that identity is always, and always has been, in process of formation: it is in a sense forever unachieved. (This, of course, does not mean that some things are not more 'absorbed' or incorporated into the place than others, nor conversely that some 'foreign' imports have not had more influence than others. Nor, more importantly from a political point of view, does it mean that no distinctions can be made, no judgements or political stances taken, on what might be the interpretation of the past or the most preferred directions for the future. These are issues which will be addressed later.) What is important to note for now, however, is that much will depend on the nature of the links made, in the construction of notions of the identity of place, between past, present and future. The identity of places is very much bound up with the *histories* which are told of them, *how* those histories are told, and which history turns out to be dominant.

## The construction of the present of places

The past is present in places in a variety of ways.

It is present materially. Patrick Wright has described a building on Hackney High Street.[8] Originally built as an entertainment palace, 'with exotic domes thrown in for orientalist effect', it subsequently became a cinema, to be converted by the 1980s into a Turkish mosque and community centre. For the older white working class of the area the place is an ex-cinema, a physical reminder of days when the High Street used to be different, when there were proper shops and a dominant, settled, long-local community (or so the memory runs).

Or the past may be present in resonance, whether actually from the past or reinserted as a self-conscious building-in of 'local character'. Words, language, names, can be important here. The significance of naming in London Docklands is notable. Is the area Docklands, Millwall, the Isle of Dogs or the Venice of the North? For self-conscious long-time locals the names of streets have been used to evoke a romance of its working-class past: all pubs and football, hard work and community. The use of the same street names today, and the careful naming and renaming of warehouses-converted-into-apartments is also an attempt to evoke a connection with a past, equally romanticised but this time in a different version. In his considerations of the worlds that were nineteenth-century Paris, Walter Benjamin writes that the only thing that remains of the increasingly rapid succession of perceptual worlds is their names: 'The forces of perversion work deep within these names, which is why we maintain a world in the names of old streets'.[9] And the past may be present in the unembodied memories of people, and in the conscious and unconscious constructions of the histories of the place.

The past, then, helps make the present. But it is a two-way process. For all these presences of the past are multi-vocal. The building with orientalist effects on Hackney High Street may for some recall days of strong local community. But what ambiguity do the 'exotic domes' produce in those from that very 'Orient', the Turkish community among others, who now live in this place? Thoughts of a history of somewhere else entirely? Distant images of some village on the Anatolian plateau? Or possibly an understanding that that Hackney local community built its self-assuredness in part precisely in relation to other places, on the basis of stories of other places, and on their interpretation of the identity of those places? The street names of Docklands, equally, evoke different meanings and can be used to different effect, when embedded in different histories. It is not just that a world is 'maintained' in the names of old streets. It is also that a (historical) world is created. If the past transforms the present, helps thereby to make it, so too does the present make the past. All of which is really a way of saying that in trying to understand the identity of places we cannot – or, perhaps, should not – separate space from time, or geography from history.

When presented with the name of a place what form does the concept take in your mind? Manchester? Germany? Hackney? Most often, I believe, when asked to think of places we think of them mainly in spatial terms. If pushed, we might indicate them on a map. It is *there;* it covers *that area.* After all, places are part of the basic subject-matter of geography. We know, or we ought to know, that they are difficult to demarcate. Where do 'the Home Counties' begin and end? Could you draw a line around the Scottish Lowlands? Where, exactly, is 'Europe'? In some cases the frontiers are deliberately maintained. The boundaries of nation-states are held in place by political power, legal agreement, physical force. They cut across a million social interactions. They are one of the many ways we have of ordering, and of subjecting to power-relations, the incredible complexity of social space.

But, more importantly, what I want to consider here is the ways in which places also stretch through time. Places as depicted on maps are places caught in a moment; they are slices through time.

Yet, not only does that particular articulation of social relations which we are at the moment naming as that place have a history (as we have seen, it is the product of the historical accumulation and combination of numerous layers of such articulations over time) but also any claim to establish the identity of that place depends upon presenting a particular reading of that history. The competing claims about the 'essential nature' of the Wye Valley were competing claims not just about its present but about its history. The differences lay in the interpretation of that history. The claims made by some for the essentially working-class nature of London's docklands depend not only upon a particular reading of that area's past but also on a particular demarcation of it: a longer period of history, for example, would have taken in other dramatic changes, not least that when the docks were first constructed and an area of agricultural land and settlements was built over in the physical manifestation of a new articulation of social relations – when a community of dockers was created.

These kinds of dispute, then, involve a contestation of claims each of which is trying to stabilise, and to establish as dominant, the meaning, not just of a particular place-on-a-map as a slice through time, but of what I call an 'envelope of space-time'.[10] The interpretation of Docklands as working class, or of the Wye Valley as secluded, depends not just on a particular characterisation of a place as it is now but on a demarcation of, and a reading of, the historically changing form of that (always externally-connected) nexus of social relations. The invention of tradition is here about the invention of the coherence of a place, about defining and naming it as a 'place' at all. It is for this reason that it may be useful to think of places, not as areas on maps, but as constantly shifting articulations of social relations through time; and to think of particular attempts to characterise them as attempts to define, and claim coherence and a particular meaning for, specific envelopes of space-*time*.

It might be easiest to illustrate this notion of places in space-time by taking as an example one of the apparently most self-evident of places: the nation state. Quite apart, for the moment, from the constant struggles to define, and to make cohere, their internal characters, what are they simply in terms of bounded spaces? Think of Poland, of Paraguay, or another of today's nation states. They once did not exist; during their existence their boundaries have frequently shifted; and maybe one day in the future they will not exist again. The boundaries of nation states are temporary, shifting phenomena which enclose, not simply 'spaces', but relatively ephemeral envelopes of space-time. The boundaries, and the naming of the space-time within them, are the reflections of power, and their existence has effects. Within them there is an active attempt to 'make places'.

The local confrontation over the establishment of a tourist attraction in the Wye Valley involved similar, though less formal, attempts to establish as dominant competing readings of a particular envelope of space-time to which that name — the Wye Valley — could be attached.

And currently before us there lies a question of place-definition which brings together all these considerations. The issue is the identity of a place called 'Europe'. This is a project which represents an attempt to impose a boundary where there has for long been a lack of distinction, or a limit which has shifted or been debated. (I was taught at school that Europe 'really' stretched east to the Urals, and that 'Africa' only 'really' began south of the Sahara.) To call the current Economic Union 'Europe' is therefore to appropriate a name with a history of a much wider resonance. It is also to claim a name for a place whose boundaries will shift in the future, as other countries join, or even leave, its membership. But more interesting than the delimitation of its boundaries are the attempts to define the character of this place. All of the attempts depend on a reading of both history and geography: what is at issue here is space-time. And each attempt at identity-definition depends on a particular reading of that history. Moreover, those claims for European identity which look set to become the dominant ones generally evoke a continuous and singular history, an uninterrupted progress to the present, and it is by and large an internal one. They seek the European character *within,* denying its constant external connections: the fact of the construction of the local character of Europe through its constant association with the global, whether invasions from the vast opennesses of the East in the distant past, the initial connections of mercantilism and imperialism (from the China Seas to North Africa to the Caribbean), or the physical presence of 'ethnic minorities' within its borders now. If the 'outside world' is recognised at all in this approach to place-definition it is through negative counterposition (this place is *not* Islamic, not part of the Muslim world), rather than through positive interrelation.

In many political struggles, writ large or small, and in many aspects of daily life, the issue of the identification and characterisation of places is a significant component. It is important, therefore, to recognise the process for what it is. First, it involves time as well as space, and their inseparable connection. Second, the characterisation of both spatial and temporal aspects can take a variety of particular forms. And third, whichever view comes to be dominant, and by whatever means its hegemony is assured, the particular characterisation of that envelope of space-time, that place, which it proposes is only maintained by the exercise of power relations in some form. The identity of places, indeed the very identification of places *as* particular places, is always in that sense temporary, uncertain, and in process.

## Concluding thoughts

The description, definition and identification of a place is thus always inevitably an intervention not only into geography but also, at least implicitly, into the (re)telling of the historical constitution of the present. It is another move in the continuing struggle over the delineation and characterisation of space-time.

On what terms, then, can it be done responsibly? Some elements of a possible 'progressive' characterisation of place have been suggested, both here and elsewhere. Thus, it has been argued, the localism/parochialism of many characterisations of place can be avoided, or at least reduced or interrupted, by recognising always the global construction of the local. Moreover, these links with the rest of the world must be characterised as positive, active, interconnections (as in Europe's active relation with its Empires, for instance, and the contribution to its identity which those interconnections provided) rather than as a relation of negative, exclusivist counterposition (as in 'Europe is not Islamic'). What is at issue here, then, is relocating this place in a positive relation to a wider space-time and thus recharacterising it by redrawing its connections.

But what of the temporal dimension? What of the relation between a place's present and its past? This essay began with perceived disjunctures between past and present. Later examples focused on competing tales of continuity. All depended, implicitly or explicitly, on notions of seamless histories and on similar notions of tradition. And one strategy is certainly to install our own version of these stories, of these relationships between past and present, which can lay an alternative basis for a (different) future: the strategy of writing a radical history. Thus, to write as I did earlier that 'the new intrusions are no more from outside, nor more out of place than were in their time many of the components of the currently-accepted character of the place' does not mean that *any* new future for a place, *any* proposed development, is equally acceptable, that no positions can be taken, no political judgements made. And conceiving the place as a radical envelope of space-time is an important means of arguing such cases.

And yet ... it is important to be aware that such histories may still depend upon the same notion of tradition, on an assumption of continuity between past and present, where the only real form of change resides in the tragedy of loss. Some of the claims of docklands communities, that this land was their land and the place somehow intrinsically working class, went precisely down this road. They evoked an essentialist, and ultimately untenable, view of the nature of place.

There are some current writers, perhaps most notably Fredric Jameson, who have interpreted the current period (usually characterised as 'postmodern') as one in which all sense of narrative, all lines of continuity between past and present, have broken down.[11] For Jameson the current era is characterised by a rootless, and for him alternately terrifying and intoxicating, sense of simultaneity/instantaneity. It could be seen as a kind of extreme version of Benjamin's monadic moment of the present, blasted from the homogenous continuity of history, the difference being that Benjamin's concept is meant to function as providing the possibility of a radical politics, while Jameson's instantaneity is interpreted rather as provoking the death of the political. Thus Homi Bhabha seems to be setting out alternatives:

> Unlike the dead hand of history that tells the beads of sequential time like a rosary, seeking to establish serial causal connections,

we are now confronted with what Walter Benjamin describes as the blasting of a monadic moment from the homogenous course of history 'establishing a conception of the present as the "time of the now"'.[12]

Yet are these the only alternatives for a history of place: an essentialist continuity or a breaking of the relation altogether? Do we have to choose, in the terms in which this is usually presented, between temporality and spatiality? Perhaps the answer lies in insisting on both, but on forging a different relation between them. Perhaps a really 'radical' history of a place would be one which did not try to present either simple temporal continuity or only spatial simultaneity with no sense of historical depth. A way of understanding which, in the end, did *not* try to seal a place up into one neat and tidy 'envelope of space-time' but which recognised that what has come together, in this place, now, is a conjunction of many histories and many spaces.

*This essay first appeared in* History Workshop Journal, *Issue 39, 1995.*

## Notes

1 Herbert I. Schiller 'Fast food, fast cars, fast political rhetoric', *Intermedia*, Vol. 20, Nos. 4-5, August-September 1992, p21.
2 Gillian Rose, 'Place and identity a sense of place', in Doreen Massey and Pat Jess (eds), *A Place in the World? Place, Culture and Globalization*, Oxford University Press in association with the Open University, 1995.
3 Doreen Massey, 'Power-geometry and a progressive sense of place', in Jon Bird *et al.* (eds), *Mapping the Futures: Local Cultures, Global Change*, Routledge: London, 1993, pp59-69; Doreen Massey, *Space, place and gender*, Polity Press: Oxford, 1994.
4 David Harvey, *The Condition of Postmodernity*, Blackwell: Oxford, 1989, p303.
5 This case is examined in more detail in Pat Jess and Doreen Massey, 'The contestation of place', in Massey and Jess 1995, *op. cit.*
6 Peter Dunn, 'Valley folk divided over "farm for tourists"', *The Independent, 7* August 1993.

7 *Ibid.*
8 Patrick Wright, *On Living in an Old Country: The National Past in Contemporary Britain*, Verso: London, 1985.
9 Derek Gregory, *Geographical Imaginations*, Blackwell: Oxford, 1994, p245.
10 Massey and Jess 1995, *op. cit.*
11 Fredric Jameson, *Postmodernism, or, the Cultural Logic of Late Capitalism*, Verso: London, 1991.
12 Homi Bhabha, *The Location of Culture,* Routledge: London, 1994, p4.

# 12

# The Geography of Power

## 2000

'Seattle' managed to establish 'globalisation' as an important, and contestable, issue on the political agenda. That debate must be kept going, but has to avoid being fossilised into static oppositions that are difficult to get out of and which finally anyway lead nowhere.

### 1

*The question of globalisation should not be posed as one of local versus global.* 'Local' may be good or bad, depending on your politics. The peasant farmers in India, being invaded by multinational companies armed with genetically modified products and bits of paper claiming patent rights over plants and seeds, are 'local', fighting to defend 'local rights'. But then so are the proponents of Fortress Europe, or those in California who vote for propositions banning 'illegal' Latin Americans from access to public services. The arguments against 'global' multinational capital's ability to roam the world, playing one group off against another, are certainly appealing. But then so are the arguments for more cultural exchange between countries and peoples. 'Going global' can be attractive or pernicious.

There has been a tendency on the left to treat the 'global' level with a degree of suspicion, partly because there is a feeling that nothing can be done about it. But this acquiesces to the dominant rhetoric – that globalisation is inevitable and we just have to work out the best ways of adapting to it. But globalisation we see at present is not inevitable, it is a project.

One example of the duplicity of this rhetoric of inevitability concerns the nation state. We are constantly being told that individual countries are powerless in the face of multinational capital, and it would be foolish to deny the changes in the relationship between capital and nation states. But many governments (and most particularly those of the US and the UK) are active participants in the promotion of the current form of globalisation. It was the governments, not the companies, that signed up to the Uruguay round of world trade negotiations. Who gathered inside the splendid halls in Seattle for the World Trade Organisation meeting? Who began the process of nations giving away foreign-exchange control? (Margaret Thatcher, the supposed great defender of our sovereignty, as it happens.) We must not cede the global level of politics to the right.

The left is also suspicious of the global level itself. This is both dangerous and contradictory. First, we need particular kinds of global preconditions to preserve the ability to act locally, to continue the recognition of local specificity. Second, we need some kind of global bodies to prevent a further slide into a politics of might is right. The fact that the current bodies (the World Trade Organisation, the International Monetary Fund, the World Bank) do not currently prevent this, and on many fronts are actually agents of the most powerful, does not mean that some kinds of global forums are not necessary. One of the biggest dangers, especially since Seattle, is the potential burgeoning of bilateral negotiations along the lines of the old Multi-lateral Agreement on Investment (MAI), and from which less powerful voices would be excluded from influence altogether.

Third, surely we want a kind of globalisation? Our political aim should be internationalist: an internationalism that respects local differences and the possibility of certain kinds of local action, yes; but emphatically not a localist future of hermetically sealed countries or cultures.

We are faced here with a problem of language. The word 'globalisation' has been hijacked to mean only the particular form of globalisation (neo-liberal and overwhelmingly concerned with the economic) that we suffer at the moment. But 'globalisation' really just means global interconnectedness, and it could take other forms, on different terms and embodying different kinds of power relations. Perhaps, indeed, there are the beginnings of ideas about how this might work in the decidedly international networks already being invented within the radical protest movements themselves. Either way, we need to wrest back the term for ourselves and argue for and imagine not the local rather than the global, but an alternative form of globalisation.

## 2

Setting up the question as local versus global is to accede to spatial fetishism. That is: imagining that 'space' or 'spatial scale' has a political meaning – to assume, for instance, that the local is always better simply because it is local. This is to side-step the real problem.

*What is really at issue is the geography of power.* The highly protected local economy of the US is immensely powerful, the opened and invaded local economy of Mozambique is vulnerable. The global mobility of multinational capital is one thing, the global mobility of the world's poor would be another. There are, then, no formal spatial rules; it all depends on the power relations embedded in the specific situation.

On the political left we deplore the restrictions on international migration, we often point to the blatant inconsistency with the fact that capital (in the form of investment and trade etc) is encouraged to roam freely about the planet, and is admired for its ability to do so. Why should people not have the same rights?

But consider the following (probably apocryphal) tale. Some time during the nineteenth century a native American chief was asked by members of his society what had been the biggest mistake of the past generations' leaders. After pondering the new society that had grown up all about he answered: 'We failed to control immigration'.

Setting the native American chief against the likes of French rightwinger Jean-Marie Le Pen makes clear that it is not possible to base one's view of international migration on a simple notion of inalienable spatial rights. There are no abstract, generalisable answers to political questions of space and place. What is at issue is not just 'space' but the geography of social, political, and economic power.

## 3

'Globalisation' is about the restructuring of the world's geography, and the world is immensely varied and grotesquely unequal in terms of power. In such a situation, not only is an appeal to abstract spatial rights inappropriate, but so also may be many kinds of universal rules, which are just another kind of 'abstract and general' approach. They assume the spatial form matters over social content. It is the two together which we must address.

Take the 'rule' of free trade. It may be invoked to allow into a Third World country the likes of agricultural goods that will lay waste to a whole region, where production had undoubtedly been 'inefficient' but where it sustained a livelihood for far more people than now are needed, and formed the basis for far more than 'economics'.

Or resistance to free trade might be mounted by a First World country and its trade unions to protect a declining sector (textiles and clothing, say) against imports from a Third World country for which this is the most promising route for development – if the First World country would open up. On the other hand, these workers in the First World country are already among the lowest paid in that economy. Or again, a newly industrialising country is forbidden (because of 'the rules') to erect protective barriers to enable a nascent high-technology sector to gain a hold. In other words, the application of such a 'rule' may be perverse from whichever position of power or politics it is viewed.

The 'universal rules' currently wielded by bodies such as the WTO [World Trade Organization] are not applied evenly. 'There are special circumstances, there are politically difficult situations, appeals must be made. And the arguments of the already-powerful (their special circumstances, their politically difficult situations) usually win the day. Free trade is not anyway in truth 'free'. So one claim that we might make, and which many do make, is that the rules be applied with fairness.

And yet we might go further and ask: in such a situation of social and cultural variation and economic inequality, can any abstract set of rules be adequate? Even the powerful find that such rules produce perverse outcomes. It is for this reason that they negotiate around their exceptional circumstances. But would absolute 'fairness' in the application of such rules be any less perverse, from more progressive political points of view? If we vote for total free movement of both trade and people, is it 'fair' that it will be the relatively poor of the First World who will lose their jobs and find their council-housing stock coming under pressure?

'Judging' between the relatively poor of the First World and the ferociously poor of the Third World shows the lack of adequate relation between these rules and the social actors, with their highly differential powers, who are the agents of globalisation. Or our (caricatured) Third World country might want, quite reasonably, to argue for free trade in clothing and textiles but the right to some protection for the new economic sectors it is trying to grow. 'Quite reasonably': because, it argues, only in that way can it lever into action the development potential it believes it has.

But there are general considerations. Trade has environmental costs, for instance. And protection can result in a monopoly for local owners. (One of the dangers of the globalisation debate is thinking of countries as undifferentiated entities. Macro-economic statistics can conceal growing inequalities within countries. The IMF can pronounce 'a success' a country in which there is increasing poverty. The elites in many a Third World country stand to gain from globalisation in its present form.) But it is to argue that the equal application of abstract rules in unequal situations can lead to unfair outcomes. So we need the possibility of a more situated response, the exercise not of a geometrical logic, or the abstract spatial fetishism of a rule such as 'free trade,' but of a practical reason.

4

This means asking what we are aiming at. There are many things that can be done: introducing a tax on financial speculation (Tobin tax), countering the decimation of public sector provision, arguing against the anti-developmental requirement of 'structural adjustment policies' for cuts in, for instance, education spending. But the big question must be: what kind of globalisation do we want? We need equalitarian, sustainable ethics of development.

We must first recognise that *almost nothing about globalisation is simply a technical issue, nor simply self-evident.*

An example is 'subsidiarity' – a word about which everyone seems to agree. Of course it is best to have government 'as close as possible to the people'. But then other questions arise. What, for instance, about the wider impact, on other people in other places, of decisions taken 'locally'? Should not such people also be consulted? Or again, keeping all decisions local can make redistribution impossible and lead to a competition between localities in which the richest, the most powerful etc, would win. The point is that there is likely to be political disagreement over how to resolve these issues. Subsidiarity, and the question of which kinds of policy can best be dealt with at which levels, is not a purely technical question.

Rules such as the one that imposes free trade on all parts of the world regardless of their very different circumstances are presented as neutral. Their 'neutrality' is said to derive, indeed, from their universality. And yet the results can be devastatingly unequal.

Perhaps we should come at this another way. Why not begin from the outcomes that are sought and make them the principles by which actions have to be guided? Free trade is a means, not an outcome.

Could there be principles (rather than universally-applicable rules) against which to evaluate particular issues, specific situations? Principles of a globalisation that might put equality and environment above some socially unexamined notion of 'growth' which in fact is no more than a calculus of assets and profits, and which might include more than the most arid definition of economics? Could we, for instance, use quality-of-life and distributional measures?

The agreements on environmental goals involve precisely such principles and aims, but nowhere have they been taken as seriously as the trade rules. What is necessary is for agreed general aims, such as the desirability of cutting back on environmental degradation, to be backed up by targets (appropriately varied between different parts of the world) and sanctions for failing to meet those targets.

Agreeing such aims will not be easy in any international forum. We shall still need global bodies, and they will still need overarching remits. There are few 'purely technical' issues in this globalisation debate, and few things are 'self-evident' either. Even the principle of democracy, which seems self-evident in the West is challenged elsewhere. And we all know that the defence of 'local cultural forms' can be a way of maintaining intra-cultural domination (the suppression of women, for instance). Nonetheless, it can hardly be an advance simply to impose Western principles on other parts of the world – they have to be argued for. What we have to accept is the 'non-foundational' nature of such principles, that taking difference (the local) seriously means we cannot assume any particular principles as self-evident. They are the subject of political contestation.

But for this political contestation to be even dreamable, the globalisation process must be opened up to democratic influence.

Disgracefully, the Uruguay round barely registered in the UK's public political debate. But post-Seattle, debate must be pursued through protest movements, while multinational bodies such as the WTO need opening up and making more democratic. Both within and between countries there needs to be democratic debate. And, once again, a formal appearance of equality (one country one vote) is not enough.

International forums must provide the conditions for a democratic opening. The current disparity in resources for the delegations of different countries makes the idea of equal negotiations laughable. Funds and facilities need to be provided to even this up somewhat (although the US, for instance, will always have more power).

In the UK we must contest the New Labour line that globalisation is inevitable; we should also contest its form. We should put on the agenda the question: what is globalisation for? What principles might we be aiming at for the international (internationalist) organisation of economy and society? Opening up that kind of a question to political debate will be endlessly difficult (and indeed possibly endless in that it may have to be periodically renewed) – but that is the nature of genuinely political debate. Learning to talk across difference in an interconnected world might be one step towards imagining an alternative form of globalisation.

*This essay first appeared in* After Seattle: Globalisation and its Discontents, *edited by Barbara Gunnell and David Timms, Catalyst, 2000.*

# Learning from
Latin America

# 13

# Nicaragua: Some Reflections on Socio-Spatial Issues in a Society in Transition[1]

## 1986

### Managua in the Nicaraguan economy

Managua, capital of Nicaragua, is a city of nearly a million people (no one knows exactly). It doesn't look at all like the standard image of a 'million city'. The centre is empty, save for some gaunt ruins, the result of the earthquake in 1972. Around the hollow centre the built-up area sprouts haphazardly, and motorway-style ringroads from the Somoza era curve between shanty-towns and wasteland. Most of the small amount of factory-scale manufacturing industry is strung out along the road to the airport. As to housing there are middle-class suburbs, of bungalows with gardens, there are working-class *barrios* of small but solid single-storey houses, and there are 'spontaneous settlements'. These last are self-built, one-room houses, made of wood, on land seized by the present occupiers. Densities are often low, and people keep pigs, and hens, and grow yuca. The housing problem which the Sandinistas inherited from Somoza was enormous. In Managua in 1979, the year of the revolution, 60 per cent of *barrios* were without piped water, sewerage or electricity, and even by 1984 20 per cent of households were without a home of their own, 15 per cent were in housing officially recognised as inadequate, and 30 per cent lived in one-roomed huts.[2] In these conditions, 'spontaneous settlements' spring up continuously. What was empty wasteland the night before by next morning has been divided up into lots, with houses half-built and people moving in, and a CDS (Sandinista Defence Committee) being organised to claim recognition and services from the government.

These rapidly-multiplying spontaneous settlements are one, particularly visible, symbol of what one might call a socio-spatial contradiction which is proving increasingly problematical for the Sandinista project of a transitional society. Managua, which was growing rapidly before 1979, is continuing to expand, both spatially (and haphazardly) and in numerical terms. In 1940 Managua accounted for only c. 7.5 per cent of the total population of Nicaragua; by 1980 this figure had risen to 28.1 per cent and today it is about 33 per cent.[3] This very rapid growth, both absolutely and relatively, is posing problems at a wider level for the development of the Nicaraguan economy and society. Most obviously, it implies enormous costs of urban-infrastructure provision. Such costs are even greater than they might be otherwise because the socially 'spontaneous' nature of the new settlements means that they are unplanned spatially and often widely dispersed. In spite of the cost, in the early years after the revolution spontaneous settlements were given formal recognition by the Sandinista government, and provided with water and electricity. Such a policy is today increasingly difficult to implement. One reason for this is the shortage of resources; in a country which is already desperately poor, around 50 per cent of national income each year has to be spent on defence against United States-sponsored aggression.

## The economy and the problem of urbanisation

But the shortage of resources for Managua is also a result, of course, of the Sandinistas' own political priorities. The Nicaraguan economy which the Sandinistas inherited was in a highly dependent position within the international division of labour. It was dependent on four export crops (coffee, cotton, sugar and beef) for the bulk of its earnings of hard currency, and that dependency was further reinforced (until the US economic blockade) by the dominance of its trade relations by the United States. The Sandinistas recognised that in the medium-term there was little that could be done to alter in any significant way the basic agro-export nature of the economy.[1] Nonetheless it is an economic structure which has run into serious problems in recent years. The problems arise from a coincidence of long-term and more conjunctural factors. Over the long term the terms of trade for the primary products which Nicaragua exports are declining rapidly. More immediately the problems this poses for a country dependent on such exports in order to be able to buy manufactured goods have been greatly exacerbated by the *recession* in the international capitalist economy. Finally, there has been the economic blockade by the US and the increasing impact of the war which it is conducting against Nicaragua. Not only does this war eat up about half the annual national budget, it also absorbs a large proportion of the already-scarce administratively and technically trained labour power. This latter has proved to be a problem particularly for the large government farms devoted to the production of export crops. Moreover the war itself is also frequently directed against economic targets – coffee harvests, tobacco fields and drying sheds.

In these circumstances the Sandinistas, while not being able fundamentally to alter the agro-export nature of the economy, have increasingly emphasised what they call a 'strategy of survival'. The focus of this strategy is the production of basic foodstuffs on rural small holdings for the people of Nicaragua. In class and political terms this means a focus on the peasantry. In spatial terms, it means a definite prioritisation of the countryside over the urban areas and especially over Managua. The objectives of concentrating on food-production are to provide everyone with basic sustenance, to save a little on foreign trade and to survive the US aggression.

In this context the process of continuing and rapid urbanisation poses an enormous problem. It increases the financial demands made by the urban areas if conditions are not to worsen intolerably. Yet they are demands which cannot be met, because the priority must be food production and consequently investment in the countryside. A further complication is that rural-urban migration drains the countryside of desperately-needed labour.

By 1985 this contradiction, between a national economic strategy of food-production-based survival on the one hand and continuing high rates of urbanisation on the other, had become the focus of a major political and public debate. There were articles about it almost daily in the newspapers, discussion-programmes on the radio, and numerous speeches by Sandinista leaders. The initial popular interpretation of the problem focussed on the new spontaneous settlements – the most visible symbol of the uncontrolled growth of the capital. The argument was that the new settlements were primarily a product of migration from the countryside. This was linked to another issue, the growth in Nicaragua of the so-called 'informal sector'. Those newly-arriving in the city, it was argued, were unable to find employment in the formal sector and therefore resorted to 'informal' activities. These were generally characterised as commercial, inflationary, and certainly non-productive. Indeed the emerging popular understanding was of a dichotomy between a productive countryside and an unproductive, indeed parasitic, city.

## Analysis of new spontaneous settlements

Such a characterisation of the issues has of course been typical of many recent analyses of 'shanty towns' and rapid urban growth in Latin America. However, this interpretation is now being questioned.[4] Certainly, it proved to be far too simple an analysis in the case of Nicaragua. Firstly, the equation between rural-urban migration and the new settlements is not a simple one. The results of surveys which we carried out in a number of such settlements, as part of a wider project, indicate clearly that the majority of inhabitants are not new migrants. The settlements are a product of the appalling housing shortage in the city more generally, and to the extent that they also result from the pressures of in-migration, they seem to do so predominantly indirectly. Most in-migrants spend at least a while living with family or friends on their arrival in the city. Secondly, preliminary surveys as part of the same project also indicate that a large section of the population in these new spontaneous settlements is not working in the informal sector, however broadly that is defined. In one smallish settlement over 15 per cent of those earning had permanent jobs with various arms of the state.

Thirdly, of course, there are all the problems of definition, and in particular the definition of 'informal sectors' and of 'unproductive sectors'. Certainly many activities often classified, because of the nature of their social organisation, as 'informal' in the Nicaraguan debate, and frequently found in the new settlements, are productive. Making tortillas, repairing machinery, making clothes, are obvious examples.

It soon became clear, therefore, that the problem was a good deal more complex than its initial schematic characterisation indicated. One early policy which had been attempted as a result of the initial characterisation of the problem was for meetings to be held with the residents of a new settlement, at which the problems of urban growth and the provision of infrastructure were presented in detail. The residents would then be offered a range of alternative 'packages', consisting of new housing, employment and land, at one of a number of locations a short distance outside of Managua. Although the policy was conducted with sensitivity, it was clearly not welcomed by the residents of the new settlements. One of the objections which they voiced most strongly was precisely that they were *not* recently-arrived peasants from the countryside but had been living in Managua for years and in many cases had been born there. The Sandinista government was clearly responsive to such complaints; indeed it was not at all clear that the policy could work in such circumstances and it was widely suspected that over time people would simply slip back into the city. In the end only two small new spontaneous settlements have been re-settled in this way, and it seems that the policy may have now been abandoned.

## A socio-spatial contradiction

But if the Sandinistas have been so readily responsive to their base, and so prepared to take on board the fact that the issue is far more complex than at first it seemed, they are now faced with an enormously difficult problem. In his article in the last issue of *Antipode,* 'Socialism, Democracy and the Territorial Imperative', David Slater argued that 'spatial dimensions *are* important and not infrequently in the examination of revolutions the general issue of spatiality is left out of account'.[5] The problems being discussed here corroborate that point, though in a rather different way from the issues presented in Slater's article. What we have here is a situation in which important elements of the Sandinistas' national-level economic and political strategy are being undermined by other social processes going on within the country, social processes in which the spatial dimension is of crucial importance. On the one hand there is a strategy which economically prioritises the peasantry and spatially prioritises the countryside. On the other hand there is a continuing and rapid process of urbanisation, an important element of which is rural-urban migration.

## Rural-urban migration

In this context it becomes important to ask why rural-urban migration is continuing at such a high rate. For even though it now seems to be clear that the new spontaneous settlements are not simply peopled by migrants arriving in the city, major migration from the countryside to Managua does seem to be occurring.[2] It is particularly challenging to investigate the causes of this in Nicaragua since most analyses of rural-urban migration in Latin America are, inevitably, done in the context of capitalist societies and the causes of migration are tied in to features of capitalist development, and especially the development of capitalist relations in the countryside. Such causes would indeed have been prominent in the explanation of rural-urban migration in Nicaragua before the revolution. The key components of an explanation would have lain in the nature of the insertion of the economy within the international division of labour and in the nature of the development of social relations in different regions of the country. Thus, in the 1950s for instance, the dramatic expansion of cotton cultivation established the Nicaraguan economy both in its agro-capitalist character and in its insertion into the international division of labour as an agro-exporting economy. That same development also implied a massive expulsion of peasantry from significant parts of the Pacific region as land was taken over for cotton production. Some of the now-landless peasantry moved eastwards to other regions, but many others migrated to Managua.

The question now is, what conditions are combining to produce, in a society which is no longer simply capitalist but a society in transition, a continued flow of rural-urban migration? It is not possible here to give a conclusive answer to this question. Research is continuing, and the issue is clearly one of considerable political urgency. Nonetheless some preliminary and tentative indications can be given.

First, there is quite simply the fact that the process is already under-way and long-established. It has a social dynamic of its own. Most people in Nicaragua, certainly on the Pacific side, have friends or family in Managua, often from previous migrations.

Second, the war is a significant promoter of migration – life is considerably safer in Managua.

Third, and more fundamentally, the revolutionary process like every social process produces its own contradictory effects and dynamics. Many of the most impressive gains of the Sandinista revolution are contributing now, as one of their indirect implications, to continued rural-urban migration. One element of this is that people's expectations of their lives have been immeasurably heightened by the revolution. More concretely, the ending of semi-feudal relations in some agricultural regions has freed many people from previous contractual and debt ties to landlords and thus to particular rural areas. In the cities, the major improvements carried out by the Sandinistas, as well as improving – as intended – conditions for people in urban areas, have also increased the attractiveness of those areas to people in rural areas. Parallel to the Agrarian Reform there is also a programme of Urban Reform. This has involved a wide range of policies to improve and cheapen housing provision, confiscate urban land held empty by large landowners, and institute emergency programmes for barrios in particular need. Perhaps most importantly from the point of view of an analysis of migration, in the years after the revolution the Sandinistas adopted a programme of 'legalising' previously unrecognised spontaneous settlements. Along with such 'legalisation', which was usually granted in response to collective organisation through a Sandinista Defence Committee (CDS), went the provision of basic services, in particular water and electricity. This process of recognition and provision continued up until 1983, and even though such spontaneous settlements are not predominantly a direct product of migration, the clear message which these policies conveyed was that the government was prepared to provide for increased living-space in the capital city. Since 1983, in the face of the fact that demand for new settlements seemed never-ending and indeed that the policy itself might be contributing to that demand, legalisation has been abandoned. The problem now is that, however much the Sandinistas insist that they will provide no more water and electricity, and can recognise no more new settlements, settlements continue to be established. This, too, is a reflection of what the Nicaraguan people have gained through and since July 1979. In the day of Somoza new overnight settlements would often be faced in the morning with the guns and terror of Somoza's National Guard; people know that this will not happen now. Further, from numerous interviews we conducted in such newly-established and still unrecognised settlements, it is clear that people do not believe that in the end the Sandinistas will be hard-hearted enough not to give in, not to recognise their settlements and provide them with electricity and water. Time and again we were told: 'it's our revolution, we made it'. Such statements are a measure of the self-confidence and sense of 'rights' which has been won through the revolutionary process. This is undoubtedly a gain, but in a situation where half of the anyway tiny national budget must be spent on defence against the largest military power in the world and where out of what resources remain the first priority must be food production not urban housing, this again also poses a huge dilemma.

### Problems of planning Managua

One element of this dilemma concerns what to do with Managua itself. *Not* to plan for urban growth increases the chaos and the costs, social and economic, of that growth when it happens anyway. But to plan for growth would be a green light to yet more potential migrants. One particular aspect of the 'planning' issue revolves around questions of the layout and density of Managua. As has been said, the present 'urban structure' is very open, with built-up areas and expanses of open land intermixed. One obvious possibility is to 'ruralise' the urban, to promote agricultural production within Managua itself.

To some extent this is being done; there are cooperative farms by Lake Managua, and in a number of barrios, and one huge agricultural project well within the city boundaries. Such developments help reduce both the problem and the image of 'the parasitic city'. Present-day Managua must represent one of the best opportunities ever of breaking down the urban-rural dichotomy at the *urban* end, and not only by 'urbanising the countryside' which has been the approach in Cuba. Yet this is an opportunity for 'urban planning' which cannot be seized. One reason is the shortage of water. Even now this shortage is such that every part of the city is without water supply (on a planned and rotating basis) for two or three days each week. Besides this, there are frequent 'unplanned' occasions on which the water-supply fails because of technical problems. The irony of this is particularly sharp because Managua is on the shores of a huge lake. But it is a dead lake, the waters of which cannot be used; all the pollution of Managua over decades has been poured into it. The cost of cleaning it, for which studies have been done, is far beyond the resources of Nicaragua, particularly in its current situation.

The problem of lack of finance lies at the heart also of the other reason for not pursuing a low-density 'agricultural' strategy for Managua – it would increase significantly the cost of providing basic infrastructure and services. Current plans for the future of Managua therefore emphasise filling in 'gaps' in the current urban structure. Nonetheless, not all those gaps *can* be filled, even in the longer term, because of the vulnerability of considerable areas to damage from earthquakes.

## Labour shortages in the countryside

The other element of the dilemma facing the Sandinistas is the one which has been the theme of this article: the sectoral and, given the arguments above about Managua, spatial, distribution of labour power. There is already a serious shortage of labour in the countryside. Here again the problem has been exacerbated precisely by the achievements of the revolution. The condition of the 'peasantry' under Somoza was so dire that few families achieved self-sufficiency from their own production. In consequence, members of a family would take up wage labour when they could get it, to supplement their incomes. Improvements in the standard of living for the peasantry since the revolution mean that this element of economic compulsion no longer exists. In consequence the available supply of wage-labour has been reduced. There are other factors too, among them, again, the war which now involves all young males in a two-year period of service in the army. The US Government is not unaware of these effects. As Wisner points out, US policy-makers 'speak openly of the "food weapon" and have not hesitated to use it.'[6]

## Political responses and political problems

One point which does seem clear in the present dilemma is that a significant part of the answer must lie in improvements in living standards, in the widest sense, in the countryside. Earlier this year (1986), in part as a response to these problems, a new stage was announced in the process of Agrarian Reform. Very briefly, the first stage in the Agrarian Reform confiscated the land of Somoza and his close associates (in a sense it was a nationalist and populist measure). A second element took over all land-holdings over a certain size which were not being used to their full productive potential (in a sense this was saying that owners at least had to be efficient in capitalist terms). Now, it is argued that even where land is being 'efficiently' used by a large landowner, other, social, criteria of efficiency might require that the estate be broken up into smallholdings for peasant food production. This, then, is a politically-significant shift towards a more radical Agrarian Reform policy. Moreover, not only the land of private owners (the maximum size of which has been further reduced) but also some state-owned land is being redistributed to smallholders for food production. The latter is part of a response to the shortage of administrative and technical skills, a shortage which is hampering production on state farms. The land is being distributed to previously landless rural people, on an individual and cooperative basis. (One disincentive to the latter at the moment is that calling yourself a cooperative significantly increases the likelihood of contra attack.)

There are, then, attempts to improve life in the countryside, at least by a wider distribution of land. In the system of food-distribution, too, the rest of Nicaragua has priority over Managua. There is a whole range of other related policies, which lie beyond the scope of this paper, dealing with pricing policy, the informal sector, and so on. Additionally there is a recent Containment Plan for Managua which suggests policies of developing local economic strategies for areas and regions outside the capital. It will, obviously, not be possible to assess the impact of these for some while. The Sandinistas are also constrained by the fact that, as Dave Slater pointed out,[7] they are not building a second Cuba. Controls on the labour market, or on migration, are therefore not policy options. But clearly, within the resource-limits of today's Nicaragua, a lot is being done.

In the meantime, however, the problems in Managua continue. The Sandinistas are very aware that the inhabitants of the urban barrios, and many of those now living on spontaneous settlements, were the key element in the urban insurrection which brought about the final triumph in 1979. Many family and friends were lost; they are right to say 'it's our revolution'. Today in these areas both left-wing and right-wing organisations (the latter including fundamentalist religious groups from the southern states of the US – no religious freedom in Nicaragua?) are trading on the discontent which people evidently feel. Yet, in an absolute sense, conditions in many rural areas remain worse; the priority *must* be food production; and, while in Managua you can often forget that there is a war going on (which also means that the privations of daily life seem less explicable), the peasantry in many rural areas is on the front line against the contra.

## Postscript

i) The argument here is necessarily highly schematic. I am currently writing up a much longer report which should be available from the Faculty of Social Sciences, Open University.

ii) There is also a significant amount of 'middle-class' migration to Managua, but this seems to be mainly from other cities. It is often related to the job-market in the new state departments and services established since 1979. It can, however, produce *reverberative* effects in a wider process of migration.

*This essay first appeared in* Antipode, *Vol. 18, No. 3, May 1986.*

## Notes

1 This paper derives from work done as part of a project currently being carried out at the Instituto Nacional de Investigaciones Economicas y Sociales (INIES), Managua, Nicaragua. The other members of the team working centrally on this part of the project were Marielos de los Angeles and Ixy Martinez. My thanks to both of them. It should be stressed that our project continues and in that sense this is a preliminary report.
2 Data from R. Drake, D. Alexander, J. Darke and A. Manogue, 'Housing in Nicaragua', 1986. Paper presented to the XI World Congress of Sociology, Delhi, India.
3 CIERA-UNRISD, *Managua es Nicaragua: El impacto de la capital en el sistema alimentario nacional*, CIERA: Managua, 1984, p10.
4 See, for instance, P. Connolly reporting on Mexico City, 'The politics of the informal sector: a critique', in E. Minigione and N. Redclift (eds), *Beyond Employment,* Allison and Busby: Oxford, pp55-91.
5 D. Slater, 'Socialism, democracy and the territorial imperative: elements for a comparison of the Cuban and Nicaraguan experience', *Antipode*, Vol. 18, No. 2, 1986, pp174-5.
6 B. Wisner, 'Geography: War or peace studies?', *Antipode*, Vol. 18, No. 2, 1986, p213.
7 See Slater 1986, *op. cit.*

# 14

# Concepts of Space and Power in Theory and in Political Practice

## 2009

It is, perhaps, no longer innovatory to state that space and power are intimately intertwined. Intuitively, for instance, there appear to be places where power is concentrated (in global cities, perhaps, or in Washington DC, US). There are those relations of power which are intrinsic to neoliberal globalisation and which tie different places together, subordinating some to the dictates of others. There are places within our own local areas which we might find it difficult to enter because they are alienating (we do not conform to the characteristics required of those who normally gain admission). And so on. Space and power imbue each other in a myriad of ways.

The purpose of this paper is first of all to reflect on this, and in particular to explore the resonances of this relationship at the conceptual level. That is to say, to explore the way in which the nature of the conceptualisation of space might be related to the nature of the conceptualisation of power. This, immediately, has political implications. However, in order to take this further, the paper then moves on to explore just one example of where this mutual imbrication of space and power has been recognised and has become a key element in proposals for political change. One reason for doing this is straightforward exemplification. It is also, however, to explore how the conceptual is itself developed in the context of political practice.

## Space and power

The way in which space is conceptualised, in intellectual work, in social life, and in political practice, *matters*.[1] It has effects, intellectual, social and political. In my own work, I have proposed three characteristics for an adequate conceptualisation of space. These are the following:

- *First*: that space is the product of relations (including the absence of relations). Space is a complexity of networks, links, exchanges, connections, from the intimate level of our daily lives (think of spatial relations within the home for example) to the global level of financial corporations, for instance, or of counter-hegemonic political activists. Taking this opening proposition seriously immediately implies that space is a 'product': it is *produced* through the establishment or refusal of relations. It also implies, as a logical consequence, that space is in its very nature 'social' (where social is taken to mean 'more than individual', rather than simply 'human').[2] If there is to be a relation (or, indeed, a non-relation) there needs to be at least more than one thing to do the relating, or not.

- This leads to the *second* proposition about the characteristics of space. This is indeed that space is the dimension of multiplicity. Without space as a dimension it would not be possible for there to be multiplicity (in the sense of the simultaneous coexistence of more than one thing). Equally, and as the mirror image of this, without multiplicity space itself could not exist (space is the product of relations within multiplicity). Space and multiplicity are mutually constitutive.

- *Third*, and following directly on from these first two characteristics, space is always in a process of being made. It is always 'under construction'. It is never a fully connected and finalised thing like the 'synchronies' proposed by structuralism for instance.[3] There are always relations which are still to be made, or unmade, or re-made. In this sense, space is a product of our on-going world. And in this sense it is also always open to the future. And, in consequence, it is always open also to the political. The production of space is a social and political task. If it is conceptualised in this manner, the dimension of space enters, necessarily, into the political (for if the future were not open there would be no possibility of changing it and thus no possibility of politics).

This bringing of the making of space into politics has been the motivation behind insisting on the importance of engaging with its conceptualisation. Space has so often (usually implicitly and without much thought) been consigned to the fixed and the dead (as Foucault had it), to the realm of the already-given. One aim of this reconceptualisation is to bring it alive. Another aim is to rescue it from its negative counterposition with time. All too often space is thought of as the dimension that is the opposite of time It is the dimension *without* temporality (hence, 'the fixed and the dead'). But if space is constantly being made, if it is the ongoing product of relationships and exchanges, then while it is most certainly a dimension that is different from time (see below) it is certainly not a dimension with no temporality within it.[4]

Nonetheless, even if bringing space alive in this way enables its more productive insertion into the political, it must be emphasised (as will be explored further below) that this is in no way to suggest that any particular conceptualisation (including this one) will lead in deterministic fashion to any particular political position. This particular conceptualisation does, however, force on to the agenda certain political questions. If time is the dimension of succession and of change, space is the dimension of contemporaneous multiplicity. For that reason, as has been argued, it is the dimension of the social.

It is space as a dimension that poses to us that most fundamental of sociopolitical questions: how are we going to live together? It is space as a dimension that offers up the challenge, the pleasure and the responsibility of the existence of 'others', and of our relationship to them.

This, then, is one side of things – the side of space. There is, however, another side to the argument of this paper, which is that, not only is space utterly imbued with and a product of relations of power, but power itself has a geography. There are cartographies of power. The concept that I have proposed, and that I continue to find most useful, in exploring this two-sided definition is 'power-geometry'.[5]

That power has a geography is something that is known implicitly – the opening brief examples implied as much. Moreover it is also the case that this proposition applies to all forms of social interaction that are brought together under this umbrella term – whether it be the power of violence, or of authority, or of seduction (the various forms of 'soft power' so commonly now recognised as being deployed, even alongside physical violence), of domination, of creativity ... (indeed, it may be that these different modalities of power have inscribed within them, as a function of their different natures, propensities towards distinct geographies).[6] Or again, the different instances of a social formation (the economic, the political, the cultural, for example) may each be analysed as having their own powergeometries, even though undoubtedly they will be related to each other, inflect each other, and quite probably reinforce each other. (In the United Kingdom, for example, it is quite possible to discern power-geometries in politics, in the economic sphere through the geography of the relations of production and distribution, and in the cultural formation. It is also undeniable that the three – each of them strongly peaking in the south east corner of the country – feed off each other and reinforce each other. The spatial centralisation of all of these power-relations in London is one of the cardinal facts of British society. It is a crucial aspect of the national democratic deficit. Most parts of the country barely have a voice.) Equally, these power-geometries exist at all spatial levels. The unequal geographies of power that underpin the chasms of economic inequality that are a product of neoliberal globalisation are only the most obvious example at the level of the international. The idea of 'power-geometries', then, is simply an attempt to capture both the fact that space is imbued with power and the fact that power in its turn always has a spatiality.

The concept has, however, a number of other significant implications. First, the very notion of power-geometry brings with it the implication that power itself is relational. This is not a question, in fact, of a geography of power, but of a geography of power-*relations*.

We should, therefore, immediately enter some modifications to the intuitive descriptions of space/power at the very beginning of this paper. It is not that all 'power' is concentrated in global cities, or in Washington DC, but rather that the power-relations are focused there. What global cities have are the *resources,* the economic weight, often backed up by political and cultural influence. Their *power* is exercised relationally, in interaction with other places (one might think of the relation between the financial City of London and a country in the global South, for instance). This in turn opens up particular possibilities for politics. In particular, it implies that a significant political task is building a politics of relations. This may be between social groups, between local places, between countries, or whatever. It also implies a politics of building alliances, maybe between political groupings or struggles in different parts of the world. It is important to note, however, that in building such alliances, or chains of equivalence, each component political grouping will itself be modified.[7] A relational view of the world entails that power is not an external relation between already finally pre-constituted entities. On the contrary, the very fact of relationality is part of what constitutes those entities themselves. Further, it is important to note what a relational understanding of power (and space) does *not* imply. For instance, it stands against those notions of energy or force that see them as internally derived; as the internally generated motive-force of being, or autarchic self-creation. Even creativity does not occur in a vacuum; rather it is necessarily social; that is to say, relational.[8] Finally, on this understanding, power will never be abolished. The aim of a progressive politics is thus not to do away with power. As Devine writes, 'Twenty-first century socialism, like any form of socialism, is ultimately about power and power relations'.[9]

## Power-geometries in action

In itself, the term power-geometry does not imply any specific form (any specific geometry). It is a concept through which to analyse the world, in order perhaps to highlight inequalities, or deficiencies in democracy. It is in this mode an instrument of potential critique. It may also, however, be an instrument through which to imagine, and maybe to begin to build, more equal and democratic societies. This point was brought strongly home to me in the spring and summer of 2007 when I received an invitation to visit Venezuela to participate in the processes of change underway as part of the Bolivarian project of building a socialism of the twenty-first century. After a resounding election victory in December 2006 this project, led by Hugo Chávez, had moved in a more explicitly socialist direction (its own characterisation) and in this context five 'motors' had been set out to carry the revolution forward. The fourth of these motors is to build 'a new power-geometry' (*la nueva geometría del poder*).[10] Here, then, a geographical concept is being put to positive political use. Indeed, as will be seen, part of what lay behind the proposal was an impressive recognition of the existence and significance, within Venezuela, of highly unequal, and thus undemocratic, power-geometries.

In its particular form of the fourth motor, the 'new power-geometry' referred to the need to reorganise the geopolitics of Venezuela, the geopolitical organisation of its territory. Importantly, however, this was recognised to refer both to the formal *geography* of its democracy and to the *form* of the power-relations that it entailed. Schematically, it is possible to spell out these aspects separately. Thus, on the more purely geographical side, the intent is to distribute 'power' and participation more evenly – to give more voice to the vast regions of the south of the country, that stretch away from the towns and populated areas of the coast towards the headwaters of the Amazon; to give more voice to smaller communities; and to give more voice to indigenous communities.[11] On the other side, there was recognition of the need also to address the nature of the power within these power-geometries. By the time of Chávez's election in 1998, the formal state apparatus in Venezuela, including its mechanisms of representative democracy, were completely delegitimised. The long period of *puntofijismo*, the subsequent chaos and farce, the extremely high levels of corruption ... all of these things meant that it was not feasible simply to continue with the forms of state and democracy that had been inherited.[12] The most important structural innovation here has been the introduction of participatory democracy 'from below'.

The mechanisms for the implementation of these changes are more complex than can be elaborated here, but a few points can be made.[13] One small and symbolic one is the proposal to call all basic-level settlements within the democratic structure 'cities'. The politics of this change revolved around the linguistic connection between city and citizenship (*ciudad y ciudadanía*) and the equality of rights and responsibilities, that inhere in citizenship, that had previously been lacking. In symbolic terms it proclaims that every geographical collectivity, however small and wherever it is in the country, has the same political status. As such, it is a small step in the building of a new power-geometry. It is also, as is much of the Bolivarian revolution, about the recognition and assertion of voice, and of a multiplicity of voices. It resonates in other words with the conceptualisation of space (as a multiplicity) that was laid out in the previous section.

Much bigger have been the changes wrought through the introduction of elements of participatory democracy. This has taken place through the initiation of a process of the formation of 'communal councils' (*consejos comunales*). These are formed by people themselves (there are posters and leaflets and so forth detailing how to do it). Each communal council brings together about 400 households (this number can be adjusted in indigenous and rural areas to conform with local customs and conditions). There is then, in principle, a successive aggregation of these councils up to national level, forming a structure parallel to that of the elected state. Broadly speaking, the aims of these councils are on the one hand to take unto themselves the collective self-management of their neighbourhoods and on the other hand to maintain pressure on the elected state (the pressure of constituent power on constituted power). In terms of power-geometries some things are immediately evident. This is an attempt (again) to shift political voice towards those who previously did not have such a voice – the poor in the cities being the clearest example. Moreover this political voice exemplifies a different kind of power-relation. It is not about representative democracy and the individualism of voting; rather it is about *collective* organisation, decision-making, management and campaigning. Moreover, this very process of self-government, the very formation of communal councils, is one that, being new, has to be learned. It is thus in itself empowering. It is part of the process of formation of *popular* power (*poder popular*, or *poder protagónico*). It is possible to see here, in other words, how both the very nature of power-relations and the geography of those relations might be changed. Truly an attempt to shift the whole nature of the national, political, power-geometries.

Let us, then, reflect briefly on this mobilisation of the concept of power-geometry, primarily at this point from the point of view of political practice but bearing in mind also the conceptual arguments elaborated at the beginning of this paper.

First, if power is relational then it is necessary to consider not just entities (such as, for instance, smaller settlements in rural areas, or communal councils) and their establishment and recognition, but also the wider relations of power within which they are set. Thus, in the case of communal councils, in any political evaluation it is necessary to take into account a host of questions such as: where is control over their recognition located? (communal councils have to be officially recognised in order to participate in the new structures) and where is control over the distribution of resources to and between communal councils located? Such considerations will influence greatly the reality of the project to distribute democratic participation more evenly. So too will the issue of resources and capabilities. If the aim is greater equality, if power is relational, and if the starting-point is gross inequality (which it is in Venezuela), then the establishment of structures and rights has to be supplemented by an expansion of resources and capabilities, human and physical, in those areas currently underendowed.

Second, there is the question of time and temporality. The intuitive image of a power-geometry might be as a kind of diagram, or map. It is essentially a spatial concept, and this map-like image of it would fit with those understandings of space that see it as a flat, finished, surface or network. As something already completed.[14] As, indeed, dead. Yet as soon as that is said it is obviously incorrect. For a power-geometry is precisely a product of relations, and relations are social processes, and very much alive. In that sense power-geometries precisely exemplify the conceptualisation of space as always under construction. The spatial as imbued with temporality.

This is richly evident in the policy of power-geometries in Venezuela, and it raises reflections both political and conceptual. It is evident in a situation, as in Venezuela, where establishing a new power-geometry is part of politics, that power-geometries are *processes*. They are not diagrams on a page; they are the evolving outcome of processes of socio-political contestation. Thus, politically, what matters is not only the initiating policy statements and formal definitions, the declarations about communal councils and the delineation of territories, but the socio-political practices of their realisation. And these practices will reflect and depend on everything from the general political culture of the nation to the behaviour of individuals (the microphysics of power).

Furthermore, in building a new power-geometry it is necessary to take account of this essential dynamism and to make it part of the politics. In particular, it is necessary to grapple with the possibility that there may be more than one temporality within a power-geometry, *and* that there may be dislocations between them. There is a very clear case of this in Venezuela. Thus, one of the most frequent criticisms of the Bolivarian process is that it is producing a situation (a power-geometry) which is too focused on the centre, specifically in the figure of Chávez.[15] One response to this is that this (acknowledged but perhaps inevitable) centralisation will be balanced by the development of popular forces through, for instance, the communal councils. Whether or not one thinks this is an adequate response, the point to be made here is that it is to attempt to balance two very different temporalities. On the one hand, the power-resources of the president can be established almost immediately, through the passage of laws. On the other hand, the power-resources of small communities in the south of the country, for instance, or in the poor *barrios* of the coastal cities, will take years to develop. From economic weight, to cultural resources, to the forming of collectivities, to the very confidence that one can raise one's political voice at all, all these things have been seriously lacking in such places and among such groups. Here the passing of legislation is merely an enabling act. The bringing to fruition of the aim will take many years and much hard work. Meanwhile, the imbalances within the emerging power-geometry are likely to persist.

A further reflection arises from the fact that in Venezuela the concept of power-geometry is being mobilised specifically in the sphere of politics. However, as was argued in the previous section, there are geometries of power in all instances of society. Moreover they relate to each other and, if there is any general tendency, it is that they are likely to reinforce each other. For that reason the real functioning of a power-geometry within the political will depend also on that within the economic, that within the distribution of educational resources, that within the cultural sphere, and so on. In the Venezuelan context, one thing this means is that other motors of the revolution will be important contributors to the establishment of a new, more democratic and egalitarian, political power-geometry. One might, for instance, cite here the third motor (*moral y luces*) with its emphasis on popular education. Most particularly, this interdependence of power-geometries within different spheres highlights the importance of economic reform – the building of what is said to be a new productive economic model that is collective and cooperative. Such a process (also likely to be long and conflictual) would contribute greatly to the reality of a new geometry of power within the political sphere.

One final, brief, reflection – and one which relates closely to recent debates within geography – concerns the role of 'place' in the building of this new power-geometry. The basic building-blocks of the new popular, participatory, forms of democracy are *places*. They are groups of households in which the grouping is through criteria of spatial contiguity (they form a neighbourhood, or settlement, etc.), and much of the task which they have been set concerns the forming of that place into a collective to address issues of local (within-place) self-management. This is typical of all such initiatives, and indeed representative democracy also typically functions through a territorial base. It does, however, raise reflections, again both political and conceptual.

In the constitutional proposals in Venezuela 'communes' were defined as the social cells of the territory, each of which is to constitute the basic and indivisible nucleus of the state ('*serán las células sociales del territorio ... cada una de las cuales constituirá el nucleo territorial básico e indivisible del Estado*'). From the point of view of the concept of space advocated here, and from that of power-geometries, space is not simply an aggregation of territories; it is also a space of flows and relations. In its turn this implies that 'places' are never homogeneous or closed. Each place is a node of relations, an internal complexity. And this in turn implies that 'places' are the products of negotiation, conflict, competition, agreement, and so forth between different interests and positions. This is in no way to throw doubt upon the proposals. But it *is* to argue that these 'basic nuclei' will, as political entities, be an evolving *result* of the process of building participatory democracy rather than a presumed already-existing coherence that one can take as an *input* to the process. (Once again, the political and the conceptual engage with each other in productive conversation.)

The political implications are significant. One aspect is, as already mentioned, that the process of building these nuclei into political entities (the *consejos comunales*) is a long, difficult, and potentially conflictual one. The existence of collectivities cannot be taken as given. On the other hand this very process is itself a learning process, and an empowering one. (It might be noted that this form of territorial base is thus in fact very different from that of representative democracy. In representative democracy the territorial base is effective only as the unit of aggregation of individuals. In participatory democracy and local self-management, however, the territorial base is required also to be effective as the scaffolding for the constitution of a collective voice. It is also different, moreover, from those autonomous communities that establish themselves, also in places, as demonstrations of the possibility of political alternatives, for in their case some kind of agreement, or commitment to the project, is assumed from the start. This is important, for it means that there is no need to confront radical differences in interests or political position. In the places of the *consejos comunales* any such differences will have to be addressed, and this is important – and positive – politically.) Furthermore, there is some evidence, for instance in the detailed empirical investigations in Caracas by Miguel Lacabana and Cecilia Cariola, that this emerging place-based collectivity is beginning in itself to give people from the poorer *barrios* a confidence and, very interestingly, that this place-basis (*anclaje territorial*) has enabled people from these *barrios* to break out of their previous territorial enclosure (*a romper el encierro territorial*) and participate more widely in the public and institutional spaces of the city as a whole.[16]

Before turning to the final section, which will reflect some more on the engagement between the theoretical and the political, there is one further point to be made. This is that, although the only way that the concept power-geometry is mobilised consistently and explicitly in the Bolivarian project is in relation to the restructuring of politics and democracy in the internal political sphere, there are of course numerous other ways in which the project is having considerable effects on other geometries of power. This is especially the case at the global level where the insistence has been on the attempt to create a world that is more explicitly politically differentiated – multipolar as opposed to unipolar. This has taken many forms, including perhaps most importantly, the moves to create a more distinguishable voice within Latin America (from ALBA, to Telesur, to PetroCaribe, to the Banco del Sur, and so on). It also included until abolished by an incoming Conservative mayor of London, an equal exchange agreement between Caracas and London that clearly challenged the neoliberal mantras that all relations between places should be those of the market and that places must compete against each other. No, it said, they can cooperate. This was an explicit politics of relations (a politics *of* place *beyond* place, as I have called it) and quite clearly a very small, but symbolic, remodelling of the existing power-geometries of neoliberal globalisation. And, although indeed tiny, its potential symbolic significance was ironically confirmed when the incoming Conservative mayor cancelled the agreement almost immediately on taking office.

## Conceptual lessons from political practice

The previous section, then, presented one small story of the mobilisation of a geographical concept in political practice. A concept being employed to do real work. This kind of deployment raises a host of questions. One of these is the issue of one's responsibility, as it were, for and towards a concept when it is deployed politically, and especially when as in this case the concept has travelled from its place of origin to be deployed elsewhere. (This latter aspect raises particular questions for postcolonial geographies.) There have been, for instance, detailed reports of how Deleuzian concepts – of smooth space and of deterritorialisation for instance – have been made use of by the Israeli Defence Forces in waging war in Palestinian settlements (Weizman, nd). It is clear that 'concepts' in themselves do not guarantee particular political usages or outcomes.

The case described in the last section was rather different from the Deleuzian one in that the concept of power-geometry was being deployed in a political context sympathetic to the purposes for which it had originally been devised. Here what was fascinating was the way in which the concept was further moulded by the very fact of its engagement in political practice. There were a number of aspects to this. First, as already mentioned, the idea of power-geometries was first developed as a tool of critique for use within the United Kingdom under Margaret Thatcher and her forebears.[17] The very fact of its use in a quite different situation – one of trying positively to construct a more progressive power-geometry – had effects. One of these was the transformation of the concept into one in which temporality, and indeed the possibility of a multiplicity of temporalities, was explicit. As academics, we write often of things being processes; it has been a long commitment of the social sciences. Marx stressed that capital is a process. And most recently the emphasis on the continual becoming of things, on verbs rather than on nouns, and so forth, has brought that aspect of conceptualisation, along with its potential political implications, once again to the fore. But it is the reality of being in the midst of a thing-as-a-process that brings home the full meaning and import of words that can roll so easily off the tongue.

Or again, witnessing the active use of the idea of power-geometries enriched the concept in a variety of ways. Thinking about how it could relate to a whole range of different kinds of power-relations – popular, participatory, collective – and appreciating even apparently small things such as the intended symbolic force of calling all settlements 'cities', gave the concept a richer, more qualitative sense. It elaborated still further, for me, the range of possibilities of what might be a 'power-geometry'.

*This essay first appeared in* Documents d'Analisi Geographica, *Issue 55, 2009.*

## Notes

1 The argument of this section on space is spelled out in detail in D. Massey, *For Space*, Sage: London, 2005.
2 This meaning of the term 'social', implying multiplicity, also enables the inclusion of the world beyond the human, from 'natural' phenomena to artefacts. This is an important extension and one increasingly addressed within Anglophone geography (see, for instance, S. Hinchliffe, *Geographies of Nature*, Sage: London, 2007). The present paper, however, does not extend into this line of argument.
3 It is important to note this, because structuralism is often characterised as being 'spatial', because instead of narratives it focused on structures. This is a grave misreading, that seriously misconstrues the spatial (as fixed, as something already achieved) and counterposes space and time (narrative or static structure; space as the absence of time).
4 Again, this argument is fully spelled out in *For Space*. Moreover, and importantly, the corollary is also true: that time, itself produced also out of interaction, requires the existence of space (see, for instance, B. Adam, *Time and social theory*, Polity: Cambridge, 1990).
5 See Massey 2005, *op. cit.* and D. Massey, *World City*, Polity: Cambridge, 2007.
6 J. Allen, *Lost geographies of power*, Blackwell: Oxford, 2003.
7 See E. Laclau and C. Mouffe, *Hegemony and Socialist Strategy*, Verso: London.
8 P. Hallward, *Out of this World: Deleuze and the Philosophy of Creation*, Verso: London, 2007 and J. Gilbert, *Anticipation and culture*, Oxford, 2008.
9 P. Devine, 'The political economy of twenty-first century socialism,' *Soundings*, 37, 2007, p115.
10 The five motors are: 1. *Ley habilitante: via directa al socialismo*, 2. *Reforma constitucional: estado de derecho socialista*, 3. *Moral y luces: educación con valores socialistas*, 4. *La nueva geometría del poder: el reordenamiento socialista de la geopolítica de la nación*, 5. *Explosión del poder communal: democracia protagónica, revolucionaria y socialista*.
11 The recognition of the multi-ethnicity of the country has been an important thread in the Bolivarian project. This has included both indigenous people and those of African descent.

12  This was one reason for the delivery of social programmes through parallel structures, such as Bolivarian circles, and missions.
13  One source is the Proyecto de Reforma Constitucional, voted on, and lost, on 2 December 2007. There is also much legislation, before and after that date, which moves in the same direction.
14  For a discussion of the connection between maps and problematic concepts of space, see *For Space*, chapter 11.
15  There are undoubtedly real issues here, but some useful light is thrown on them by Ernesto Laclau's analysis of populism (E. Laclau, *On populist reason*, Verso: London, 2005).
16  See C. Cariola and M. Lacabana, 'Globalización y metropolización: tensiones, transiciones y cambios', in *CENDES-UCV: Venezuela visión plural: Una mirada desde el Cendes*, Cendes: Caracas, 2005.
17  See Massey, forthcoming.

# 15

# Learning from Latin America

## 2012

This article is born in part out of exasperation. I am fed up with having to defend the so-called pink tide in Latin America when in fact there is so much that we 'over here' could be learning from the experiments that those progressive countries are undertaking. So I want to turn defence into positivity.[1]

But apart from my impatience there is a serious conjunctural reason for making this case. If, as we have been arguing in *Soundings*, the economic crisis of neoliberal capitalism might provide the conditions for a wider ideological and political challenge that could engender a moment of real rupture, then we need all the resources we can get. At such moments, it is vital for the left to have examples of – and for the right to eliminate – any practical operational possibilities for a progressive way out from the troubles besetting the hegemonic settlement.

During the last such period of potential breakdown, with the collapse of social democracy in the 1970s and 1980s and the battle over what would follow, there were experiments in left alternatives. They were hesitant and not without problems, and neoliberalism of course won. But the left alternatives were taken seriously enough by the right to be very vigorously attacked. Among these ways out to the left there was the innovatory municipal politics of the GLC and the Metropolitan Counties (they were simply abolished). And there were experiments in the global South, among them in Nicaragua. I remember to this day, having left London where I'd been working with the GLC, sitting in Managua and watching a speech by Ronald Reagan, broadcast in this Sandinista capital, in which he told the world of the threat posed by Nicaragua. (This was why he was backing the Contra war.) Behind him, a map of Central and North America, plain save for the boundaries of countries, showed a small red patch at the bottom – Nicaragua. And as he talked, the red patch bled north, through Central America, through Mexico, to lap on the banks of the Rio Grande. Threat? Three million people; no oil; no nuclear weapons; we didn't even have chocolate or enough biros.

It was the threat of a good example that Reagan feared. One of my arguments here is that right now, with the neoliberal settlement in at least economic crisis, the emergence of a range of progressive experiments in Latin America holds out the possibility for us to point to, and learn from, a way out to the left.

There are many things we could learn, but the focus here is on just three areas, all of them probably unexpected – 'democracy','the media' (aka the freedom of the press) and 'space'. The first two are important because it is on these that most criticism of Latin America has been levelled. In both cases not only are the criticisms often downright wrong; they also offer lessons that we in the North could learn from, if we are to improve our own pallid democracies and dysfunctional media.

Moreover the very fact that these are the areas where we find the dominant lines of attack itself reflects the nature of the articulation, under neoliberalism, of those two old incompatibles liberty and equality. 'Liberty' has won out over equality.[2] So Venezuela is attacked for its supposed lack of liberty while there is no mention of the strides that have been made in addressing poverty. Indeed I would argue that the attack on grounds of lack of liberty is precisely *designed* to obscure the advances on the equality front. In this mindset, 'liberty' is usually referred to as democracy. But a prerequisite of democracy is equality. So the case crumbles on a multitude of grounds.

A discussion of 'space' is here for rather different reasons. The political left in Latin America has taken this issue more seriously than is customarily the case in Europe. It is one of the more unusual spheres of politics in which progressive Latin America has been especially imaginative and in which it might provide another provocation to our own political imaginations.[3]

## Democracy

You would not know it from the European or US press, but one of the innovative experiments in left Latin America is the enrichment of democracy. All these left governments came to power through elections. But what has been going on since is the emergence of a host of new relations between the representative state on the one hand and participative and proactive grassroots movements on the other. This includes, though it is not confined to, attempts on the part of the elected state itself to provide enabling conditions for a more direct engagement of people in politics and in the very constitution of society.

The reasons for this are multiple. Many of the elections were won on the basis of existing social movements. In some of the countries the organs of the inherited state were corrupt and delegitimised, and often continued to be staffed by foes of progressive change. But it has also been a matter of both political principle and political necessity. As Temir Porras (Vice-Minister for Foreign Affairs in Venezuela) put it in an address in London in April 2011, the commitment to enriching democracy comes both because it is believed in for itself and because it is a necessity for the revolution – for pushing on further with progressive political change. The choice is between a democratic revolution and the restoration of the ancient privileges. The form and depth of these new democratic relations varies (contested relations between the PT and social movements in Brazil; constituent power and communal councils in Venezuela; indigenous democratic forms in Bolivia; barrio-based councils in Nicaragua ...), but this is a detectable theme. It is also experimental, and hotly contested within each of the countries (and not only by the right but also within the left). And it is largely ignored in commentary 'over here'.

In some cases these developments were set in train through the calling of a national constitutional assembly. There is much stress on grassroots *protagonism* (the power to initiate) rather than mere participation. So multiple forms and sources of democratic power coexist. Neighbourhood self-management groups, such as the communal councils in Venezuela, work through direct rather than representational democracy. Such organisations, and social movements more generally, provide arenas for the development of horizontal relations between people, and for the development of *collective* democratic power and voice, as opposed to the individual power of voting. In many cases – also in contrast to the power simply to vote – self-management and campaigning organisations develop the power to *do*. These evolving structures are therefore in themselves materially and subjectively empowering – people learn how to hold meetings, run budgets, negotiate with the elected state, and a host of other things. All this provides the possibility of each person being placed in a more complex and collective mesh of social relations through which new political subjectivities can emerge.

There are certainly difficulties on the path of this development. Participatory democracy has its own problems. There are issues of how to relate to party-political structures, and to the power of personality. There is resistance within the inherited organs of the representative state to the emergence of new sources of voice and initiative. Most of all there is the question of the balance of power between the state and these grassroots organisations. On the left there is criticism that this relation can be a way not of developing but of containing grassroots power; that the latter may be used but not responded to; that there are problems of favouritism. What, in other words, happens to autonomy? On the other hand, without enabling structures put in place by the elected government, some of these organisations would either have had less influence or would not have existed. Even more importantly, many of them are only meaningful because of the investment of public resources they have received – for equipment, training, etc, and for countering already-existing inequalities. (Without such investment any process of local 'decentralisation' – a tepid word, this is much more than that – risks reinforcing existing inequalities.) So, this tension, between the autonomy of the base and a progressive elected government, is not necessarily a problem; rather it can be integral to the dynamic of progressive politics themselves.[4] At best, the multiple forms of democracy can hold each other to account.

This enables the raising of new voices. But it involves more than including new voices into old structures; it is beginning (only beginning, for this will be a very long cultural change) to reimagine the structures of democracy themselves. It is this that has most outraged the regional elites, challenging their long-held assumption of their right to rule.

Given the dereliction of European and US representative democracy, our rule by markets and now explicitly by technocrats, and the way in which neoliberalism itself works against democracy, we could do worse than to look to Latin America for inspiration, including to its fierce and sophisticated debates.

Meanwhile the US, sensing the danger in all of this, pours resources into right-wing oppositions, sanctions elections in Mexico widely seen as stolen, connives at coups ... and vilifies these resurgent countries to its south as undemocratic.

## Media

These experiments in democracy are hardly reported in our media. The overwhelming majority of the media in Europe and in North America is implacably hostile to what is going on in Latin America, and systematically misrepresents it.[5] The misrepresentation is particularly ironic because one of the chief lines of attack on the progressive governments of Latin America is that they are opposed to the existence of 'a free press'. This is a key element in the general characterisation of these countries as lacking in liberty.

There certainly are huge issues about the press and the media more generally. First, in nearly all of these countries the media are overwhelmingly dominated by corporate interests, either themselves embodying or powerfully representing the interests of the right-wing opposition. In Ecuador Rafael Correa has called the press 'the real opposition'. In Paraguay an important element in the continuing power of the old elite is the press. One constant across all these countries in which a movement to the left is being attempted is that their elites remain entrenched; and crucial in their armoury is the press. Second, then, the tale usually told of state domination is the opposite of the truth. In Venezuela, the country most criticised in this regard, the same is true – newspaper and television outlets are dominated by private interests. Third, elements of this press play active political roles. In 2007 Hugo Chávez did not renew the licence of RCTV. The Western press screamed in horror. This was the TV channel that actively prepared the ground for the coup in 2002, and then famously showed Hollywood films as Chávez was restored to power. The story of this is well documented, but you'd hardly know from our media.⁶

However the purpose of this article is not to defend against misrepresentation but to talk of positive things from which we might learn. For in fact there are in Latin America positive strategies towards the media, particularly broadcasting. Thus in some countries (Argentina, Venezuela) the aim is to redistribute the airwaves, with a third for state/public, a third for private ownership, and a third for community production.⁷ Within the private sector there would also be attempts to reduce the concentration of ownership. The development of the community sector is well under way in Venezuela, and not just as part of media policy but as a further contribution to the wider enablement of voice and democracy. What most impressed me when being interviewed by community radio in Caracas was that they were interested in very wide-ranging political issues, which is really important because there is always a danger that neighbourhood-based grassroots politics will focus only on 'local' issues. This was plainly not the case. And it must enrage even more those from the richer parts of the city whose right to voice has hitherto been unchallenged. We could learn from this.

And yet, in spite of all this, the media story is all about clamping down on democracy and on the freedom of the press. And it is important that this *is* the message. Of Venezuela, Stoneman writes:

> Chávez's brand of radical nationalism had managed to displace the previous imaginary of the nation and extend it to wider social and racial groups. He had captured history … and replaced the old idea of the nation with a more egalitarian one. The opposition sought to shift the basis of the argument to other grounds. Evidently it is easier to win a debate set in the clear-cut terms of 'democracy vs dictatorship' than in the contentious terrain of arguments about the social division of wealth and power (p62).

The cynicism is breathtaking. And it is a line cravenly followed by the media here, whose own misrepresentations reach the absurd. It has been reported that the US State Department between 2007 and 2009 paid several million dollars to Latin American journalists, particularly in Venezuela.[8]

## Space

It is only rarely that space makes a serious appearance within political debate in this country. Yet space and power are intimately related, and spatiality is crucial in the construction of the social and the political. In progressive Latin America, sometimes implicitly, sometimes explicitly, there seems to be recognition of this, and some attempts to imagine, and to create, socio-political spaces that are more democratic and more egalitarian.[9]

Thus, for example, although these are each nationally-based projects, the very definition of the nation has come under scrutiny in a number of countries – it has not been taken simply as a given. Chávez first won elections at the head of the Polo Patriótico but, as already pointed out, at the heart of the Bolivarian project in Venezuela is the struggle to install a *new*, more democratic, imaginary of the nation. What is invigorating about this is the recognition that 'national identity' is not to be 'found' by searching for (ever more bland) common characteristics. Rather, it is an object of political contest, of hegemonic struggle. The debates about Britishness and Englishness could learn from this. Further, either constitutionally or through new legal structures, the multi-ethnic nature of these countries (Ecuador, Peru, Bolivia, Venezuela) has been explicitly recognised. This process has been taken furthest in Bolivia with its concept of *'plurinacionalidad'*, which goes way beyond the paper recognition of 'difference': difference here is something that is actively contested and developed through fraught political practice. And that practice includes dispute over the very meaning of terms within the political project. For example, the TIPNIS conflict over a proposal for roadbuilding set indigenous groups against each other, against *campesinos*, and against the government.[10] It has thrown into sharp relief differing conceptions of indigenous rights, development, landholding, and the whole national notion of *'vivir bien'*. The media and the right took advantage of this, using the conflict to undermine Evo

Morales. The road has now been cancelled, but the issues rumble on to such an extent that Morales proposed a national debate on the future direction of the national agenda. A summit was called to which social movements, but not representatives of political parties, were invited. One item for discussion, proposed by social movements, is the problem of 'the media'.

Furthermore, the recognised importance of social movements and the attempts to develop protagonistic democracy engender a very different imaginary of the internal political geography of the nation. All this, particularly in its understanding of the relation between spatial organisation and power, could challenge and enrich our own debates about 'localism'.

Or again, there is a reimagining, and an active reconstruction of the spaces, both of Latin America as a whole and, even more widely, of Latin America together with the Caribbean. New political spaces, and I would argue new *kinds* of political spaces, are being constructed. The very subcontinent is being re-worked through the gradual accumulation of a complex mosaic of intersecting and overlapping alliances and institutions. There is MERCOSUR, the Banco del Sur, Telesur, ALBA-TCP, Unasur, PetroCaribe, CELAC ... and a host of more project-based relations. Each of these new institutional spaces is in itself interesting. None of the economic alliances is simply a free-trade area.[11] They involve principles of solidarity, equal exchange and mutual aid. ALBA is beginning to incorporate cross-national engagement between social movements as well as at the normal governmental level. But it is in the multiplicity of these alliances and their complex overlapping that the real strength of this new spatial thinking can best be seen. It is a structure that is constructing a solidarity between nations, but a solidarity that allows for variation in historical trajectory, economic strength and political project. It is a genuinely experimental spatiality, and it is lending to this group of countries a new sense of their own collectivity and collective sovereignty. The latest addition to this mosaic is in fact more all-inclusive. CELAC (the Community of Latin American and Caribbean States), inaugurated in 2011, is the first ever grouping to include every country in the Americas (and that includes Cuba) *except for* the USA and Canada. It is a mark of a new confidence and sense of identity.

## The importance of the current moment

In a recent meeting about Latin America, a colleague asked why the West, its governments and media, were lending such support, from blank cheques to military intervention, to the Arab Spring while directing such hostility towards progressive developments in Latin America. It was an ironic, rhetorical, question, and there are many possible elements to an answer. While Latin America has been retold as a story of authoritarianism (obscuring the socio-economic progress), the demands from the streets of North Africa have been one-sidedly interpreted as solely electoral (obscuring the claims about poverty and inequality). The Arab Spring on this (mis)reading represents a desire to follow 'us'. Progressive, and already democratically elected, Latin America has made plain its desire not to do so. The Andean nations especially have been vocal in their denunciation of neoliberalism, and of capitalism tout court. (In fact, though structural changes have been made, these are still capitalist economies. They have had the luck of the (now ended) economic era – oil in Venezuela, soya in Argentina – and this has enabled significant gains for the poor without – yet? – a frontal assault on capital or indeed, economically, on many of the rich.) Their collective voice against the Washington Consensus has been strong, and it has been heard. So far, too, apart from the opposition coup in Honduras, it must seem out of the control of the neighbour to the north. In contrast, the attempt is still on to turn the Arab Spring into a trajectory amenable to the West's economic and political interests.

Latin America, however, is ploughing its own furrow, and huge gains have been made, in poverty-reduction, health, education, and social and political confidence and voice amongst the previously disenfranchised. There is more that we could learn from than I have touched on here.[12] These are 'good examples' on which we can draw in the current crisis and the search for an alternative way ahead.

Thirty years ago, when the British social-democratic settlement collapsed, the majority of the Parliamentary Labour Party had no alternative to offer. Ways out to the left were invented outside of parliament (in the cities, in the global South). Most of the PLP seemed as hostile to the GLC as were the Tories, and in the end they caved in to neoliberalism in its Blairite incarnation. There is a real danger that the same will happen this time. In another recent meeting, a left-leaning former Labour MP described the continuing power and destructive activity of this Blairite formation. (It is no wonder Ed Miliband has such difficulty propagating the bigger arguments he clearly wants to construct.) Latin America demonstrates that a way out of this crisis, to the left, is possible. As this speaker pointed out, it was under neoliberalism for longer than anywhere (since the coup against Allende in 1973) and is searching for ways to reject it through both electoral politics and popular mobilisation. Openness, or not, to Latin America, he said, is a real guide to the divisions within the Labour Party; and the touchstone is the position on neoliberalism. 'Learning from Latin America', then, is bound up with our own political debates.

Meanwhile new threats mount to the gains made in these countries. In the US even more viciously hostile appointments have been made to the Foreign Relations Committee and to the position of spokesperson on Latin America, while the fact of presidential elections in 2012 is likely to lead to yet more right-wing positioning. In Europe, the victorious Spanish right has vowed to denounce the curse of left-wing 'populism' in Latin America. The combination of this, together with the hostile interventions mentioned earlier, and the difficulty of continuing, in a period of economic problems, with what has been so far an essentially redistributive model, presents real threats to pink Latin America.[13] These countries need our vocal support and engagement as much as we need to learn from them.

In the 1970s and 1980s the countries of Latin America went through debt crises that had many structural similarities to the situation facing European countries right now. 'Over there', as here, the response of the right was the imposition of neoliberal policies. The result was '*la década perdida*', the lost decade. But out of the wreckage which that wrought emerged these new progressive alternatives. It is (is it?) too much to hope that we could pursue a similar path? At least we could look and learn.

*This essay first appeared in* Soundings, *50, 2012.*

## Notes

1 This does *not* mean being uncritical (see below). One of the problems of 'debate' in Europe and the US about Latin America is its tendency to polarise into pro- and anti-camps with little constructive debate between them.
2 See D. Massey, 'Economics and ideology in the present moment', *Soundings*, 48, 2011.
3 What follows is not detailed empirical analysis – there are many excellent books and articles that do this (the problem being that they tend to be read only by the already committed). What I do here is frame an argument.
4 See D. Massey, in A.G. Gonzales (ed), 'Espacio y sociedad: experimentos con la espacialidad del poder y democracia', *Latinoamérica, laboratorio mundial*, La Oficina Ediciones, Madrid, 2011.
5 The most honourable exception I know of is *Le Monde Diplomatique*.
6 See G. Wilpert, 'RCTV and freedom of speech in Venezuela', 3 June 2007, at www.venezuelanalysis.com; R. Gott, 'The battle over the media is about race as well as class', *Guardian*, 7 June 2007; R. Stoneman, *Chávez: The revolution will not be televised*, Wallflower: London, 2008.
7 At continental level there is also the development of Telesur.
8 J. Bigwood, 'Buying Venezuela's press with US tax dollars', *Report on the Americas*, New York, September/October 2010, cited in W. Robinson, 'Latin America's pink tide', *Le Monde Diplomatique* (English Edition), November 2011.
9 See Massey 2011, *op. cit.*, 'Espacio y sociedad', as above.
10 See the regular news briefings from the Bolivia Information Forum: enquiries@boliviainfoforum.org.uk.
11 See, for instance, C. Katz, *El rediseño de América Latina*, El Perro y la Rana: Caracas, 2007.
12 Though – again – this does not mean that our supportive engagement should be uncritical. Solidarity works both ways. And indeed there is much thoughtful and sophisticated, and very fierce, debate within each of these countries.
13 The forthcoming elections in Venezuela mean that these threats will intensify. Francisco Domínguez will write about this in our next issue.

# Occasional Writings

# 16

# Liverpool's Football Activists are Part of a Wider Social Movement

## 2010

The ownership of football clubs, writes Martin Kettle, does not matter. The ownership of Liverpool Football Club, in particular, ranks among those things 'about which one does not care and which don't matter either'.[1] I don't care whether or not he cares, but it does matter.

The current nature of ownership of many of our clubs is a particular manifestation of the larger recent dominance of the economy by neoliberalism and financialisation. It is one way those huge shifts in economy and society touch people's lives. And it is through such specifics that people encounter, and learn to address, the more general political issues. If we are to build opposition to this society in which everything is for sale and everything has a price, then it has to start at ground level, from the myriad concrete ways in which people are affected. The ownership of our football clubs is one of them.

A social movement has grown up around Liverpool FC. It began, of course, with opposition to Hicks and Gillett. Its activities are multifarious and imaginative: rallies, marches, email campaigns, lobbying, banners, songs, videos, fanzines and an attempt to take ownership of the club through establishing a credit union.

One day in Manhattan, Hicks was spotted by a fan, a financial consultant. Guessing that Hicks was there seeking funds, the fan sent images to his partner, who put them on Twitter, where they were picked up by a cabby in Liverpool, who posted a form letter online. In an hour, emails were flowing in to the financial institutions on that Manhattan street. It was all written up in the Wall Street Journal.[2] A small example.

This is a movement that certainly has its internal disagreements, but it is remarkable for its social mix, its international nature, its careful tone (and debate over this), and its depth of knowledge. As SaveLFC says, in calling for people to lend their skills, 'Ordinary people did all this'. This is an organic creation drawing on and developing a popular and collective expertise. Stand on the Kop, read a blog, walk down a train on the way to a match, and you'll find it being developed.

Still, isn't it all over now? The club's been sold. One set of Americans has gone, another installed. The debt has been cleared.

First, for many of us this was not just about 'Americans' or even 'foreign' ownership. There are certainly localist hostilities, but the club's fanbase is global, the campaign itself international. The supporter-based ShareLiverpoolFC, facing geographical restrictions on where it could offer shares, appealed to Norwegian fans, especially lawyers, for information about financial regulations there. An optimistic reading is that it is in movements such as these that some of the tensions of local/global are being addressed.

Second, what's at issue for me and many others is the whole model of ownership. Spirit of Shankly – ShareLiverpoolFC have long called for democratic supporter ownership of the club and this remains their long-term goal. For now, they are pressing for 'supporter-ownership through a direct equity shareholding in LFC, in partnership with new owners, giving the supporters real and meaningful representation'. In this, fans are challenging 'the laissez-faire stance of the football authorities' so well described by Andy Green on Comment is free.[3] The arguments learned here could be carried into a wider movement against a form of economy in which nothing has value, everything has a price, and all that matters is short-term gain.

*This essay first appeared in the* Guardian *on 28 October 2010.*

## Notes

1. Martin Kettle, 'Shed No Tears for Liverpool Football Club', www.theguardian.com/commentisfree, 14 October 2010.
2. David Enrich and Gregory Zuckerman, www.wsj.com, 24 September 2010.
3. Andy Green, 'Liverpool Football Club Sell Out', www.theguardian.com/commentisfree, 8 October 2010.

# 17

# Exhilarating Times

## 2016

*Soundings* has been arguing for a long time that Labour should 'take a leap', that it should challenge the dominant terms of debate: that, rather than accepting the established political terrain, it should be marking out distinctive territory of its own. Just before the last election we bemoaned the party's lack of inspiration, arguing that this was a 'moment crying out for some political bravery'.[1] The whole point of the Soundings *Manifesto*, likewise, has been to argue the political necessity of challenging the currently hegemonic common sense and to establish new ground.[2]

The election of Jeremy Corbyn as leader of the party may herald the possibility of such a brave leap, and so we welcome it enthusiastically. But, as we also reflected in Issue 59, 'being politically brave is a gamble … and like any gamble it may not pay off' (p7). We are currently in the choppy waters of precisely such a gamble and it is engrossing. These are exhilarating times.

There are certainly signs that the terms of the debate are shifting. There are the big things of course, like opposition to austerity, which are fundamental. And there are also small things which may be equally significant: the use of the word kindness; the insistence that the task is to work for victories not just electorally for Labour but emotionally in society as well (a counter to Margaret Thatcher's 'battle for the soul'?). There is the engagement with the weasel word 'aspiration', but the immediate pulling away from the competitive individualism which that usually implies, in the argument for collective endeavour.

Then there was the response to the attack – from those who are on most days routinely misogynist – that there were no women in the 'big' posts. Came the reply from Team Corbyn: 'It's you who thinks these are the big jobs. Most people look to Health and Education'. What a response! Post-hoc rationalisation? Who knows? But it was a brilliant turning of the tables of the debate. Indeed it reflects a wider interest across the left in 'social reproduction', and our long-standing arguments that health and education, as *investing*, not just 'spending', departments, are central to the construction of a better society and economy.[3]

And there is the simple fact that the words 'capitalism' and 'socialism' are being uttered in the mainstream media. What is going on here can be understood as the putting out of feelers towards a way of expressing what might be elements of a different common sense. It is also something we believe to be of crucial importance: the beginning of the construction of a new political frontier.

Another clear indicator that Corbyn is establishing new terms of debate is the incomprehension and bafflement of the establishment, certainly at the time of writing. Even the supposedly progressive media are finding themselves without a language, or a set of concepts, through which to understand what is going on. They find themselves lost in a political landscape which is in the process of being redrawn.

We are not talking here of already achieved political gains. Far from it. 'Shifting common sense', 'changing the terms of debate' and 'shaping a new political terrain' can only be part of a long and multi-faceted political project; and, most importantly, any new common sense must be able to reach out to, and in some way engage, parts of society way beyond the self-described left. But seeds are being sown. There is somehow a feeling of possibility.

## The specificities of the new terrain

The landscape within which this political earthquake has happened has as its immediate background the long decline of European social democracy, within the context of hegemonic neoliberalism, about which we have written extensively in these pages and in our *Manifesto*. The convergence of social-democratic parties with neoliberalism, and the extraordinary thinness of their democratic element, have been much analysed.

This has been figured, especially by mainstream commentators, as the decline of the purchase of party politics (a proposition now possibly being challenged), even as a 'post-political' age, the end of interest in politics *tout court*. Certainly, recent decades have given us little choice between the main parties. Politics has been reduced to technocratic administration and arguments over (relative) detail. There has been little confrontation between contesting political positions. And there has certainly been – as a result of all this – a crisis of representation. This in turn has opened up a space for populism: for the emergence of a different kind of voice – anti-establishment, grassroots, imbued with passion, producing meaningful talk and action. We have seen these eruptions on the right and the left across Europe and indeed in the US. As Sirio Canos from Podemos put it at a recent *Soundings* event, 'when you suddenly have a party that doesn't talk to people as if they are stupid, everyone else has to step up their game too'.[4]

This is the context in which we understand the Corbyn phenomenon – as an element in a bigger picture. The neoliberal establishment (or however it is characterised) is undoubtedly still hegemonic. But it is having to engage in a succession of fire-fighting exercises as opposition to its rule breaks through in one place after another. Each of these eruptions of frustration and discontent, these upwellings from beneath the carapace of neoliberal hegemony, is distinct. Even among the left-wing uprisings within Europe there are differences. In Greece and Spain they took place through the emergence of social movements and parties outside of the hegemonic political structures. And the differences even between these two are marked. In Scotland the discontent came to be articulated in relation to an establishment party (though also beyond it), but around a – contested – nationalism. And so forth. The case of Corbyn is different again – in ways that are encouraging, but which present different challenges.

In this case the new was born within the old social-democratic party itself – a party that those of us on the left have variously seen as the great obstacle in the path to real change; as the necessary but frustrating vehicle to any small change at all; as the only political voice for the labour movement; and as the party which – recognising that the world was changing – called itself 'New' and responded in precisely the wrong way. The Labour Party has been the great 'thing' that had somehow to be dealt with. And now it has somehow given birth to this.

This is a situation that is full of contradictions, but in ways that, in the end, can be turned to our advantage. It means that this new voice comes into the world inheriting all the institutional resources of an established party – even if those structures and processes are often archaic and part precisely of what needs reforming if politics is to be done differently. It means that there is already in place a huge constituency, in one way or another 'signed up' – even if there is within the very same party a quite visceral hostility from the right that wishes to see the experiment fail. It means, as some have it, that the Labour Party itself must be opened up to become a social movement, which is indeed important – but social movements and parties are distinct animals and that distinction must be recognised: this difference, and the nature of relations between parties and movements, will be challenging aspects of the construction of a new more democratic politics (and there is much to study and learn from in this regard in the experiences in Latin America, Greece and Spain).

This new voice also has strong and positive relations with the organised labour movement. The number of unions that backed Corbyn, and the union experience now represented in the shadow cabinet, is a great asset. But here too there are lessons to be learned. Thus, at our event Sirio Canos welcomed the constructive nature of the discussion with Simon Dubbins of Unite – which was in contrast to many of the difficulties between Podemos and the unions in Spain – while Simon himself acknowledged the differences of approach that can sometimes cause problems between unions and social movements.[5] Working together takes persistence, patience and much listening – but it can be done.

We also know that enthusiastic support from unions in the UK may be a point of attack by the right (ironic given the aims of the new voting system). But the great hope is that this could again be a moment – and a locus – in which (as in that moment in the 1980s when the new urban left met with the NUM, as so brilliantly dramatised in the recent film *Pride*) the (very) different elements of the left can come together and learn to talk to each other.

The main point, though, is that all these characteristics give this particular UK eruption of the new politics specific characteristics that we must understand and build upon.

## Some ideas to work with

It is certain that achieving wider success for this new politics will take work, with each of us making different kinds of contributions (and of course active participation as opposed to commentary alone is essential). For our part, we believe that a journal like *Soundings* – and the network of engaged and thoughtful conversations that take place around it – has a number of ways of contributing. Firstly, it should be a place for the development and exploration of ideas for alternatives. This work was begun with the *Manifesto*, and will be taken further in a new series that will be inaugurated in the next issue. We hope that in the new political atmosphere there is now a greater appetite for such debate within the Labour Party. Secondly, *Soundings* can continue to play a role in standing back a bit in order to better understand the wider and deeper dimensions of what is going on. And a third role is to try to bring to the project the resources of the intellectual labour that has been underway on the left even during all these years of what – in this country – has often seemed like a political desert. There is much to take up here, but two particular things immediately come to mind.

The first is the importance of a move away from any form of determinism (particularly by the economic, or by class) in the construction of political positions. Rather, what we have gradually come to understand is the significance of pretty much every aspect of society, and of daily life, in the forming of political attitudes, moods and constituencies. The critical point here is that political positions are not automatic. They are a product of, and a part of, hegemonic struggles. This understanding grows out of Gramsci, out of the work of Stuart Hall on Thatcherism as a hegemonic project, and out of the thinking of Ernesto Laclau and Chantal Mouffe.[6]

The degree to which New Labour failed to grasp this essential point was astonishing. It recognised that the world was changing, but saw its role as merely to be a passive reflector of those changes. It had no sense that new times meant finding new ways of constructing a democratic and hegemonic politics. Maybe here Labour's history as the party of an already-constituted labour movement proved to be a disadvantage. It had had a constituency that was already made and given – indeed that had given rise to the party. There had therefore been less need actively to intervene and campaign to change the soul of the nation; less need actually to create a political constituency for the values it said it stood for. (This too is an aspect of the specificity of the UK.)

It is this that formed the backcloth to the emergence of what has been termed retail politics, the framing philosophy of which is to give the electorate what it already wants.[7] Hence the endless focus groups and so forth. There is no notion of campaigning to *change* what the electorate might want, to argue for values and understandings of the world, that may not be popular now but are what the party (says it) stands for. The result, of course, is that you end up working within the terms of the established hegemony (for this is evidently what the electorate says it wants). With this approach there is no chance at all of countering the currently dominant ways of thinking, no chance at all of challenging the current common sense and beginning to construct something new. No chance at all of taking a leap, changing the terms of debate.

*Soundings* has always worked within this general framework of understanding. But the financial implosion and its aftermath threw this set of issues into high relief. The crisis of the economic did not produce in the subsequent period any serious fracturing of the dominant ideology or politics. It was recognition of this that provoked us into our project of revisiting the ideas of conjunctural analysis – and subsequently into producing our *Manifesto*, in which there is a strong focus on the formation and contesting of common sense.

Now, however, with the possibility of a challenge to the prevailing hegemonic terms of debate, there is more work to be done. How, exactly, can we subvert the dominant common sense? What elements of 'good sense' can be drawn out into the political light and be positively built upon? How can the energy and arguments of the emergent politics filter out into, and give confidence to, wider sections of society?

Second, there is the question of what kind support this is. What kind of social and political forces are at issue here? In this arena too there is much theoretical/political work that we can draw on.

Jeremy Corbyn is frequently characterised as a conduit, a focus, a canvas upon which a host of different strands have painted their discontents and desires – a lightning rod. This characterisation is correct in many ways. Corbyn has burst into power on a wave of pent-up frustration with the way that neoliberalism systematically hurts the non-rich, and particularly the poor, the sick, and the young. The great strength of this politics is the degree to which it breaks – in both substance and style – with the smooth technocratic Westminster bubble, which has refined a style and a set of policies that is far removed from the vast majority of the population. It is also, of course, his enemies' target.

There is no doubt that Corbyn's support draws together many flows. It draws together young and old, long histories and new initiatives. It encompasses elements both of the labour movement and of new social movements. It is definitely not only 'the young', as it was initially, rather lazily, labelled. The presence of young people is marked, but so too is the presence of the over-60s (a potentially positive constellation that might help get us beyond the supposed battle between generations). It brings together Generation Rent – priced out of the housing market and let down by the Liberal Democrats over university tuition fees; disillusioned Labour voters coming back to the fold after years in the Blairite wilderness; and people who marched against the war in Iraq only to feel that it had made no difference. Then there are those in 'the squeezed middle' who see their standard of living dropping year on year whilst that of the wealthy mushrooms; the environmentalists who see the chance to move climate crisis higher up the actual political agenda; the ballooning precariat who are no longer buying the line that it's their fault; people who see corporations not paying their tax, and the privileges of the 1 per cent swelling, whilst everyone else pays through 'austerity'. There is a politics here that speaks to people using food banks, pensioners whose pension is not enough to live on, and victims of social cleansing forced to move away from their homes. And there are more constituencies than this, many of them overlapping.

Among these new constituencies there are also connections with some of the most innovative moments in socialist democracy over the past fifty years: the anti-racism, feminism and peace movements from the 1960s onwards; that great experiment in popular democracy, the metropolitan counties of the urban left and the GLC (Greater London Council); and the contemporary wave of experimental activism, from alter-globalisation to Occupy.

This support is multifarious, possibly inchoate. Can it be given a shape that can channel into a more focused energy, and a coherent – even while open – set of political purposes?

Here it might be possible to draw on some of the ideas of Ernesto Laclau, especially his work on populism.[8] In a moment like this, when there is (or has been) a serious crisis of representation of significant sectors of society, a figure such as Jeremy Corbyn, who has emerged as the locus of a whole range of pent-up demands, might be characterised as a 'signifier'. (Laclau makes a distinction between empty and floating signifiers, but that need not detain us here.) The point is that he stands for, in some way, that range of diverse demands. In these early moments, neither the full nature of the diversity that has been brought together nor the precise way in which the demands can be related to each other and embodied is at all clear. There are, therefore, political tasks. One of these lies within the political base – what are the different demands? What is the nature of their articulation to each other? Do they have common enemies which might form the basis for exchange and alliance? (and if so what/who are they?) In other words, is there any way in which – without in any way abandoning the particularity of different demands (housing, environment, trade union rights ...) an identifiable commonality can be found among them – at a higher structural level if you like – that would enable them to form what Laclau would call a chain of equivalence? The question then becomes whether or not the signifier can 'represent' the commonality of these demands; and this is a question of process – a two-way process, and one which is ongoing. Here Corbyn's commitment to democratic engagement and openness, and to doing politics in a different way, as well as his rejection of individual celebrity status, is a real strength. All this will continue to shift the terms of political debate if it is possible to maintain the current combination of confidence and integrity, pithy acuity (cutting through the neoliberal spin), and, crucially, democracy – humility, genuine inclusiveness, and awareness of the need for new ways to democratise politics, all the way through from PMQs to electoral reform to Labour Party structure.

These kinds of tough analytical and political engagement are necessary to the creation of a successful movement. They are essential, too, for the construction of a political frontier. There is a real question in the UK today of exactly how we would characterise this frontier and who/what is 'the enemy'. 'Capitalism' is too general and has little immediate popular purchase, while to focus on, for example, 'housing landlords' is too specific. How about something that captures the dominance of finance and financialisation in our lives and society? If the experience of Podemos is anything to go by, this will be a long-debated issue. They decided on '*la casta*' versus '*el pueblo*'. But the identification of a political frontier needs to be a product of a response to the specificity of time and place. This is a task that should be addressed. Recent discussions in the New Economy Organisers Network (NEON) have made some suggestions on this front; and we need to think further about it.

### The emerging international left

We have enjoyed many places and moments of hope in recent years – in Latin America, Greece, Spain, Scotland, Turkey, even with Bernie Sanders in the US – but we have also encountered setbacks. For many of us, Latin America has provided ideas and inspiration, and it still does, but the attacks that progressive governments there have come under, combined with a difficult economic climate, mean that today all are labouring to keep alive the initial fervour. (It is notable that Jeremy Corbyn has been a consistent and solid supporter of this Latin American involvement. Indeed openness or not to Latin America is a real guide to the divisions within the Labour Party: and the touchstone is the position on neoliberalism.[9]) Syriza has certainly suffered reverses, and faces hard times ahead, though holding its own in the September election was a significant achievement. Podemos is facing heavy weather in Spain. Nonetheless the viciousness of the response to each of these popular breakthroughs by the hegemonic forces is itself a measure of the potential they carry. The panic of the British establishment in the face of the Scottish insurgence was extraordinary. The financial terrorism against Argentina has been cold-blooded calculation. The brutality of the attempt to annihilate Syriza in Greece was horrifying. There are many ways of persuading us there is no alternative.

But the eruptions will not go away. And the energy around Jeremy Corbyn's campaign is the latest manifestation. Magma is erupting from beneath the carapace of neoliberalism in place after place. 'They' have to be on constant alert to put out all the fires.

Among the most uplifting responses immediately on Corbyn's victory were the messages of support – from Latin America, from Syriza, from Podemos … there is a network of ideas and solidarities here. In an extremely interesting article on the situation in Europe, Podemos Secretary for International Relations Pablo Bustinduy Amador has argued that – in spite of everything – Syriza has succeeded in opening up cracks in the neoliberal front, and that Europe is a crucial space for the confrontation of forces.[10] Spain, he argues, must now, through Podemos, take up the baton. Maybe the UK can now join in. Corbyn and McDonnell have made a number of commitments: first, not to give Cameron a free ride in negotiations, especially in relation to employments rights and TTIP; second, to develop in the UK a left critique of the EU; and third to convene a cross-Europe conference of those who oppose austerity.

So, times may have been hard, and there have been recent defeats as well as victories. But even five years ago most of these European challenges to neoliberalism could not have been imagined. They can now. Maybe there is here the potential fracturing of the ideological and political hegemony of neoliberalism that seemed so absent in the immediate aftermath of the financial crisis.

It may be that Jeremy Corbyn will somehow be hounded out. If he is, and if the party returns to the comfort zone of pale imitation of the Tories – in a context whereby the centre will inevitably move yet further to the right – the Labour Party may well face extinction as any kind of progressive force. We must do everything we can to keep this initiative growing and to play our part in the wider movement that keeps on bubbling up.

*This essay first appeared in* Soundings, *6, Summer 1997.*

## Notes

1 *Soundings*, 59, Spring 2015, p4.
2 See Stuart Hall, Doreen Massey and Michael Rustin (eds), *After Neoliberalism: The Kilburn Manifesto*, Lawrence Wishart: London, 2015, especially the framing statement and chapters 3 and 11.
3 *Ibid.*, chapter 7.
4 Sirio Canos, 'European alternatives', *Soundings*, 60, Summer 2015, p19. In our next issue we address crises of representation, populism and the relation between movements and parties in a translation of sections from a new book by Íñigo Errejón and Chantal Mouffe, *Construir pueblo: Hegemonía y radicalización de le democracia*, Icaria: Barcelona, 2015.
5 *Ibid.*, p27.
6 For an introduction to Gramsci, see Roger Simon, *Gramsci's Political Thought: An Introduction* (third edition), Lawrence Wishart: London, 2015. For Stuart Hall's writings on Thatcherism see the *Marxism Today* archive at www.amielandmelburn.org.uk/collections/mt/index_frame.htm. For Ernesto Lacau and Chantal Mouffe see *Hegemony and Socialist Strategy: Towards a Radical Democratic Politics*, third edition, Verso: London, 2014.
7 See, for example, the interview with Jon Cruddas in *Soundings*, 6, 1997.
8 For an introduction to some of these ideas see David Slater, 'Ernesto Laclau 1935-2014: an appreciation', *Soundings*, 58, 2014.
9 See Doreen Massey, 'Learning from Latin America', *Soundings*, 50, 2012, p139.
10 Pablo Bustinduy Amador, 'Grecia: reflexiones después de la batalla', Publico.es: www.blogs.publico.es/dominiopublico/14481/.

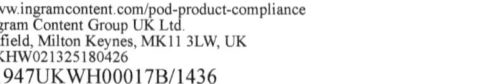